Performing Power in Nigeria

For decades, Pentecostalism has been one of the most powerful socio-cultural and socio-political movements in Africa. The Pentecostal modes of constructing the world by using their performative agencies to embed their rites in social processes have imbued them with immense cultural power to contour the character of their societies. *Performing Power in Nigeria* explores how Nigerian Pentecostals mark their self-distinction as a people of power within a social milieu that affirmed and contested their desires for being. Their faith, and the various performances that inform it, imbue the social matrix with saliences that also facilitate their identity of power. Using extensive archival material, interviews, and fieldwork, Abimbola A. Adelakun questions the histories, desires, knowledge, tools, and innate divergences of this form of identity, and its interactions with the other ideological elements that make up the society. Analysing the important developments in contemporary Nigerian Pentecostalism, she demonstrates how the social environment is being transformed by the Pentecostal performance of their identity as the people of power. This title is also available as Open Access on Cambridge Core.

ABIMBOLA A. ADELAKUN is Assistant Professor in the Department of African and African Diaspora Studies at the University of Texas at Austin where her research focuses on the politics and performances of Pentecostalism. She is the author of articles in journals including the *Journal of Women and Religion, Jenda: Journal of Culture and African Women Studies*, and co-editor of *Art, Creativity, and Politics in Africa and the Diaspora* (2018).

T0372707

African Identities: Past and Present

General Editors
Toyin Falola, *University of Texas at Austin*
Carina Ray, *Brandeis University*

African Identities: Past and Present offers scholars a unique publishing platform for exploring the multivalent processes through which collective identities have come into being. Books in this series probe the work that African identities have been made to do, the varied investments that historical and contemporary actors have made in them, and the epistemological dilemmas and intellectually fraught politics of writing about such contingent categories of being. The focus on African identities makes clear the series' commitment to publishing histories of the complex and ongoing processes of identity formation through which Africans have taken on shared senses of being. This series calls upon its authors to unpack the flexible, fluid, contingent, and interactive nature of collective African identities, while also exploring how historical actors have alternatively sought to delimit, expand, or otherwise challenge the boundaries of such identities.

Performing Power
in Nigeria

Identity, Politics, and Pentecostalism

ABIMBOLA A. ADELAKUN
University of Texas at Austin

CAMBRIDGE
UNIVERSITY PRESS

University Printing House, Cambridge CB2 8BS, United Kingdom

One Liberty Plaza, 20th Floor, New York, NY 10006, USA

477 Williamstown Road, Port Melbourne, VIC 3207, Australia

314–321, 3rd Floor, Plot 3, Splendor Forum, Jasola District Centre,
New Delhi – 110025, India

103 Penang Road, #05–06/07, Visioncrest Commercial, Singapore 238467

Cambridge University Press is part of Cambridge University Press & Assessment,
a department of the University of Cambridge.

It furthers the University's mission by disseminating knowledge in the pursuit of
education, learning, and research at the highest international levels of excellence.

www.cambridge.org
Information on this title: www.cambridge.org/9781009281744
DOI: 10.1017/9781009281751

First published 2023
Reissued as Open Access, 2023

A catalogue record for this publication is available from the British Library.

Library of Congress Cataloging-in-Publication Data
Names: Adelakun, Abimbola Adunni, author.
Title: Performing power in Nigeria : identity, politics, and Pentecostalism / Abimbola
Adelakun, University of Texas, Austin.
Description: Cambridge, United Kingdom ; New York, NY : Cambridge University Press, 2021. |
Series: African identities: past and present | Includes bibliographical references and index.
Identifiers: LCCN 2021023784 | ISBN 9781108831079 (hardback) | ISBN 9781108923194
(ebook other)
Subjects: LCSH: Pentecostal churches – Nigeria. | Pentecostalism – Nigeria. | Identification
(Religion) | Identity (Philosophical concept) – Social aspects. | Performance – Religious aspects –
Christianity. | BISAC: POLITICAL SCIENCE / American Government / General
Classification: LCC BX8762.N6 A34 2021 | DDC 289.9/409669–dc23
LC record available at https://lccn.loc.gov/2021023784

ISBN 978-1-108-83107-9 Hardback
ISBN 978-1-009-28174-4 Paperback

For Marcel, Iyunola, and Irawoola

Contents

This title is part of the Cambridge University Press *Flip it Open* Open Access Books program and has been "flipped" from a traditional book to an Open Access book through the program.

Flip it Open sells books through regular channels, treating them at the outset in the same way as any other book; they are part of our library collections for Cambridge Core, and sell as hardbacks and ebooks. The one crucial difference is that we make an upfront commitment that when each of these books meets a set revenue threshold we make them available to everyone Open Access via Cambridge Core.

This paperback edition has been released as part of our Open Access commitment and we would like to use this as an opportunity to thank the libraries and other buyers who have helped us flip this and the other titles in the program to Open Access.

To see the full list of libraries that we know have contributed to *Flip it Open*, as well as the other titles in the program please visit www.cambridge.org/fio-acknowledgements

Acknowledgments

In Nigerian Pentecostal churches, "testimony time" is an integral part of worship. Someone comes forward to publicly testify to the goodness and faithfulness of the Lord in their lives. Or, as they tend to put it, "I have returned to give God all the glory." When they are done with the narration that led to their eventual triumph, they thank God for what he has done. Some do not stop there. They also thank the human agents – family, friends, acquaintances, and even strangers – who participated in making their testimony an eventual reality. Underlying this public performance of gratitude to God and their community for what He has done is an acknowledgment that divine deeds require human vectors. My heart bursts with gratitude to everyone, from family and friends to various institutions, who supported me all through the process of writing this book.

First, I must thank my family for all the support I have received so far. I am greatly indebted to my aunt, Funmilola Akintobi, to my cousins, Damilola, Kemi, and Tobi Akintobi, who took the great burden of childcare off my hands while I carried out the fieldwork for this research, starting when my child was only six months old. I had to leave her with my aunt and cousins, and I never had to add worries of my child's welfare to the challenges of carrying out fieldwork. All through the years that this work took, they were always there to support me by providing childcare. I have not yet found enough words to express the depth of my gratitude. I should also thank Adeola Emasealu, "Sister D," for the help and support all through. She has always been there for me as a friend, sister, mother, defender, lawyer, advocate, and adviser.

My gratitude also goes to the people of various Pentecostal churches that I worked with throughout this project. I owe you for all the time you committed to interacting with me, and demonstrating your commitment to helping me succeed. I am also grateful to the pastors of various churches who not only acted as resource persons, but also connected me with those in administration and church departments. Without all that support, I would not be here. I am deeply grateful to Pastor Mike Bamiloye for his help and support. Also, thanks to Daddy Freeze (Ifedayo Olarinde), Oladipupo Daniel, and Olufemi Michael for the interaction.

In the time this project gestated, I have been blessed with the wisdom of my teachers and colleagues who committed intellectual and moral resources to this work at one point or another. Thanks to Dr. Joni Omi Osun Jones, whose nurturing hands shaped this work and its author; I am grateful to Dr. Charlotte Canning, Dr. Paul Bonin-Rodriguez, and Dr. Lisa Thompson for their support. In the years of working on this project, I have racked up a lot of debt to my teacher and now colleague, Dr. Toyin Falola. His interest in this publication work right from the day I concluded my doctorate has been unflagging. Without all his support, moral and material, none of these things would have happened.

My special gratitude also goes to Dr. Nimi Wariboko. It was not until I met you that I fully understood what Nigerian Pentecostals mean when they pray to meet their "destiny helper." You have been a great source of help to me. When I count my blessings, I count you thrice: at the beginning, at the end, and then I go back to the middle, and count you. Many levels of thanks to my wonderful oga, Dr. Ebenzer Obadare. At first, it was merely serendipitous that I met you in Ibadan that day. Over the years, I have come to see it as divine arrangement. Thanks for all the support.

To my friends who helped me in one way or another, I thank you all. I, however, cannot fail to mention Monisola Onaolapo, my dear friend of many years, for all her support. Thanks to my research assistant, Kalu Chibuike Daniel, for the work he did for me each time I called upon him. I cannot forget my friend, colleague, and editor, Amy Guenther, who pushed me to be clearer in my assertions as I worked on this project. Thank you, Amy. I am equally grateful to the friend community I refer to as "The Famous Five" Tolani Ogunsanya, Adenike Adeoye, Joannah Otashu, Angela Eluwa, and me. Thanks for all the laughs and the witticisms that helped to dilute all the tension of writing this work. Thanks to my friend and brother, Adedoyin Ogunfeyimi, the uber brilliant scholar. I will always be grateful we are friends. I am thankful to colleagues in the Department of African/African Diaspora Studies of the University of Texas at

Austin like Lisa Thompson and Cherise Smith for their generosity of spirit. At critical times in this work, they came through for me in ways that were really touching. I am grateful to you. My gratitude goes to Dr. Omoniyi Afolabi and Dr. Moyo Okediji. Thanks for always sending notes of encouragement and good wishes.

At some point through this work, I have enjoyed some benefits offered by institutions and the people who run them. I am grateful to colleagues that I met at *The Mellon School of Theater and Performance Research* in 2016, especially Rebecca Kastleman and Martin Puchner, for really invigorating sessions. Thanks to the American Association of University Women (AAUW) International, for the support that helped me at a crucial stage of this work. I am also grateful to the John Warfield Center in the University of Texas at Austin for the financial support. Thanks also to Jacob & Frances Sanger Mossiker Research in Humanities for supporting me when I needed it.

Finally, I am grateful to my husband, Marcellinus Ojinnaka, for his unflagging support. He not only encouraged me to push beyond myself when and where necessary, he also gave me the gifts necessary for this work to be done: the time and the space I needed to work for extended hours, undisturbed. Thank you for being a wonderful helper, lover, friend, and supporter. I could not have asked for better!

To all of you that helped and supported me, I say thank you over and over again. You are part of my testimony. You are my testimony.

Introduction: Power Identity: Politics, Performance, and Nigerian Pentecostalism

When I began the fieldwork for this research in Nigeria, one of the questions that I frequently confronted from the Pentecostal Christians to whom I introduced myself as a scholar of performance studies was the correlation between Pentecostalism and my academic discipline. In those moments, reeling out academic studies that have variously established that theater and religion have always been interwoven from as far back as Ancient Egypt and Greek societies would have, at best, elicited an indifferent shrug.[1] I could also have mentioned that religious rituals in African societies have always had dramatic elements; that in both profane and sacred settings, the communication of meaning to both human and divine witnesses takes place through repetition of symbolic actions. However, as someone raised in the Pentecostal culture myself, I knew that kind of academic explanation would likely backfire. Nigerian Christians, generally, are sensitive to allusions that their religious practices have any African syncretic elements. Pentecostals especially do not take kindly to the insinuation that their practices are not purely divinely inspired. To draw lines that connect what they do with "rituals," a terminology they associate with "pagan" practices rather than as a form of symbolic communication, was to lose them.[2]

The answer I often provided was that worship activities such as singing, dancing, preaching, speaking in tongues, miracle performance, hand laying, prophetic utterances, prayers, ecstatic worship,

---

[1] See, for instance, McDonald & Walton, *The Cambridge Companion to Greek and Roman Theatre*; Wise, *Dionysus Writes*.

[2] Albrecht in *Rites in the Spirit: A Ritual Approach to Pentecostal/Charismatic Spirituality* notes the same about Pentecostals in the USA, although they have a slightly different reason for the disavowal of "rituals." He says that to them, "rituals represents something 'dead', meaningless or even 'unscriptural', and 'unscriptural' mechanical religion." Rather than such a niggling term, they use less-charged expression such as "worship services," "spiritual practices," or "Pentecostal distinctives."

and so on were all performative in nature.[3] It is, therefore, worth studying these ritual activities as performance acts to understand the various rites through which people communicated with God, and how they navigated their identity as both Pentecostals and as political subjects. What they did within their churches mattered if one wanted to understand the contemporary Nigerian social character. Sometimes, I supplemented my answers with Bible verses. Often that was enough, although in some other cases I was further prodded to clarify. They could understand studying Pentecostalism as religion or sociology, but performance?

I learned to recalibrate my standard explanation to convince people that my conceptualization of Pentecostalism as performance was in no way pejorative or belittling of their faith practices. In fact, the approach underscored my taking them seriously enough to understand how they generated meanings through their actions. I tried to simplify my research by saying the disciplinary tools of performance studies are to critically investigate Pentecostalism: what they do, why, and what factors they contend while doing. My characterizing Pentecostalism as performance, I explained several times and in various ways, was in no way a judgment of the boisterousness of their worship activity or their general activities. It was so I could use the right analytical approach to examine their actions, the thoughts that created them, their assumption of their identity as social actors, and the transformations that occur when the truth of social conditions are dramatized through acts of fervent worship.

One of the pastors that I approached, a senior administrative member of one of the most prominent Pentecostal churches, was not to be easily moved. He said, "Performance?! You think we are playing here? No, we are not performing here. We, are making power happen. Even when you see us sing and dance, we are not playing. If we are performing anything at all, it is power! Power! We are a people of power! Power is our identity!" I was momentarily taken aback by the characterization of a religious identity category that sidestepped familiar essences of theology or doctrines, and pivoted straight to its ambitions. To say that for

---

[3] The range of activities are general to Christianity, but these listed activities are almost peculiar to Pentecostals. The Pentecostal liturgy and worship are quite diverse, and too inflected by local contexts for one to homogenize or universalize them successfully.

Pentecostals, power is the distinct marker and their means of self-differentiation means power is not only capable of activating social processes and coercing situations but also stands in the place of the "self," the one whose performances enacts or actualizes. The "I" of the identity is an embodiment of power and the body itself as a place of power inscription. His response gave me pause, and I was prompted to further think of his answer in several ways. My engagement with his response formed the direction I pursued in this book. I follow this self-conceptualization that construes identity primarily through the point of its desire, power, and expresses as much in multiple sites of social relations. Consequently, I explore seven theses on power throughout this book.

First, by telling me that power is the Pentecostal identity, he clarified how Pentecostals operate within a social milieu that affirmed and contested their desires for being, and how their faith practices continuously imbue the social matrix with saliences that also facilitate their performances of power. I was used to sights of people praying; eyes closed, fists bunched like a hammerhead and swung to crush the air and all the oppressive forces it harbors while they chanted "Power! Power! Power!" However, by directly stating that power was their identity, he had helped me apprehend the ideology that distinctly underwrote their ritual actions. At that point, I could fold up the research and go home since he already handed me the answer that I sought. However, I still had more work to do to clarify certain questions. If power is the identifying marker of the Pentecostal, what cultural practices constitute it? What are the histories, desires, knowledges, tools, and innate divergences of this identity, and how do they interact with other ideological elements that make up the society? How is the social milieu being transformed by the Pentecostal performance of their identity as the people of power? In talking about power as the Pentecostal identity, he also challenged me to consider its organization and performance across various levels. Definitely, that power cannot be uniformly performed across every stratum of the Pentecostal demographic. It would be instructive to see how people who stood at the social margins feel empowered through Pentecostalism.

Second, by using the present tense to tell me what they do – *we are performing power* – he alluded to the ritual activities through which they strove toward their desired status as permanently ongoing.

Cultural studies have typically explored identity along the lines of cultural sameness and strategic differentiation, raising questions of how people choose to see themselves in relation to other groups. As much as identity is construed based on the many ways that history is instrumentalized to generate an essence and mark the positioning of the self against an *other*, what makes it perceptible is the performance aspect. Its beingness requires a consistent series of action and stylized behavior to become what it is, or what it purports to be. Identity is not a given; its recognizability as a distinct category also depends on the consistency of performing it. If power is that distinctive marker of Pentecostals, it also means they act in a series of determining ways to articulate their striving to attain and embody that power. From an internal conviction of divine form of empowerment now conjugated into an external determination of identity, they impersonate an ideal through which they also intuit their "cosmically empowered identities ... a singular poetic impulse to bring self into being and manifests in acting."[4] Power performed is not only inscribed into the body, the persona too becomes all about power itself and all its actions are oriented toward confirming that defining identity. There is no thought or action that is not about acquiring and performing power.

Third, the nonstop nature of this identity performance also registers the flimsiness of power as it is performed. As I will show in the forthcoming chapters, the moral authority generated through Pentecostal power performance is continuously contested by various other people who seek their own power within the construct of Pentecostal power. The sense of immediacy and continuity in "we are performing power" also suggests a restless grasp for more power on the part of these subjects who become the place of power inscription. That coincidence of site with the end goals means they cannot *not* perform power. Their activities are means as much as the ends, and the Pentecostal subject has to be seen performing power perpetually. In discussing the power and authority Pentecostal leaders embody, political theorist Ruth Marshall, noted, "the authority and fortunes of pastors rise and fall. They are subject to close and critical scrutiny on the part of converts."[5] The social and ritual

---

[4] Mason, *The Performative Ground of Religion and Theatre*, 8–9.
[5] Marshall, *Political Spiritualities*.

activities that engender their power is transient, too fleeting and too variously challenged for it to be broadly accepted as a foregone conclusion. That fragility necessitates their performing power to sustain their perception as people of power.

The possibility that the power they gain can be lost just as easily means there is an element of paranoia always underlining their actions. They stoke anxieties that generate the impulse to develop more power to sustain what is already attained. Power identity is fluid and can be easily disassembled. Those for whom power has become their identity also have to keep doubling down on power practices to maintain that identity. Power has to be performed unceasingly because of the frequent destabilizing threats this identity faces from social forces. As power is hierarchical, it also has to compel both adulation and reverence, and remind people of its existence and what it can do. The repetition of these processes can lead to authoritarianism and crudeness in using the instruments that produce power. If performing power transforms one's social status and informs one's identity within a society, the processes by which that identity is established can also be the means of its disestablishment. The constant need to perform power will run into social conflicts and impasses that will delimit that power.

Fourth, production of the empowered self through performance is personally transforming and has social implications. As a religious movement whose doctrinal practices and vernacular are quite pervasive, especially in the urban areas, their social practices also condition political impulses. To a large extent, social practices also condition political impulses. Their theology of domination is explicitly confirmed in the way they try to control the social sphere, and their self-identification as the "people of power" thus makes complete sense. The cultural realm, notes historian Christina Klein, is that "privileged space in which politically salient meanings can be constructed and questioned, where social categories can be defined and delimited, where shared values can be affirmed and contested."[6] In that same cultural realm, indices of identity are established, performed, transferred, memorized, and reiterated.[7]

---

[6] Klein, *Cold War Orientalism.*
[7] Here, I allude to performance studies scholar, Diana Taylor, who said "performances function as vital acts of transfer, transmitting social knowledge,

Fifth, despite Pentecostal proponents having never hidden their intention to dominate the cultural arena, it is still striking that a faith movement can be defined by the will to power. Pentecostal ethicist Nimi Wariboko, speaking about the Pentecostal understanding of power that rationalizes a fixation on power is a form of identity, said, "knowing that … reality is split between the seen and unseen world … and extracting knowledge from the invisible realm to explain, predict, and control the visible world is an important identity marker for Nigerian Pentecostals."[8] Their fixation with supernatural power creates real-life consequences through manipulating the invisible. This was expected as Pentecostalism developed in the context of various kinds of crises of modernity, development, and identity.[9] For the youth population that poured into the urban centers in the 70s, Pentecostalism provided an identity by which to bypass provincial identities and embrace a new life in Christ along with other promises of upward mobility. Pentecostal faith not only "reconstituted the Christian identity under the hammer of failures and shortcomings of the Nigerian state and under the pressure of immense difficulties of economic survival,"[10] it also transcended a mere identity label of "Christian." Pentecostalism promised that the processes of conversion and transformation could "reconstitute their experience of the world."[11]

Sixth, power in Nigerian Pentecostalism is informed by inherited notions of power: the belief that supernatural forces undergird the manifestation of everything tangible, and access to this form of power will determine every other form of power, whether social, political, or economical. Nigerians have watched, and therefore implicitly understand, how these various forms of power have been performed through the years of authoritarian government and how the hegemonic performance of power reached into the transcendental to maintain its hold on the public. Pentecostals particularly have learned the dimensions of power – to achieve certain goals, as a condition of existence, and as a form of identity – and embodied the understanding that these three coexist, cofunction, and are mutually determining. When the pastor

memory, and sense of identity through reiterated, or what Richard Schechner has called 'twice-behaved behavior.'" Taylor, *The Archive and the Repertoire*, 2.

[8] Wariboko, *Nigerian Pentecostalism*, 39.
[9] Vaughan, *Religion and the Making of Nigeria*.
[10] Wariboko, *Nigerian Pentecostalism*, 32.
[11] Marshall, *Political Spiritualities*, 141.

said "power is our identity," he meant that the faith movement's pursuit of goals through various ritual and social performances has, over time, become both their unique self-presentation and self-recognition, as well as their existential condition. Both their goals and the conditions of their existence are reciprocal presuppositions that are diagramed and performatively enacted by identity. Pentecostals' identity not only points to these but also participates in their power and glory.

Finally, I consider the simultaneous rejection and acceptance of my characterization of Pentecostalism as a performance as equally instructive. This pastor's reaction, which Western theater scholars might identify as an "antitheatrical prejudice,"[12] (that is, the intuitive aversion to acts that are theatrical partly because its mimetic nature is associated with the art of "deception"), was understandable. If one viewed his objection as protecting his faith from being discounted as mere frivolity or artifice, it made sense that he resisted the idea of construing Pentecostal practices as play or ad hoc constructions of spectacle that might fall apart under a critical gaze. Yet, his unease was telling in other ways too. What repulses people and how they show it can effectively dramatize the social conflicts, tensions, and power negotiations ongoing in that society. The stage, whether the proscenium one of the traditional theater or the banal one on which we perform everyday life, can magnify broader historical struggles, the cultural shifts and political contentions that created such sensibility.[13] His acceptance that they do perform – although what they do is power – leads me toward the social history of Pentecostalism as a faith movement that has undergone several epochal shifts and has evolved to the point of describing itself by what it has achieved.

Performing Pentecostalism, Pentecostalism as Performance

At the early stages of this research, much of the study of Pentecostalism was being carried out in anthropology, history, religious studies, and political science. The were producing important work on techniques of Pentecostal religious practices ranging from invocatory prayers to mediated liturgies. While some of them touched

---

[12] Barish, *The Antitheatrical Prejudice.*
[13] Freeman, *Antitheatricality and the Body Public*, 2.

on the dramaturgical aspects of Pentecostal worship, and even applied performance theories in their studies, the elaboration of the creative dimensions of these performances that performance theory engagement would have highlighted was often missing. The religious social activities still out of range of scholarship focus are ones crucial to understanding the nature of the movement because they help critical reflection on the production and reception. The ones that I highlight here show Pentecostal religious performance are not all about collective obedience and social compliances to religious authority. Instead, they demonstrate more nuanced ideas of Pentecostal identity constructions. With the malleability of its theoretical constructs and applicability to virtually every cultural product, performance studies presented the best methodology to examine Pentecostal aesthetics, embodied actions, and political consequences.[14]

Excitingly though, ongoing studies in performance scholarship literature have begun to explore the nexus between the discipline and various religions, opening up more channels of understanding how the performative nature of religion – and its rituals – facilitates belief and seals believer identity. These wide-ranging works prompt us to pay close attention to how believers themselves increasingly understand religious activities – from worship to proselytization – as performative, and astutely use that level of conceptual awareness to their advantage.[15] Theater studies, these studies rightfully note, has always engaged the aspects of religion through a critical analysis of mutually evolved history and shared elements such as spaces, lighting, embodiment, aesthetics, and the dramaturgy of liturgy. Recent work by theater studies scholar David Mason, for instance, critiques the approach of theater and religion that takes one as reflecting the other to open up a path for understanding how their imbricated foundations powerfully express their mutual truths.

Several works from performance scholars have compellingly studied the relationship between theater and (mostly) Christianity just as theater scholars are engaging religion critically and providing a grid of thought broadly applicable to performance studies.[16] For instance, theater scholar Elizabeth Schafer has looked specifically at the

---

[14] Bial & Brady, "Introduction" in *The Performance Studies Reader.*
[15] Palacios, "Introduction: Performing Religion."
[16] For instance, there is Jill Stevenson's study of how the belief systems of evangelical Christians in the USA inflect their engagement of performance genres.

relationship between theater and Christianity, exploring their complex intersected histories as they navigated the borders of the real and realism.[17] She noted that theater can deliver an appearance of what is real through stagecraft, and that ability to mimic the real might unsettle belief. While scholars have trained their focus mostly on Christianity (especially in its nondenominated forms), others in the growing corpus of scholarship construe the category of religion in more encompassing ways.[18] Performer and scholar Cia Sautter, in exploring the performance of religion and the attendant effectual power of the sacred, attempts to free the sacred experience that can come through the performing arts from the compartments of the Western mind that experiences religion and performance as disparate.[19] In a similar vein, for performance scholars Claire Chambers, Simon du Toit, and Joshua Edelman, the meaning-making practices of religion do not only happen through abstract or formal theology, but performed ritual acts.[20]

These works are critical in understanding how contemporary scholarship is finding fresh convergences in the imbrication of theater/performance and religion beyond looking at the thrill of the former as a religious experience, or the rites of the latter as merely construed to satisfy instincts for entertainment.[21] Indeed, virtually any cultural or public practices can be studied as performance events, and the multiple perspectives of these works have been quite illuminating.[22] By collating the depth and intricate details of actions used to express one's faith, these works disentangle overlayered structures of meaning and point us to the larger imports of embodied religion being acted out in sacred and profane contexts. However, much work that purports to reconcile theology with embodiment and performance reveals itself as still wedded to classic Western ideas of construing religion as formal liturgy and practices of faith as lacking spontaneity. Approaches toward

---

[17] Schafer, *Theatre & Christianity*.

[18] An example will be Marvin Carlson's study of the conjunction of Islam and theater.

[19] Sautter, *The Performance of Religion*.

[20] Chambers, Edelman, & Toit, "Introduction" in *Performing Religion in Public*, 1–2.

[21] Childers, *Performing the Word*.

[22] Although not primarily a performance scholar, political theorist, Ruth Marshall, vigorously engaged the performative component of spiritual warfare by Pentecostal/Evangelical in her investigation of their modeling of truth. Marshall, "Destroying arguments and captivating thoughts."

performance of religion and spirituality that deploys performance as a methodological tool to free religion from the abstraction of dead-rigid dogmas supposedly challenges the binary between faith and reason, personal experience and rationality. This rediscovery of the liveliness of religion reflects concerns that are peculiar to Western societies and do not consider the ways African Pentecostal practitioners, for instance, have long abandoned orthodoxy and built livelier theology through their creative performances whether in the sacred space of church or just in daily life. Religious practitioners in the Pentecostal denomination self-consciously create for the worshippers, the "experiences designed to foster embodied beliefs that respond to specific devotional needs and priorities."[23]

While some of the contemporary scholarship of religion and theater/performance still grapples with how the theories of the latter can adequately illuminate the study of the former, Pentecostals have been unabashedly borrowing the tools and techniques of theater/performance to curate livelier religious experience and encounter for worshippers. Pentecostals, especially in Africa, may recoil at any suggestion that their activity has something to do with "theatre," "performance," or even "drama," yet, even a superficial study of their activities as they plan worship activities that would take place within the church (as well as online) and their reflexive analysis of each worship session says otherwise. Their careful construction of their religious leaders as persons who embody the power of God to the degree to which it appears in the church and among the congregation, their use of modern technology to enhance embodied experience, and the general ways they try to shape the event of church services, show how much they innately grasp their faith practices as a performance event.[24] Their attitude of seeing worship as a performance and planning accordingly (for both their present congregation and even prospective members) shows how much they appreciate the rich potential of performance to generate conceptual frameworks that motivate people and ultimately establish their power identity. With that in mind, it now behooves the researcher to

---

[23] Stevenson, *Sensational Devotion*, 4.

[24] This phenomenon, of course, is not limited to Africans. For instance, anthropologist James Bielo, explored how fundamentalist Christians created a theme park in Kentucky where the Bible story of creation is staged into an experiential encounter for the purpose of religious conversion, education, and of course, entertainment. Bielo, *Ark Encounter*.

study the level of political intelligence and aesthetic appeal at which they aim when they perform their faith through worship and social practices. Since they enrich their worship activities with similar instruments used by performance artists, scholars would only be taking their efforts seriously if their actions are examined from the critical lens of the theater/performance traditions and the artifices they consciously appropriate. To treat their creative output as performance is not to inquire about their ability to entertain, but to acknowledge the artistic and political intelligence of their efforts.

In recent times, the flexibility of performance as an analytical tool has made it more pronounced as an increasing number of works from across interdisciplinary aisles corral its theories to analyze social and political phenomena. From the social commentators who borrow the terminologies and deploy them rather casually, to academics who are pushed to reclaim ideas and refocus arguments, performance has become the go-to paradigm to explain the actions of politicians whether they are on television or Twitter, various sporting events, daily life, Instagram photos, news broadcasts, and weather reports. With so many possibilities, it is exciting to be a part of this conversation of burgeoning discoveries. Yet, the promiscuity makes the scholar of Pentecostalism hesitate to divine Pentecostal practice as performance without subordinating ineffable and elusive spiritual realities to theoretical paradigms that view all politics as theater merely created to be witnessed by an audience. As the pastor I mentioned earlier said to me when I told him that I was studying Pentecostalism as a performance, "You think we are playing here?" The righteous indignation that underlay the question has kept me mindful about how I read the discursive practices of worship and the political actions that emanate from them. As rites and social behavior are usually done as an act of faith, I understand the insistence on them being seen as inspirations that stem from their spirituality, rather than their spiritual practices evaluated as mere outward representational exchange.[25]

In this book, my conceptualization of Pentecostalism as a performance is an analysis of how the techniques and aesthetic effects of colorful Pentecostal practices inform practice, resonate with their subjective experiences, persuade, and elicit the behaviors that turn into political actions. Embodied faith propels the body to move in certain

---

[25] Dox, *Reckoning with Spirit in the Paradigm of Performance.*

directions, and performances carried out by a mass of people who subscribe to a faith movement such as Pentecostalism, necessarily moves even the body politic in radical ways. Such movements generate the spiritual forces that trouble, corrupt, disrupt, affirm, and ultimately restructure society's ethos. However, my interest in Pentecostal performance is not restricted to activities within church venues alone. This work also critically looks at the various sites of their action, where both the sacred and the profane combine into political behavior with transformative consequences. I employ performance as a framework for studying social situations and by "viewing them as performances, thereby facilitating a new sort of thinking about them."[26] By focusing on phenomena that clarify social interactions in Pentecostal culture, I also explore the creative means by which people express their identity as people of power and even expand the cultural ideas of empowerment. The evocative force of Pentecostal performance has had an inscriptive effect on the Nigerian social character. Faith has created acts and spectacles, and by engagement with them, have also highlighted the conflicts and social struggles that drove people to summon spiritual forces to transform reality in their favor.[27] Subsequently, they perform power to challenge discursive authorities that rule their lives.

Performance studies offer a unique approach to understanding how Pentecostalism, a faith movement deeply invested in drawing the power of the indwelling Spirit to determine temporal circumstances, to "live out" their faith in practical terms. Through performance, we can also conceptualize how the "micro-level of individual shows and the macro-level of the socio-political order ... productively interact."[28] As performance is primarily about bodies in action and the ways we witness them, this work explores the experiential and phenomenal dimensions of Pentecostal practices – both within and outside the church, but all of which are mounted in the propagation of their faith.

"Power Is Our Identity": Pentecostal Self-Recognition

Scholars of performance and power tend to locate the latter within a system of interactive signs embedded within the backdrop of social

[26] Shepherd, *The Cambridge Introduction to Performance Theory*, x.
[27] See, for instance, Asamoah-Gyadu, *Contemporary Pentecostal Christianity*; Ukah, *A New Paradigm of Pentecostal Power*.
[28] Kershaw, *The Politics of Performance*.

culture, and continuously stoked to hook into familiar structures of meaning. For my purposes here, I will focus on only two modes of performing power as they occur between the dominant and the dominated class, and then go on to demonstrate how both forms lead us to notions of power among African Pentecostals for whom "the object of political power is wealth and control over the channels of accumulation creates a logic in which the struggle for power at *every* level has to become a zero-sum game."[29] While Nigerians, as a modern nation-state, might not have a central organizing myth that binds its disparate ethnic and religious identities, yet there exists the mythos of power – that it ultimately flows from a transcendental source and the source legitimizes the human agents that possess it. By foregrounding both forms of power before describing Pentecostal power, I show how belief in the power in the name of Jesus drives Pentecostals to use the supernatural to coerce natural forces. When the contemporary wave of the Pentecostal movement burst on the Nigerian social scene around the 1970s, it came with promises of revival for those on the margins of society. Over time, the movement would acquire power of its own and even come to recognize itself by that power. To Pentecostals, power is the ability to transcend the limit of one's human ability, and it is essential to relationship between humans and God.[30]

The first form is the efficacy that occurs because a display of ritual activity has been presaged by myths and mutual beliefs in the ability of that power to perform. Power in this sense is not a thing or a material object, but is indicated through social constructions of reality and the structures of meaning built into the society. This structuring determines the bodies and the objects that will be considered sacred, which people's lives matter, boundaries of identities, and the ability to marshal the intensity of the forces of collective feelings toward certain causes and give those issues the weight of social importance. Usually vertical, this form of power reposes in institutions or in charismatic political figures who direct the rituals of investiture that legitimates authority, and public demonstrations of the command *of* and control *over* the public spaces, and also blend people, history, and events. The holders of symbolic power get to select what makes up social reality from an endless stream of historical materials, public memories, and

[29] Marshall, "Power in the Name of Jesus."
[30] Akinade, "Holy Dilemma," 154.

symbols. They also use institutional authority to curate what will be identified as culture, ethos and norms, and collective understanding of reality.

Power performance is a precursor to its coercive uses, and that is why witnessing such displays is important. The public's participation constitutes their identity as political subjects within a centralized political system, reinforces the moral order, and also confirms their understanding of who wields power within society as well as the specific members of the society that embody part of that power. Expression through dramas and spectacles provides the epistemological context whereby members of a community sense their place within the social order. In a study of how performances shaped politics in pre-modern societies, anthropologists and archaeologists Takeshi Inomata and Lawrence S. Coben, noted that "performance is characteristic of all known societies and ... theatre and spectacle are the contexts par excellence where power relations are alternatively established, celebrated, mocked and subverted."[31] Thus, they note, "theatre and spectacle are commentaries about the contemporary social order and metadiscursive acts."[32] Performances constitute the social order because the phenomena people are compelled to witness contain dense symbols that demonstrate the degree of their social relevance within the mix of signs and systems of power.

How power is performed and/or received depends upon the degree of the cohesiveness of the social backdrop. When sociologist Jeffrey Alexander describes power and the modes by which is performed in society, he elaborated on how it happens against the backdrop of the structures of culture, how they inform actions and also give them meaningful resonances.[33] These meaning-making processes are not to be taken as permanently stable; they are regularly enhanced through a spectacular restaging of those symbols. For holders of political powers especially, the augmentation of social symbols is sometimes dramatized through pomp and majestic displays that speak powerfully to people because, "the audience, its concentration on the impending performance channeled and sensitized by a strong emotion, is in a better position to be influenced, persuaded or manipulated by the actions they witness."[34] It is this illustrative display of performed

---

[31] Coben & Inomata, *Archaeology of Performance.*   [32] Ibid., vii.
[33] Alexander, *Performance and Power.*   [34] Garlick, *The Final Curtain.*

power that brings people to regard political power as almost sacred, and they normatively yield to the force of its authority.[35]

An instantiation of how power holders in the society try to create a cohesive system of signs is what historian Andrew Apter illustrated in his study of the second World Black and African Festival of Arts and Culture, FESTAC '77, that held in Lagos, Nigeria, in January/February 1977.[36] The grand festival celebrated global black art and culture during the years of the oil boom when international economic forces aligned in favor of the country and brought almost unprecedented prosperity. Through its captivating force, the grandeur of the gathering of black people and their diverse performance cultures from different parts of the world was a project of retrieving African history and pride. On one side, the splendor of the festival would erase what Africa had lost to the humiliating years of slavery, colonialism, and other historical events that have culminated in underdevelopment. On another side, Nigerian leaders who were at that time military dictators could – through the songs, dances, drama, and celebration of black spiritual essence – also sell themselves to the rest of the world as the holders of black power, wealth, and glory. Thus, FESTAC '77, with ostentatious black cultural displays, was purposely spectacular because of the political ends it needed to fulfill.[37] It is rather apposite that the bridge between tradition and modernity, an imperfect African past and the utopic future

---

[35] See, for instance, Nimi Wariboko's analysis of the nurture of sacred kingship through the rituals and festivals that regularly take place in Ile-Ife. In responding to Jacob Olupona's *City of 201 Gods*, a book that studies the various sacred activities in the city of Yoruba people's origin, Wariboko demonstrates how the power of the king is regularly deepened in the consciousness of the community through the myths and rituals that are publicly staged all year round. Olupona, *City of 201 Gods*; Wariboko, "The King's Five Bodies."

[36] The first one took place in Dakar, Senegal, in 1966.

[37] The splendor of celebration of FESTAC '77 festival illustrated how Nigeria intended to objectify newly found power along racial lines. The production of these performances extracted from local stories and myths, the global Pan-African ideology of black destiny, and also took place at a temporal juncture when international forces were productively interfacing with their economic trajectories resulting in excess of revenue that boosted the power of the nation-state. By showing the Nigerian and foreign audience different stunning displays, the holders of power within Nigeria also produced the specific images which people's imaginative faculties would further multiply to eventually discern the full extent of their coercive forces. The various public exhibitions that a nation-state's agents occasionally put up in the celebration of political power are efficient mechanisms of performing power.

that Nigeria and its leaders desired to illustrate the country's emergence as a nation rapidly moving to modernity, culminated in the building of a grandiose theater structure, the National Theatre, in Lagos.[38]

As performance studies scholar Diana Taylor noted in her study of public spectacles in Argentina, such displays by state agents are a powerful efficacious technique of forging an inherent notion of national identity. They stir a longing in the people (and also manipulate it), bring the spectators insight into what is being enacted, invite them to move between the demarcating lines between actor and spectator. The state can do all this and still deny people access to power.[39] These public events and rituals condense the symbols that people already know and understand, and strengthen existing meanings and their interpretations. They also act to "build(s) up those continuities of language and performance that locate and or, by means of the event of the drama, the storyline of retrieved history, and the logic of a projected future, a reconstitution of the body politic."[40] This form of power often seeks to normalize hierarchies. For sociologist David Apter, when these performances are at their best, they also "enable politics as theatre to endow a particular space with a certain clarity, miniaturing, focusing, concentrating and intensifying public attention, by magnifying a symbolic register."[41]

The various staged displays put up during those festivals are not the "power" itself; these spectacles and spectacular performances are both an objectification of power and an arrow pointing toward the sources of power in the society. According to postcolonial theorist Achille Mbembe, state power creates

through its administrative and bureaucratic practices, a world of meanings all of its own, a mastercode which, in aiming for a primary centrality, also, and perhaps paradoxically, governs the logics of constitution of all other meanings within these societies ... attempts to institutionalize its world of meanings ... to make that world fully real, turning it into a part of people's common sense.[42]

---

[38] Apter, *The Pan-African Nation.*   [39] Taylor, *Disappearing Acts."*
[40] Apter, "Politics as Theatre," 227.   [41] Ibid.
[42] Mbembe, "The Banality of Power and the Aesthetics of Vulgarity in the Postcolony."

It was not altogether surprising that the national theater, a huge architectural monument put up to host the spectacular performances of FESTAC '77, would metonymize the power of the military government in power at the time.[43] In 1973, General Yakubu Gowon signed the contract for Bulgarian engineers to build Nigeria a theater that looked like "a giant crown rising out of the earth, as if linking the wealth of the land – its chthonic traditions and subterranean oil – with national territory and sovereignty."[44] By the time the FESTAC '77 festival took place, Gowon had been ousted in a coup, but that did not stop the diadem that made up the architecture of the theater from being nicknamed "Gowon's cap." The image of him and his military cap had been inscribed into the minds of the populace so much that his apparition appeared in the site where military government forces staged culture to miniaturize their power.[45]

This conflation of performance space with the power of the military government shows that the public dramatizations are quite efficacious in impressing an audience. But it does not end there. The drawing out of public acts and scenes in these grandiose performances can reveal those who are marginal to the construct of the culture being symbolically staged. Such theater, along with its ritual ceremonies and pageantries, is ultimately about celebrating of some kind of victory – whether won or needing to be sustained – and that is why marginalized people experience these displays as clarifying moments. By watching the plaited components of the performance and "contemporary ideological traditions with the voices of that tradition as the exemplars of the public," they also realize their contributions to the polity and other civic demands placed on them are "radically disconnected."[46] Even though staging of splendor can be entertaining, it can also evoke terror and revulsion when it dawns on people that the myths being staged in the public sphere are exclusive of their histories and realities, and it is upon their bodies the victories being celebrated have been – and will

[43] The design of the national theater was a replica of a similar one in Bulgaria, the Palace of Culture and Sports in Varna. See https://nationaltheaternigeria.com/h3/about-us/
[44] Apter, *The Pan-African Nation*, 47.
[45] By the time the festival took place, there was another military administrator in place, General Olusegun Obasanjo, whose head too would come to metonymize the National Theatre. During Obasanjo's time, the theater was called "Obasanjo's head."
[46] Coleman, "Elections as Storytelling Contests," 175.

continue to be – tested when the holders of this power need to push beyond allowable limits to preserve the integrity of the articles of this power.[47]

This insight produces a crisis that leads to a breakdown of constructed social cohesion and ultimately leading to the second form of power performance: the marginalized rise to demand their right to power through radical performances. Having now been inspired to be an active participant, they try to wrench their suppressed narratives out of the suffocating grip of official power even at the cost of the total destruction of traditions and social practices, and the public artefacts that monumentalize them. Confronted with the violence, marginality, erasure, and disempowerment that underwrite the public performance of power, these underdogs get restless and begin to push a counter-performance with which political power has to reckon. Performance is a particularly powerful medium for this self-assertion as – according to postcolonial performance scholar Nandi Bhatia – its "visual focus, emphasis on collective participation and representation of shared histories, mobility, potential for public disruption, and spatial maneuverability impart yet another layer to the cultural investments of colonial and postcolonial texts in framing, organizing and presenting alternative stories."[48]

What thus follows are radical acts by the excluded to denaturalize their places within the canon of social influences, and also arouse the public to their existence and the importance of their epistemologies too. They, the disempowered, resist their subjugations by turning their marginalized conditions into innovative forms of performance that counter existing performances of power. These counter-performance s take an unruly turn, comprising minuscule everyday revolutions to slash through the forces of ideological and hegemonic power.[49]

---

[47] In Nigeria, it is said that the marginalized people of the Niger Delta community did not know how badly they had been robbed of their natural resources that had been taken to fund Nigeria until they arrived in the nation's capital during a national rally, saw the splendor the country could afford at their expense, and they took to militancy. It is not enough to assert that the "emotional responses of the participants and audience are never homogenous, and they may at once involve positive and negative feelings, as well as disinterest," these instants also illustrate to them – as the Niger Delta case illustrates – that they were being shortchanged. Coben & Takeshi Inomata. *Archaeology of Performance*, 15.

[48] Bhatia, *Acts of Authority/Acts of Resistance*, 3.

[49] Scott, *Weapons of the Weak*.

Without being as disruptive, polemical, confrontational – or as scholar of black performance, Thomas DeFrantz puts it, "to sing against the grain of the other instruments"[50] – they would more likely swim unnoticed within the fast-moving streams of other cultural practices. With mental and moral clarity of their positions, they are spurred to innovate dissident tactics, eccentric actions, renegade behavior, insurrectional acts, transgressions, manias, and various other antisocial and anti-normative cultural expressions to undercut the totalized powers of symbolic authorities. Since the goal is to challenge existing ideologies that exclude their realities, there has to be a destabilization of the normative order. Performance, whether the theatrical one enacted on stage or as a series of cultural practices, becomes a site of contesting power and political struggles against the ruling order.[51] They demonstrate their power as agents through their dramatized resistance politics that rupture the stable meanings embroidered into the social fabric.

While dominant power stages public spectacles to instruct on who is to be feared and what will be done to protect authority, the oppressed's counter actions and provocative critiques of powerful forces curtail absolute authority. Social acts that confront the performance of authority with resistance delimit norms, call attention to social evils, and incite the public to a yearn for a new order through mobilizing toward transformative actions.[52] One of such instances is the case of East Africans who turned the colonial Christian theater and its pacification agenda on its head and subversively used the same theatrical traditions and morality lessons colonizers bequeathed them to center their own local stories.[53] By making use of indigenous traditions and

---

[50] DeFrantz & Gonzalez, "Introduction" in *Black Performance Theory*, 6.

[51] In the critical and creative works of theater scholars/practitioners such as Bertolt Brecht, Ngugi wa'Thiongo, Femi Osofisan, Augusto Boal, Wole Soyinka, and August Wilson, the political transformation ignited on the theater stage has radical potentials that can carry over to social and political life. The eyes of the dominated, having been opened by witnessing displays of power, makes it a mission objective to denaturalize the despotic visions that has tucked them within the marginal corners of the social spheres and designate such as their "natural" lot.

[52] Bhatia, *Acts of Authority/Acts of Resistance*, 3.

[53] Okagbue, *Resistance and Politics in Contemporary East African Theatre*. Also see Samuel Kasule's similar study that showed how theater continued to be a useful form of political engagement in postcolonial Uganda where, faced with a murderous and absolutely tyrannical government, people instrumentalized theatrical performances to stand up to a brutal government.

culture, the colonized subjects also ingeniously made political performances of resistance meaningful at an instinctual level for those steeped
in the culture.[54] Another example of such resistance politics is the
"tactical performance" of civil rights advocates in 1960s USA. These
protestors demonstrated their power even within a social sphere
actively trying to obliterate them. They came up with innovative techniques, such as passively letting themselves be beaten without fighting
back, that subverted the tactics authorities pulled up from institutional
memory and used to suppress dissent.[55]

For scholar of black performance studies Daphne Brooks, this
quest for calling attention to one's difference in the worldview of
crushing political authority takes the strategic forms of anti-realistic
cultural expression and innovation techniques that rupture or override the placid surfaces of a normative sphere. She says of black
cultural performances and its unique radical approaches, "rather
than depending on conventional realist methods to convey the
humanity and value of black subjectivity ... black producers ...
perform narratives of black culture that resist the narrow constraints
of realist representation."[56] As these actors occupy a marginal position within the structures of power in society, they truly have to
resort to unconventional methods to assert their presence. Without
nonconformism, their action will not get past the deadweight of
traditions and self-justifying bureaucracy. Thus, such performances
typically comes with excess—which could be in form of noise or
vulgarity. Whenever the society eventually re-fuses, it is sutures up
into its cultural fabric the dissident elements its marginalized subjects
bring to the mix.

This last detail brings me to the boisterous ways contemporary
Pentecostalism is performed in the Nigerian social sphere, and through
which they spectacularly demonstrate their fixation with obtaining
power. Pentecostal performance of power encompasses both the totalizing actions of the dominant and the confrontational tactics of the
dominated. On one hand, it mimics the trappings of power as exhibited
by the privileged power class and, paradoxically, also inhabits the
space of the marginalized to push for more power. This ability to be

---

[54] Odom, *Yorùbá Performance, Theatre and Politics.*
[55] Bogad, *Tactical Performance.*   [56] Brooks, *Bodies in Dissent*, 6.

simultaneously powerful and to still fight for power from the position of an embattled party has enabled their continuous dominance in various cultural realms—political, economic, and cultural—and consequent shift in social relations.

As have been noted by its historians, the current wave of Nigerian Pentecostalism gained traction around the 1970s in university campuses where young people began to form church fellowships. These young people would enter public transport vehicles or stand in street corners to loudly proclaim the gospel and urged people to be "born again." What they lacked in formal theological training, they made up for in passion and their belief in the authorizing power of God's Spirit. In his account of the Pentecostal and Charismatic revivals in Nigeria, one of the pioneers of campus evangelism in Nigeria, Austen Ukachi, noted how the FESTAC '77 celebration was, to them, an open invitation of demonic forces into the country. Rather than see a festival of black grandeur the military leaders intended, what they saw was a celebration of African paganism and solicitation of demons from all over the black world into Nigeria.[57] To them, this festival that celebrates African culture along with its "pagan" practices represented a moral and temporal retrogression. The historical festival—particularly its featuring of black religious and spiritual culture in the diaspora—although meant to capture the essence of black cultural power and proudly celebrate it before the world, registered to them as demonism. Rather than racial pride, they saw a conflation of transcendental and political power, and how wielding the composition could truly make things happen, but against them as Christians. With the mentorship and nurturance of missionary Rev. Sydney G. Elton, they motivated fellow Christians on the necessity of praying for Nigeria over issues such as "revenue allocation, national elections, and at other times encourage Christian

---

[57] The festival was a month-long event and it featured a spectacular celebration of African music, art, and religions. The event attracted thousands of people from Africa and the diaspora, with about fifty-six countries represented and famous artists like Stevie Wonder, Miriam Makeba, and others performing. For Christians, however, the celebration of African indigenous religions at the festival was considered to be a deification of satanism, a glorification of idolatry. Nigeria's subsequent economic misfortunes and corruption have been attributed to this misadventure with evil spirits and has become the popular lore. Ukah, "Emplacing God," 351–368.

students to participate in campus politics."[58] From campus politics, this group would graduate to contend national politics where the power that was at stake had far more potency in coercing social realities.

For a faith movement whose formative contours took place within the context of political instabilities, the Pentecostals that emerged, especially from the 1990s to the present, were more politically conscious. They appeared on the cultural scene with a confrontational attitude determined to contend for the power with which political authorities had dehumanized society for so long. The divine mission was to cause some seismic shifts and also move the tectonic plates of culture and history in the direction of God. There was no question of them appearing as genteel Christians who had come to respectably negotiate an inscription of their existence into the collective ethos. Any other approach except the one that sought domination would have been impractical in Nigeria's postcolonial context where power is variously contested in every sphere as a war. Besides, power and politics in Nigeria are treated as warfare, with a clear definition of who is a friend and who is an enemy.[59] Without power, one lacks access to "extracting and allocating resources from the *commons* that are needed to live a fully human life."[60]

Powered by the name of Jesus, they punctuated the atmosphere with noisy prayers, evangelical outreach programs, their beliefs in the metaphysical, and the victorious shouts of hallelujah over those dark forces.[61] Church historian Ogbu Kalu noted that Pentecostal youths arrived on the cultural stage to contest the traditional ways of obtaining power – through witchcraft, sorcery, ancestral cults, and covenants. Partly because they were largely also disempowered political subjects, they angled for a form of power and authority that "rests on divine inspiration, and not on an influential position in society."[62] Their mission was to contend for the amalgam of political and spiritual

---

58   Ukachi goes on to narrate how, partly in response to the demonic invasion of the
      country by the proponents of the festival, they formed the Christians Students
      Social Movement of Nigeria (CSSM now CESM) on May 7, 1977. They began
      to hold prayer conferences to sensitize believers on the need to pray. Ukachi, *The
      Best Is Yet to Come*, 297.
59   Wariboko, *Nigerian Pentecostalism.*   60   Ibid., 45.
61   Adeboye, "Explaining the Growth and Legitimation of the Pentecostal
      Movement in Africa," 25–39; Ojo, "Pentecostalism and Charismatic
      Movements in Nigeria."
62   Kalu, *African Pentecostalism*, 113.

power that the country's authoritarian leaders wielded.[63] As the pros- elytization efforts undertaken by the earliest converts began to gain ground, the movement's growing power became evident through the compelling spectacle of a massive sea of heads that gathered at crusade grounds to hear the word of God and pray. Gradually, as their estab- lished churches boomed and sought divine power to challenge the crisis of meaning and the futility of existence in postcolonial and post–civil war Nigeria, their activities became quite noticeable. This movement sought to recreate reality and drew from their repertoire of social and spiritual epistemologies to create the scope of meanings that would reconstruct social ethics. Such political action was meant for them "to begin anew," to instigate a fresh start since the re-fusion of the ruptured opened liminal spaces to them. Given how much Pentecostals are invested in using their embodied actions to reverse contrary social cir- cumstances, there is no performance of the self in everyday life for them that is not simultaneously a performance of power, a distillation of their conviction – who they are, what they do, and their efficacy to change the world – into quotidian actions. With such gravity of belief in their ability to coerce even intractable existential reality in their favor, their social behaviors become a symbolic investment in the economy of transform- ing faith. They not only identify as people *of* power, they also identify *with* power, particularly political power whose apparatuses and affect- ive force they frequently mimic. In the coming chapters, I reflect on Pentecostalism's emergence as a cultural force at the intersections of faith and power. By demonstrating the kinetics of their identity politics, and their brokerage of the power they have found in the name of Jesus, I narrate how their performance of their social and sacred selves has defined the Nigeria social and political culture.

The Researcher as a Pentecostal

Being a Pentecostal for a long time was greatly beneficial in pursing this project. Having joined a Pentecostal church at age fifteen when I first

---

[63] Jeffrey Alexander also observed in his study of performance as a generating force of power that, "Power comes into being when social actors exercise their agency. It is subtle and complex, often of exquisite indirection, a process that is not all that different from how dramatic actors project the power of their characters in a play." Alexander, *Performance and Power*, 3.

followed my mother to a church in Ibadan that she had just discovered and was enthusiastic about, I had been part of the faith movement long enough to understand certain dynamics. Thus, I began my fieldwork among family and friends who introduced me to other people, especially those who had administrative roles in their respective Pentecostal churches. Most of them were quite welcoming, and our relationship got better each time I proved my Christian bona fides. But Also because I was no longer based in Nigeria, I also used a research assistant, Kalu Daniel Chibuike to conduct some interviews for this work, particularly the ones with the artists in Chapter 5. Sometimes Kalu would conduct an interview for me, and by the time I returned to Nigeria, I would have had enough insight on an issue to do other rounds of interview. That model saved me some transatlantic trips and the hassles of having to frequently call interviewed people back to clarify one or two things. This network of family and friends kept working for me until year 2020 when I finally put the last full stop to the writing of this book. Some of the interviews featured in several chapters, I must note, were anonymized to protect the identity of the respondents.

Another factor that helped this work advance was my weekly news-paper column with *PUNCH* Nigeria, which I have been writing since 2008, and I have some reputation as a result. In my weekly articles, I have been an unsparing critic of leadership and political power in Nigeria and Africa. I have criticized both political and religious leaders whose actions have been a major impediment to African growth and development, and my criticisms affected – both positively and negatively – the way some people related with me while I was carrying out the fieldwork. The positive aspects were the times prior recognition opened some doors for me, while the negative parts were those few times some people connected the columnist with the researcher and instantly became defensive about their country, religion, identity, and religious practices. In some cases, someone I just met would give me a rejoinder to a past article I had written and there were a few times that some of the interview responses felt like they were responding to me the columnist, not the researcher. Over time and as I had repeated discussions with some people I surveyed, I noticed some of that attitude smoothened out considerably.

Chapter Breakdown

In Chapter 1, Demons and Deliverance: Discourses on Pentecostal Power, I use a close reading of staged/fictional performances allied to the Pentecostal movement to lay out the history and nature of Pentecostalism, describe its preoccupation with power, and also showcase the successes of performing power identity. This chapter also argues that understanding Pentecostal performance of power identity entails not just looking at the practices conducted in the church or the structure of religious activities, but also within the theatrical activities and drama productions about demonic encounters that are staged to boost the faith of Pentecostals. The mediatized accounts of spiritual warfare narrated to Pentecostals by drama ministers are often morality tales, but they are also strategic to the reading of Pentecostal social history and ritual actions. Through them we can discern the demons that haunt the social body at a particular period of history, and let their demonic specters give form to the anxieties that irk people. In this chapter, I chronicle the Pentecostal trajectory and their demonstrated desire for power through two television dramas about deliverance from satanic attacks, *Agbara Nla* (The Ultimate Power) and *Abejoye* (The King Maker). Both were produced by the same Christian film company, the Mount Zion Faith Ministry, across about three decades. The differences in how both dramas capture the performance of exorcism are instructive in understanding how far the Pentecostal faith has traveled as a social practice and how they have achieved their power identity over this period of time.

In Chapter 2, "What Islamic Devils?!": Power Struggles, Race, and Christian Transnationalism, I explore the dynamics of political theology as it crosses the bounds of nationhood. Pentecostalism understands that spiritual and social power without political power is limited in its ability to coerce, and so it contests for power through spiritual warfare and active partisan politics. This chapter is an exploration into the nitty-gritty of the politics of Nigerian Pentecostal spirituality: confronting Islam, the other religion that contends power; the local politics of faith and ethnicity; and how all these dynamics of sustaining the power identity manifest in their adoration of the forty-fifth president of the United States, Donald Trump. Sociologist Ebenezer Obadare already argues, we cannot understand the ways Pentecostalism has impacted Nigerian politics without going back to where "the dawn of democratic rule in 1999 coincided with the triumph of Christianity over its historical rival, Islam, as a political force in Nigeria."[64] While

[64] Ibid.

Pentecostals in Nigeria and leading religious authorities might have taken up considerable power since 1999 – the beginning of the Fourth Republic in Nigeria, that is – they still have to contend for it along the matrices of ethnic and national identity. This chapter takes the idea of Pentecostal Republic across space and time by looking at the roles of powerful pastors in the 2015/2019 general elections, how the election was "lost" and how a congregation deprived of a key source of symbolic power instruments derives vicarious joy from looking to Trump as the "Christian president" Nigeria missed in 2015.

In Chapter 3, "Touch Not Mine Anointed": #MeToo, #ChurchToo, and the Power of "See Finish" is an analysis of what could happen when the performance of power identity through the production of image is ruptured. Here, I look at how a pastor stages his power identity through visuality, and how in the wake of the global *#MeToo* movement, his flow of visual signs and symbols to the audience was crucially undercut by the counter-power of women's stories. The necessity of continuously being in the public eye and performing one's power means the inscription of power identity on collective psyche also facilitates a critical reception of their persona. When leaders perform power by regularly thrusting themselves or their virtual images in front of their audience, they also become overexposed. The "#MeToo" events in Nigeria also show how people who have performed power to the point of embodying power will double down on the use of power to sustain their identity.

In Chapter 4, Everything Christianity/the Bible Represents Is Being Attacked on the Internet!": The Internet and Technologies of Religious Engagement I move toward the public contestation of power with powerful pastors through a crucial aspect of asserting power: money. This chapter illustrates a revolt against pastors through the critical examination of the aftermath of what was dubbed "The Great Tithe Debate," a battle between Online Air presenter, Ifedayo Olarinde (known as Daddy Freeze), and most of the famous Pentecostal pastors. If the identity of Pentecostals is power, then the rise of modern technology has provided the means for which ordinary people on social media can duel with religious authority. Pentecostalism has frequently studied pastors' influence, and one of the focal points of analysis is their ability to build immense financial power through skillful solicitation of their congregants' generosity. With the ubiquity of technology, contenders threaten pastors' authority to build financial capital through the established ways of operating symbolic means. These contenders stage their own shows, demonstrating how they have equally been empowered to tap into the same symbolic instruments that generate power for their leaders. This development troubles not just the Pentecostal pastorate but their followers as well.

In Chapter 5, "God Too Laughs and We Can Laugh Too": The Ambivalent Power of Comedy Performances in the Church, I investigate the trend of Nigerian Pentecostal churches interspersing church programs with comedy performances. I look at performance of power beyond acquisition and contestation to how power identity of authority figures could be affirmed publicly and contested privately. Comedy performance has consistently been treated as a site of resistance by the marginalized subject, but my study of comedy in Pentecostal churches shows some complications in this analysis of the art form. Using both ethnographic methods in my various fieldwork interviews with "gospel comedians" (as some refer to themselves), I consider exchanges that constitute power identity whose radicality is not found in the public sites but in the backrooms where negotiations take place between the artist and the producers.

In Chapter 6, "The Spirit Names the Child": Pentecostal Futurity in the Name of Jesus, I show how naming rituals are a source of Pentecostal power and influence, and how this will remain strong for a long time as its values are invested in children as futurity. Much of this book is about a politics of identity that is not primarily construed along the lines of ancestry and the familiar markers such as ethnicity, nationality, class, etc., but the object of desire. This chapter shows that Pentecostals do not entirely dispense with ancestral or familial modes of identification; they supplant them in creative ways that show their power within social culture. To illustrate how the Pentecostal power is invested in the rhetoric of naming, I study an aspect of Pentecostal identity-building – giving both oneself and one's children names that include "Jesus" (or "Jesu" in Yoruba) to fully embed the social and spiritual atmosphere of the society with their values. The Pentecostal onomastic, I note, is thus a sonic and systematized politics of societal ordering and contestation of spaces. The antiphonies of names as a process of "call and response" is the interaction of the many "transcendences" of Africa: histories – past and present; worlds – human and supernatural; cultural beliefs systems – indigenous and appropriations; all of which jumble and are manifested through Pentecostal onomastics.

In the concluding chapter, Power Must Change Hands: COVID-19, Power, and the Imperative of Knowledge, I note that the COVID-19 pandemic broke while this book was being completed and, therefore, I offer my reflection on the pandemic and Pentecostal power. In my description of how the Pentecostal establishment responded to the pandemic, I argued that what that apocalyptic event revealed was that the forms of power invested in and acquired over the years did not anticipate the world-changing event of the COVID-19. As a result, leaders showed they had no immediate answer for the situation other than resort to conspiracy theories and myths of their embattlement that did not quite stand up to the scale of the demands of the historical event.

As a cultural movement, Pentecostalism has brought together millions of Nigerians, both within the country and the diaspora, united by faith in the Son of God, Jesus Christ, and the empowering ideology of the embodied power of the immanent Holy Spirit. The conviction of empowerment has had an animating force. Along with other cultural factors, it propelled them to actions that marked a shift in how they experience or engage diverse political issues of the day. This dynamic Pentecostal interplay of religious and political actions has invigorated the social and political spheres, and actively reshaped the ways various politics is engaged at various levels. Performance artist and scholar Lance Gharavi noted in his argument that religion is not separate from social life but imbricated into the cultural context. Both are, he says, "formed by and through that context, its performances and discourses."[65] Indeed, as an ineluctable part of the cultural context, faith has been comprehensible by watching its public staging in the divergent social spheres that Pentecostals occupy, understanding the identity complexes of those who witness faith acts being performed, and the diverse effects produced in spectators across the social spectrum. In reading faith as performance, other aspects of social culture – such as the organized pattern of sentiments, dictating impulses, moral inflections, and the actions that make us amenable to other actions – are equally highlighted.[66] Throughout this book, by bringing the analytical tools of performance studies to analyze Pentecostal events, I have explained how these private convictions translate to public performances, calcification of identity, formation of subjective ideals, and even contestation with religious authority.

---

[65] Gharavi, "Introduction" in *Religion, Theatre, and Performance*.
[66] Shapiro & Barnard, *Pentecostal Modernism*.

1 | *Demons and Deliverance: Discourses on Pentecostal Power*

She was the about the most familiar diabolic spectacle of the Nigerian 1990s, a distinctive cinematic creation that combined decades of folkloric and popular cultural imagination of the devil and its operation in human spaces. Yet, she felt uniquely novel in her emblematizing of evil within the coordinates of Christianity, an African supernatural milieu, and the cinematic engravings of the perception of good and evil.[1] Ayamatanga – that was her name – was made up to have a moderately dark visage. She was not only polylingual, she also mixed human languages with that of demons. Ayamatanga possessed a raucous and mocking laugh that spoke the voices of a legion of demons through millions of TV sets.[2] For those who followed the TV series by the Mount Zion Faith Ministries International, *Agbara Nla* (1993), Ayamatanga was an image of the evil demonic specters that they had always known existed in the supernatural sphere. The television series and its representation of the devil transformed evil into an apprehensible human character, evoking similar feelings of dread derivable from watching a horror film. So compelling was the teleseries that the streets would empty out every week as people sat in their homes to watch the next installment. The Ayamatanga effect on public imagination at broadcast time was quite impactful.[3]

---

[1] As Rosalind Hackett notes, during this period, works by popular American deliverance specialists such as Derek Prince, Rebecca Brown, Marilyn Hickey, and Lester Sumrall were also widely available. All of these influenced local cultural producers of demonic encounters. Hackett, "Is Satan Local or Global?," 113.

[2] The impact of *Agbara Nla* was also partly due to the paucity of TV entertainment content at the time. *Agbara Nla* preceded the liberalization of the media and subsequent private ownership of media houses. There were quite few television channels in 1999, mostly government owned. With viewing options constricted, the drama and its original storytelling circulated across the country and became quite popular.

[3] Adelakun, "Pentecostal Panopticism and the Phantasm of 'The Ultimate Power.'"

Ayamatanga had possessed the body of a covetous born-again Christian, Bose. Through the somatic agency of Bose, Ayamatanga explained her motives to both Bose's pastor and the viewing audience. Her persona's contemptuous malevolence of divine power – and to an extent, her ability to repel prayer – made Ayamatanga fascinating enough to be launched into the public imagination as a material representation of evil. She was "an experience of dread,"[4] the haunting fear of finding oneself in a place of helplessness, and the threat of what could befall those that slipped through certain margins of spiritual protection. The climax of the series came when Ayamatanga had to be exorcised. God told her pastor that He had already converted a sorcerer, Isawuru, who lived in a village called Muwonleru, for that purpose. Isawuru, now called Paul Esupofo,[5] was the chosen "deliverance minister" for Bose. Both the pastor and Bose's husband went to the village to fetch Paul Esupofo and bring him to the city, in Lagos.

Paul Esupofo, played by the young actor Mike Bamiloye made up as an old man with grey hair and costumed in a simple attire of a village dweller, entered the house. He was shown the sparsely furnished bedroom where Bose lay on the bed with her hands tied to the bed poles, and her face covered with blood from her self-inflicted wounds.[6] The demon, noticing the power Paul Esupofo embodied, was threatened enough to put up some fight to intimidate him right from the door. Paul Esupofo would not be frightened. He had come in with the confidence of a man whose years of sorcery had given him an insight into the entire gamut of the devil's mischief. Now he had found a new source of agbara – power, that is – in Jesus Christ, and it was the ultimate one.

As anthropologist Robin Horton indicated in his study of the Aladura church movement – precursors of the Pentecostal

---

[4] Alford, *What Evil Means to Us*, 3.
[5] (Meaning: Esu – which Yoruba translate as "the devil" – has come to nothing). As has been variously argued, Esu, a Yoruba local deity, is not the equivalent of "the devil" as conceived by Judeo-Christian theology. Substituting Esu for the devil in translating the Bible might have made the Christian theology more relatable and eased the work of missionaries, but it destroyed the whole ethical system on which the concept of Esu was based. Christians, especially, have continued to translate Esu as the devil. As is evident in this name, "Esupofo," Esu is still being judged for a crime he did not commit.
[6] This scene is reminiscent of the film *The Exorcist*. In my interview with Mike Bamiloye, the founder of the Christian group that made the series, he confirmed that the scene was inspired by *The Exorcist*.

movement – although agbara translates to "power" in English, it also has a traditional meaning for those who speak Yoruba. Power is transcendental and coerces reality to one's ends. When translated into the semiotics of Pentecostalism, it is "the power of God and the spirits as manifested in the space-time world, either directly or through the medium of religious leaders."[7] Power is a compelling force, but it is also understood to be in gradations. As they say in Nigeria, "power pass power." The Pentecostal quest is, and always has been, to embody power at its highest level. For instance, when the English-language version of the series later made for non-Yoruba-speaking audiences and African internationals was released, it was titled *The Ultimate Power*. "The ultimate" quantifies the degree of power they are fixated on: the one at the apogee.

In the episode, Paul Esupofo engaged Ayamatanga in a fierce spiritual interaction that saw him praying fervently on TV, and reeling out invocatory scriptures from the Bible to disarm the kingdom of the devil in both the film and also in the imagination of the enraptured viewer.[8] As Paul Esupofo prayed, he was shown to transcend into the kingdom of evil where Ayamatanga and other demon spirits lived. In the spirit realm, he appeared wearing an all-white costume, his head wrapped in a white headdress, and holding a sword. The demons were costumed in red and black, with a shiny star embroidered on their attire. Ayamatanga herself was wearing a long red dress, her long woven hair reaching as far as her waist.[9] There, Paul Esupofo fervently prayed with the sword in his hand raised to the heavens as he instigated the power of God to release Bose from the hold of those captives. As the Bible already metaphorized the word of God as "the sword of the spirit," having a sword in his hand as he invoked the Bible before the legion of demons intensified the point that this was a literalization of spiritual

---

[7] Horton, "African Conversion," 88.
[8] The series has been uploaded to YouTube: www.youtube.com/watch?v=zLrqn6GJxso
[9] When the series ended, Ayamatanga – as a hail of the devil – continued echoing in the public imagination until it became a byword and popular slang for beautiful women thought to imperil the social order through their propensity for evil. As Olubitan shows, it is part of the legacy of *Agbara Nla* that "Ayamatanga," a name its creator insisted was purely inspired by the Holy Spirit, symbolized personified and transcendental evil, and has become subsumed into urban lore.

warfare.[10] Paul Esupofo prayed to disarm the demons in their kingdom. When Bose was eventually freed from their captivity, even the viewer who had followed the series and whose insides had tightened with the tension of that contest felt a cathartic purge.

Some twenty-six years later, the highly charged melodramatic scene was replayed in a different teleseries by the same production company that made *Agbara Nla*, the Mount Zion Faith Ministries International (MZFMI). This second series is also produced for television and titled *Abejoye* (2020) or *The King Maker*.[11] Although the plot also featured personified good challenging evil, something had changed in the conception of spiritual warfare. The character that confronts the devil is the same actor – Mike Bamiloye – who played Esupofo in *Agbara Nla*. In *Abejoye*, his character, Olayiotan, is an older man who has traveled from his village in Nigeria to visit his son and his family in Dallas, Texas. He had arrived in the USA as a sorcerer but he was soon converted to Christianity by the family's Nigerian pastor who ran a church for immigrant Nigerians. His character in *Abejoye* was unlike the humbly dressed the old man in *Agbara Nla* whose environments in both the village and city were relatively modest. Olayiotan was more richly attired in all-white. In contrast to the house where the Bose's deliverance in *Agbara Nla* took place, this family's abode is in a Dallas suburb, from the visual takes of both the interior and the exterior, showed the trappings of an American middle-class life.

In this more recent scene, Olayiotan is lying on a bed when he is visited by a demon figure sent from his village. He rises abruptly as soon as he senses the presence of the devil. The rather striking blackened visage of the devil slowly emerges through the plain-colored bedroom wall, and

---

[10] The sword comes up frequently in Nigerian prayers, and while the weapon is mostly an image called up during prayers, it also compels some theatrics. For instance, Nimi Wariboko notes of a West African prayer that goes thus: *Holy Ghost, sword, shear, shear, shear*. Wariboko says that when people pray this prayer, they have taken up the sword (of the spirit) in their minds already, and saying "shear" repeatedly while moving their fingers as if they are cutting the air means they are already fighting the battles psychologically and their bodies are moving to the rhythm. He says, "The punning meaning that arises as a his hand becomes a physical sword as well as a spiritual sword of God – and his voice duplicating the killer-sound of the sword-hand – brings together images, sounds, and words in an associative freedom that is both liberating and threatening in its embodiedness." Wariboko, *The Split God*, 160, 161.

[11] Season 2 of the series was released in 2020, but I got a preview copy a year earlier.

Olayiotan instantly confronts it with the sword of the spirit—that is, the word of God. This time, though, he has an actual Bible in his hand. Unlike the days of *Agbara Nla*, however, the old man character does not stop at calling up God's word to overpower the devil. While the chant with which he tells the devil he cannot be harmed because of his new status as the child of God began with scriptural invocations, as characteristic of such rituals, he also slips in commentaries meant to induce some laughter. The climax of this scene comes when man and the devil face each other, the camera swirling around them and alternately showing them from the back and the front. With one costumed in white and the other in black, the contrast of light and darkness, good and evil, God and devil, righteousness and decadence, is quite apparent. The Bible still in his hands, Olayiotan continues invoking its verses at the demonic figure, and gradually, his prayer turns into a song. Still standing before the devil figure that was heaving its body, Olayiotan sways his own body in a light dance. The devil too, in a rather unusual move, begins to mirror Olayiotan's dance. Olayiotan commands the devil to dance for Jesus, and both characters move rhythmically to the sound of Olayiotan's voice. Still facing each other, they both dance together for a moment before Olayiotan commands the devil to disappear![12] Amidst the characteristic seriousness and tension of the banishing of the devil, this moment of frivolity where the spiritual warrior dances with the devil is quite significant. Unlike the potent and ravaging possessing force of Ayamatanga, this demon appears domesticated; its threat is far less compelling. While Ayamatanga spoke her grievances through Bose's body and provoked the viewer to a moral judgment of issues, this demon has no voice and the fight within it is rather too quickly extinguished. It barely posed a threat to the Christian patriarch who easily subdued and literally house-trains it by making it conform to the kinetic rhythm of his empowered Pentecostal body. There is spiritual warfare, all right, but the apocalyptic anxiety with which it haunted the social imaginary in *Agbara Nla* is lessened.

Certain symbolism in the deliverance scenes in *Agbara Nla* and *Abejoye* are consistent enough to draw a schematic map of how the notion of spiritual warfare that rests heavily on the imagination of Nigerian Pentecostals has shifted through cinematic and real time and

[12] www.youtube.com/watch?v=axcxui10wYA

expresses their evolving aspiration of power. First, there is an old man character who is a recent convert to Christianity from occult practices – typically represented with the aesthetic and the poetics of African traditional religious beliefs. He is brimming with the fire and enthusiasm of his newfound knowledge of Christ and relationship with God, and has been empowered to expel a demon through the rituals of spiritual warfare. This character has also moved from the rural and essentialized African spaces—symbolized by the "village"—to the urban area to vanquish a demon in an interior(ized) space such as the body or the bedroom. Having been a part of the occult, he implicitly understands its operations and can control demonic agents in the name of Jesus. This recent convert also self-consciously marks his identity as a new creation in Christ to distinguish between pre-Christian life and the present.

However, other aspects of the narration of the diabolical have changed: the patriarch who banishes the demon in *Abejoye* has grown physically older. Mike Bamiloye, who was made up to look older in *Agbara Nla*, is actually advanced in years when he plays Olayiotan. Visible signs of material comfort associate religious faith with upward mobility and prosperity. Viewed from an extra-diegetic angle, MZFMI itself has acquired material resources over the years. Understandably, it represents economic upgrade as compatible with faith and power. The cinematographic quality of the more recent *Abejoye* shows far more technological and aesthetic sophistication than *Agbara Nla* that was shot with, "the kind of amateur camera they use for birthdays."[13] Expansion from a rural and urban Nigerian territory to a suburban home in one of the largest cities in the USA shows a transcendence of the provincial, a geospatial shift that also indexes other kinds of changes. Then, there is the function the devil fulfils; as a comedic spectacle in *Abejoye*, a departure from Ayamatanga as a source of abject terror which needed to be urgently expunged. Because the devil did not go away – it *never* does; it is an open-ended narrative template that fills up with contemporary anxieties – its feature in both series is quite instructive.

With the similarities and differences in the characterization of the devil figure and the mode of the devil's vanquishing in *Agbara Nla* and *Abejoye* highlighted, this chapter reflects on Pentecostalism and its

---

[13] Personal interview with Mike Bamiloye.

evolution through the years using the teleseries' depictions of spiritual warfare to illustrate the social evolutions that their narrative elements convey. While demonic encounters are a staple in MZFMI productions, I have chosen these correlated scenes from *Agbara Nla* and *Abejoye* because they have narrative similarities that illustrate the historical arc of the Pentecostal movement even though the two series' broadcasts span almost three decades. The Pentecostal movement has a longer historical arc, but since the focus of this book is mostly on the present era, I have bracketed the historical period covered here with the two television productions that stretch from the 1990s to the 2020s. Rather than a direct historical analysis of Pentecostal evolution to narrate their power identity, I chose to look at the archived stories of demonic confrontations told at certain junctures of Nigerian social history to see how they express the times and the spirits that haunt them.

The teleseries that carry these stories of human encounters with demonic specters illustrate the desire for power, the quest for it through spiritual means, and how the eventual attainment of cultural power became the crucial distinguishing mark of the Pentecostal identity. To ensure their *being* within Nigeria's disempowering political economy, they reached for the ultimate spiritual power as a means through which other forms of power could be acquired. Through their faith in the name of Jesus, ritual prayers, mass congregational gatherings, Bible schools, prosperity gospel teachings, and collective mobilization toward economic, political, and social ends, they worked toward becoming people of power. Power identity is permanently signifying; it keeps beckoning at social and historical situations as it seeks to establish its essence. The more Pentecostals performed their power identity, the more they were transformed and revealed as people of power. This desire for power and the perennial obsession with being identified by power would map unto the Pentecostal subject until power identity came to name the circumlocutory process by which the desired objective and its pursuer mutually identify. However, for power identity to be confirmed, it has to enter into the political realm where its constituents are tested and attested. One of the ways the Pentecostal subject negotiates their way through the thickets of the political sphere is through the instrumentalization of the demonic. These specters condense the symbols and myths of an irredeemable evil opposition, and they are a quick reference to understanding the nature of confrontation in processes and places of power exchange.

Thus, demonic encounters are a rich site of cultural and historical knowledge because their appearances – or even the instinctual sensing of their presence – awaken a primal instinct in those whose sensibilities have been attuned to see them as radical evil. As Pentecostals think of spirits in the literal and metaphorical sense, spectral appearances are not only spiritual, they are also political because they illustrate a quest, a haunting, an incitement to demonstrate power. In the realm of the political, bodies contest against each other to determine who will control the symbolic and material resources necessary to live as fully realized human beings, and also who – the "other" against whom the "self" identifies – needs to be diminished for this aspiration to be unambiguous. As Pentecostal ethicist Nimi Wariboko stated, "Politics is haunted by what it excludes, combats, expresses or represses. There is always the possibility of specters intruding into the contest and exchange of power even as the specters of possibility float over the site of contestation" and politics is therefore, "spiritual warfare, a struggle between *one power of being* against another that determines the *who* of the contestants' humanity. The spiritual is the inner dynamics of political in all spheres of society or public life."[14] Accordingly, specters appear in power contestation to shift the struggles from abstract contentions to more apprehensible depictions of evil. Their deployment into social struggles impels antagonistic transactions in the political sphere where the "militant site of the agonistic transfer and control of power" occur.[15] In Nigerian politics the process of power exchange is "akin to warfare, with clear, concrete definition of friends and enemies," and "the possession of power means control over resources, meanings, and the power of being, political processes and sites are patrolled and pervaded by spiritual presences."[16] Their haunting presence turns political contestations for power into spiritual exercises, and the sites of spiritual exercises reveal the dynamics of political machinations as various blocs that struggle against one another for the control of power express their desire for control through spiritual exercises.

Since these teleseries producers are a part of the Pentecostal movement themselves, the stories they tell about the devil and its expulsion

[14] Wariboko, *Nigerian Pentecostalism*, 145.   [15] Ibid.   [16] Ibid.

approximate how they imagine Pentecostal power. It is also telling how they characterize threats to the body of Christ from the social body, and what a Pentecostal needs to do to overcome. In narrating those basic stories of the agonistic contests between good and evil, they "stage an enchanted world in which spiritual powers are perpetually present, and in which the struggle between good and evil within the self mirrors an epic struggle against the demonic forces at large in the world."[17] They also provide other kinds of illumination of a period through the physical setting of their stories, aesthetic choices, and the politics of the era. The intertextual character development arc of Esupofo and Olayiotan from the early '90s to the 2020s, for instance, shows a level of growth and maturity in the MZFMI's outlook. Even from the basic elements, one could see that the narrative identity of the Pentecostal movement has evolved from the ascetic new convert of Paul Esupofo who dwelled in an African village and traveled to the city to deliver its inhabitants from haunting demons, to the richer and more cosmopolitan character of another new convert, Olayiotan, whose territories – spatial and otherwise – have been widened across continents. Yet, the quest for power through staging demonic encounters remains consistent.

Abejoye's depiction of a Nigerian Christian family in a US suburb is also the story of the Nigerian professional class's migration to the new world in search of greener pastures. Not all of those in Paul Esupofo's generation confronted the devil with the sword of the spirit. While some stayed behind in the country and sought to transcend the limitations of their economic situations through the blessings of the prosperity gospel that Pentecostalism would later popularize in Nigeria, others fled to the far more prosperous metropolitan cities of the world. Some migrants would become "reverse missionaries" whose religious activities have contributed to an intensification of Christianity in a secularizing West.[18] One such migrant was the pastor who preached to Olayiotan and urged his conversion to Christianity in *Abejoye*. These migrants graduated to global spheres with their religious practices reconfigured to match their identity in tandem with their new locales.[19] Yet, they also remain haunted by African demons who, they say, need no visa to travel across space and time to haunt them

[17] Marshall, "The Sovereignty of Miracles."
[18] Olupona, "The Changing Face of African Christianity."
[19] Adogame, *Religion Crossing Boundaries*; Adogame, "Transnational Migration and Pentecostalism in Europe"; Asamoah-Gyadu, "Mediating Spiritual Power."

and who take the guises of evil in the repertoire of issues that
immigrants face.[20] As *Abejoye* showed, the demons also track immigrant Christians to their new abodes through familial connections and
the spiritual breaches that occur due to the sins of the fathers of the
house. To battle them, African immigrants gravitated toward their
churches. This choice also keeps them "rooted locally and in the land
of origin, but also into an intra-communal web linking them with
different places across the globe."[21] Their modes of confronting and
understanding of the demonic are, therefore, also narratives of social
history.

The Social and Political Life of Demonic Specters

The demonic encounters in *Agbara Nla* and *Abejoye* are both, at the
root of their narrative, an illustration of historical knowledge and
sensibility during a period of Nigeria's history. While they might not
immediately appear as a rational discourse on history, the rationale
for conjuring a spectral presence in religious or social rituals is
a function of both the temporality and the ideology underwriting
the religious imagination. Demons too have a social life, and the
contingency of their social effects can make them become "true"
and "self-evident."[22] In every demonic encounter are assembled the
anxieties that haunt the social body within a period, but which are
beyond quantifiable proof or empirical demonstration. As people get
caught in the ground-shifting changes in the ethical structures of their
society, as their familiar lived realities give way to new structures of
social experience, they betray their shifting orientations through their
behaviors, imaginings, and insights – all of which builds up and is
articulated through intangible and spiritual entities. Therefore, the
spectral appearances of demonic figures are configurations of social
encounters.

MZFMI featured a devil figure, Ayamatanga, popularly received as
a foreboding specter of evil.[23] Almost three decades later, the same

[20] Adogame, "The Anthropology of Evil," 433.
[21] Butticci, *African Pentecostals in Catholic Europe*; Cherry, Stephen & Ebaugh,
      Global Religious Movements across Borders; Miller, Sargeant & Flory, *Spirit
      and Power*, 193.
[22] Blanes & Santo, *The Social Life of Spirits*.
[23] Women seen as unruly and nonconforming came to be labeled "Ayamatanga."

drama company reenacted a similar scene of deliverance from malevolent evil. Given how popular *Agbara Nla* and the Ayamatanga character were, they returned to haunt the present rendition of the demonic conquest of *Abejoye*. As theatre and performance scholar Marvin Carlson explained theatre and cultural memory, each staging of a show brings something familiar back to us. There is a "ghostly quality" to theatre productions as "a simulacrum of the cultural and historical processes," and that is because it produces a sense of haunting that viscerally awakens glimmers of memories that have already been incorporated into the body politic.[24] *Agbara Nla*'s account of the deliverance of a demon-possessed body, like other religious drama, is a public lesson in the struggle between God as the force of good, and the devil as that of evil and sin.[25] When a replay of its iconic demonic encounter was brought back in *Abejoye*, it aroused not only the ghostly quality of what has been staged previously in *Agbara Nla*, but also the era and all the feelings it evoked in those of us who watched it. The ghosts of past demons also coincided with those of the present, and both sites of demonic encounter cohere the mood of the present.

Although the modes of expelling demons in both scenes demonstrate consistent belief in the agency of spirit beings, they also display other shifts in the social dimensions of haunting. The figuration of the devil, their breach of either the body or interior spaces, and the kind of harm they cause are a part of larger social trends. In *Agbara Nla* and *Abejoye*, different periods of Nigerian social history and the changes that have occurred are emblematized in these cinematic representations along with the demons that the appointed ministers of God encountered. While the cultural effect of demonic beings is a useful framework for an understanding of the social forces that brought the specters into being, these encounters also document social histories. For instance, the period and the spaces and places where these encounters occur and reoccur, and the degree of fervency displayed during demonic expulsions, are also important for understanding the culture that bred these representative stories.

The assertion that evil can be destroyed for good from the inside of the human body also raises the question of the components of the inside of the human destroyer or the exorcist and the moral authority that

---

[24] Carlson, *The Haunted Stage*, 2.   [25] Van Dijkhuizen, *Devil Theatre*.

legitimizes this agent of "good" to carry out the deliverance. Theatre scholar Nahidh Sulaiman pointed out that exorcising demons enlarges the belief that the problem of evil can be supernaturally treated while also affirming belief in human interiority.[26] How the details are conceived in the social imagination, and the political and moral consequences, all unfold in their cinematic representations. In both *Agbara Nla* and *Abejoye*, while the spectacle of a devil with a darkened visage is consistent with the idea of evil as semiotically black, the "good" foil, the human representation of the conquering God, appears as the patriarch. This character dramatizes its contrasting purity against the darkness by dressing in white. Whether in a modest city homestead in Nigeria or in a suburban home in Dallas, Texas, surrounded by the props of middle-class financial contentment, the consistency of the depiction – in both, he also first goes through a process of conversion from a village sorcerer to a born-again Christian – shows a normative mindset of the nature and trajectory of good and godliness, and the embodiment of supernatural power. In both TV series, the deliverance minister is the quintessential Pentecostal convert. He had to be someone who left a past life of sorcery to embrace Christ and whose Christian identity evidences power and authority in the name of Jesus Christ.

The methodological choice of interrogating Pentecostal character from the perspective of a film/drama company such as the MZFMI is strategic. MZFMI has an institutional progression arc that both exemplifies and aligns with the Nigerian Pentecostal movement, and the stories they have told through the years express the spirit of the times. We cannot talk about Pentecostalism from the '90s upward in Nigeria as "the most important source of religious and cultural creativity in the continent ... channels for harnessing spiritual and social resources for members' aspirations to modernity"[27] without also locating the creative sites where the affective images that buoyed the church messages were concurrently produced. Narrations of faith are backgrounded by the spiritual and social atmosphere in which people are presently embroiled, and their tales are meant to both speak *to* and speak *of* their experiences. Nigerian Pentecostalism did not arrive on the global scene all by itself. MZFMI was – and still is – one of the tributaries that

[26] Sulaiman, "Theatre of Exorcism," 180.
[27] Wariboko, "African Pentecostalism," 21–23.

poured into Pentecostal imaginaries, and their activities give a moral shape to the Christian social life. MZFMI has not only evolved with the faith movement, its advancement as a cultural institution also epitomizes the evolution of Nigerian Pentecostalism.

Performances, particularly when popular, isolate the spirit and the sensibility that rule a period. Their reverberation with the public effectively indexes the traumatic pangs society goes through as its new realities are being birthed. If even a word can condense and "register all the transitory, delicate, momentary phases of social change,"[28] stories such as popular TV shows and series are cartography of experiences, feelings, and sensibilities that rule an era. We can fully understand why *Agbara Nla* and its stories of demonic encounters resonated with the public when we enter "the interior domain of politics, to the structures of feeling, the habits of the heart, the worlds of moral sense and perception"[29] that gave the story so much traction and made it one of the most popular Nigerian dramas ever. Performance scholar Richard Schechner explained cultural productions through the methodological lens of performance:

Whatever is being studied is regarded as practices, events, and behaviors, not as "objects" or "things" . . . . Thus performance studies does not "read" an action or ask what "text" is being enacted. Rather, one inquires about the "behavior" of, for example, a painting: how, when and by whom it was made, how it interacts with those who view it, and how the painting changes over time.[30]

The graph I plot through this chapter with the two teleseries parallels their creation with the Pentecostal trajectory. To understand the Pentecostal implosion and its rapid growth, one must look beyond the structures of their religious activities or the managerial acuity that raised the massive cathedrals. The dramas concomitantly staged within the same period as Pentecostalism grew are representative of issues that needed addressing to heighten people's faith. The idea is to locate the how and the where that "multiple elements reach a density that condenses various social interests into a movement with confrontations

[28] Voloshinov & Bachtin, *Marxism and the Philosophy of Language*, 19.
[29] Alexander, *The Performance of Politics*, 278.
[30] Schechner, "What Is Performance Studies?," 3.

and systemic features, the elements of which are not exactly repeatable, but do resonate onward from its early phase."[31]

Following Schechner, I inquire into the "behavior" of the two series, the social and political context of their making, how the politics of their era coincided with their reception, and how the encounter has changed over time. From around 1990 when they first started making television dramas, the various MZFMI productions resounded with the audience.[32] As a youngster growing up in Ibadan in the '90s, I recall how much each weekly episode of *Agbara Nla* informed public under-standing of demonic influences.[33] Even though various MZFMI series were – and still are – popular, *Agbara Nla* remains their touchstone production. A veritable classic, its enduring popularity owes to the topicality of its message in the era it was produced.[34] The plot of *Agbara Nla* spoke about virtually everything Nigerians could relate to regarding the imbrications of political and spiritual power. From *Agbara Nla's* depiction of Abuja (as the Federal Capital Territory and the nation's capital is popularly labeled) as a seat of corrupting power that seduces Christians away from the love and the work of God, to stories of mysterious women who wield economic power to recruit other vulnerable women into the sinful vanity fair province of urban spaces, the teleseries was an all-encompassing exegesis on competing forms of power. Power, a permanent fixation of Nigerian Pentecostalism, could be construed as a character in the story because the quest for its possession drove the entire series from beginning to end. Viewers soon found themselves rooting, not for the characters' deliverance from militating forces of evil, but for the power they embody. For those viewers whose various conversion stories to either a Christianity or to Pentecostalism parallel that of Paul Esupofo – from a great sinner to a great believer –the manifestation of power across the

---

[31] Shapiro & Barnard. *Pentecostal Modernism*, 55.

[32] Adogame, "To God Be the Glory."

[33] On this one, I have also relied on memory of peers and acquaintances for information. In interviews and our joint recollections of our growing years, we deduced how much *Agbara Nla* influenced our ideas of the demonic. Most of us grew on a joint diet of TV programs, not just because we were of the same generation but also because we had narrow choices at the time. In 1993 Nigeria, the few television stations in the country were run by both the federal and the state government and they tightly controlled what could be viewed.

[34] This is particularly true of southwestern Nigeria where many mega Pentecostal churches are also currently located.

thirteen episodes of *Agbara Nla* were a dramatization of the processes by which their power identity was established.

Having taken astute advantage of the various political, technological, and economic changes at the end of the millennium to build a film industry that can be described as a generator of modern Christian mythology, MZFMI became a household name, especially among Christians. Their stories translate religious messages, as preached in the church and from interpretations of the Bible, into video/film productions. The agenda is to expand the faith sensibility already ascribed to believers by the church and to exhort the religious imagination through morally sanitized entertainment. One of MZFMI's specialties which they have repeatedly explored is the demonic imaginary, and this is quite understandable since fantasy has a strong hold on the public mind. The MZFMI transmutes demons to cinematic forms, and also creates a mythopoeia of demonic actions through their staging of human nature. Thus, both the church and filmmakers form a circular route through which supernatural reality and its imaging on the screen unearth latent beliefs, ideas, visions, and ethics that are translated into cinematic images – consumed, validated, and recirculated into the public moral imagination. Staged and fictional performances allied to the Pentecostal movement such as *Agbara Nla* and *Abejoye* were some of such performance art practices that captured the sociocultural impulse. Given the force of its reverberation with the viewing public, also shaped the lineaments of faith.

MZFMI started as a traveling theatre group of young evangelists, performing mostly dramas on church altars they turned into makeshift theatre stages.[35] These were done during interludes in church services, both as a supplement to the sermons and also as "safe" entertainment for Christians who have to live in a culture riddled with other vain worldly distractions. By 1990, the company started producing TV dramas, videos, drama series, and much later, action thrillers. As a Christian film company, it straddles two creative Nigerian "enterprises" that have demonstrated, globally, the people's resourcefulness

---

[35] Though they shy away from the provenance, Christian drama artists who mutated into video filmmakers are also inheritors of an older tradition of artistic productions by legendary Yoruba artists such as Hubert Ogunde, Duro Ladipo, Moses Olaiya, and Isola Ogunsola. Drama ministers grew to become an integral part of the Pentecostal material culture who use their artistic skills to shape the religious and public moral imagination.

to organically build entire industries with little material start-up capital and more of the intangible resources of zeal, faith, and sheer grit – the Pentecostal movement itself and the Nigerian film industry popularly called Nollywood.[36] When the story of Nollywood's founding around the same early '90s is narrated, there is typically a focus on the ingenuity of the earliest practitioners who saw an opening created by the coincidence of global technological resources and a local taste for familiar stories.[37] Then there is a discrete focus on the aspect of Nollywood popular cinema that oriented toward the propagation of Pentecostalism and whose preoccupation was the imagination of modernity through a Christian (Pentecostal) lens. While the promotion of Jesus and Christian religious power in the Nigerian film industry have considerably tapered off,[38] the ideological underlay of Nollywood films remains partly wedded to preoccupations with the morality play format that came about through its relationship with the Pentecostal movement in the '90s.[39] The other part that does not quite feature in these narratives of mega successful enterprises of the Nigerian film industry is the chronicles of the likes of MZFMI founders.[40] Artists

[36]   On Nollywood, see, for instance: Adesokan, *Postcolonial Artists and Global Aesthetics*; Haynes, *Nollywood*; Ugor et al. *Global Nollywood*. Okome, "Nollywood."

[37]   In the era in which *Agbara Nla* was produced, many Nollywood films of the "halleluyah genre" were proclaiming a similar message of deliverance from evil forces and unabashedly pandered to Pentecostal Christian sensibilities and middle-class consciousness. *Agbara Nla*'s visualization of evil felt credible because it had an added advantage of having being produced by African Christian evangelists who supposedly know – through lucid divine revelations, cultural embeddedness, and sheer intuition – what "evil" religious people who practice African religions do in their covens. By simultaneously depicting Christian supremacist attack and also pandering to an Africanist worldview through theatrical aesthetics, the message of the play resonated with a viewership that cut across social strata and religious divides. On the halleluyah genre, see: Kumwenda, "The Portrayal of Witchcraft, Occults and Magic in Popular Nigerian Video Films."

[38]   One reason could be that those storylines have become commonplace, and the audience would rather have more nuanced and less didactic stories.

[39]   See, for instance: Meyer, "Praise the Lord."

[40]   Today, the MZFMI is arguably the most prominent and dominant Christian film production company in Africa with a grass-to-grace story that Pentecostals enjoy testifying about. They have become an organization that has made dozens of films, built a drama institute, run an online streaming site and a movie channel on satellite TV, and made films in different countries in the world including a Hindi-language film that was shot in New Delhi and featured a cast of Indians. When *Abejoye* was first released, it premiered in over 360 locations, most of

like Mike Bamiloye also saw an opening – a yearning for stories about Christian lives told by actual Christians – that needed to be filled, although their motives for going into the business of filmmaking were primarily about evangelism rather than just profit.[41] As a cultural producer, MZFMI played a crucial role in the forming of the Pentecostal identity, the contouring of the religious imagination, and the construction and enforcement of conservative values and ethics. With performance as a medium, MZFMI propagates religious values with their depictions of Christian social and family life, and demon vanquishing.

When I interviewed Mike Bamiloye – the founder of MZFMI, and the person who also acted the characters of Paul Esupofo and Olayiotan – one of the several lasting impacts of *Agbara Nla* that he described was how the drama boosted the faith of church field workers. He talked at length about how the church missionaries who had been sent to rural areas testified that the vigor of the screen visualization of Christian triumph over evil heightened their faith in what they could accomplish in the mission fields.[42] Deliverance ministers too testified that watching Ayamatanga eventually cast out intensified their faith that the power of God could exorcize the most malicious of all devils. The evangelists and revivalists that churches sent to carry out fieldwork in many rural areas would screen the series to people before asking them to give their lives to Jesus.[43] These fieldworkers claimed that the

which were the Pentecostal churches in Nigeria, Africa, Australia, Europe, and the US. The stories they tell, whether on screen or as their religious corporate success narration, are also a personal testimony to how far they have come.

[41] Asonzeh Ukah, in his study of Christian films, uses the "religious economy" model to describe the neoliberal model that explains the how and why the cultural marketplace has been amenable to the success of these films and how their creators make "profitable" choices. While the model helpfully illustrates the push and pull of economic forces and the fervent capitalist imperatives that helped the Christian film industry thrive, that secular conceptualization also risks eliding the sheer evangelical zeal that drove companies such as the MZFMI. Following *Agbara Nla*'s astounding success, MZFMI recalibrated the size of its vision demonstrating astuteness in deciphering social trends influenced by the discernment of spiritual needs. With such perspicacity, the company could catapult itself from a band of struggling drama evangelists into respected artists that are sampled all over Africa and beyond. Asonzeh. "Advertising God."

[42] Personal interview with Mike Bamiloye.

[43] As Bamiloye told me, prior to Christians making films, what evangelists used to screen to prospective converts was the Hollywood story of Jesus, *Jesus of Nazareth*. Because many of the audience could not understand the language or

missional exploits of the evangelists in the drama gave them a renewed stamina about the urgency of their missions to witness to all and sundry. With their eyes open to another level of the spectacular display of God's power, their feet were quickened as they hastened to harvest the souls of the spiritually unsaved and the politically disenfranchised. In later sections, I will elaborate more on the Nigerian political context when *Agbara Nla* was produced and why its spectacular elements of the demonic captivated public imagination.

As Bamiloye shared with me at his residence in Ibadan, one of the biggest factors that contributed to the success of MZFMI's evangelistic mission is that people view its dramas mostly in the intimate spaces of their homes. Their organizational mission has been to minister to this social unit by telling relatable stories that depict spiritual warfare as it takes place on a cosmic scale and also affects people at individual and family levels. Unlike other – and more public – church outreach programs, these dramas transmit the gospel directly to people's homes where family members cluster and bond around their TV sets. Their persuasive messages are directly broadcast to an entire household, the unit of the society that will carry out the social reforms the play intends. As anthropologist Katrien Pype also noticed of similar Pentecostal Christian television series in Kinshasa, the cultural producers of these materials and their works do not stand apart from the society; their goals connect to the extant social reality they aim to transform through their artistic productions. Pype noted, "As such, the evangelizing TV actors are mediators. They try to negotiate between lived realities and what they think is the best way to actualize a better society."[44] For Kinshasa, embroiled in extensive social conflicts, the teleseries tell of people in search of redemption and renewal. The stories on their TV that feature conversion to Christianity are a discourse put forward toward the possibility of social progress – ending chaos and social disorderliness – and ultimately "produc[ing] the good, the orderly, and the healthy."[45]

The audience's reception of these stories primes their hearts for the sermons of personal and social transformation they will encounter in churches and in other evangelistic outreaches. With prior reception of

---

follow the accent, someone narrated the storyline to them over a microphone. With MZFMI making films, they started showing local stories that resonated with audiences quite well.

[44] Pype, *The Making of the Pentecostal Melodrama*.   [45] Ibid.

relatable stories of supernatural encounters rather than abstract theological issues, people become more amenable to receiving the salvation
messages preached in churches. The churches too find that thanks to
the teleseries and the live performances "drama ministers" stage in
church, their task of convincing people about the workings of the
power of God are easier, and so they conscript both teleseries and
also live drama performances into their church activities. Churches
not only sponsored drama organizations like the MZFMI to bring
live stage productions to church, some developed their own "drama
department." They have brought in well-known "drama ministers" to
perform during church services or hired professional drama directors
to make plays for the church. So, Nigerian Pentecostalism has also
thrived and become one of the most important cultural movements
because it co-opted one of the most powerful devices for ideologically
fine-tuning a society: narratives, and their dramatization through various media forms.[46]

Bamiloye attributed the wide acceptance of *Agbara Nla* among
Yoruba people in the southwestern part of Nigeria to the "richness"
of the language and culture with which the story was visually and
oratorically rendered. Because of the language, he said, people understood the message at an instinctual level. He said the story elements
such as "the evil power residing in the village, evil powers in the city,
occult powers, spiritual powers, and the diabolic power of witchdoc-
tors" were all relatable.[47] When they made the English translation, *The
Ultimate Power*, the elements of the story's demonic encounters were
familiar enough within the universe of the African worldview for the
story to resonate across cultures. "Almost everyone in Africa could
relate to the story's elements," Bamiloye said. "The compelling message of victory, deliverance as the solution people are looking for … all
of these are relevant to the African life."[48] Their drama productions
consciously created cultural forms that resonated, and can be said to
have "freed Christianity to be more at home in local situations."[49]
Through various methods that instrumentalize the demonic, they div-
ined unfulfilled spiritual longings and ideals, and created explanatory
spiritual paradigms for phenomena in the natural sphere. Their legacies

[46] Meyer, "Picturing the Invisible"; Meyer, "How Pictures Matter," 160.
[47] Personal interview with Mike Bamiloye.   [48] Ibid.
[49] Robert, "Shifting Southward," 53.

as "drama ministers" include how their cinematic approach to demonic encounters shaped a template for the social imagination of the Pentecostal cosmic world. Particularly in Nigerian Christian films, the MZFMI dramaturgy of spiritual warfare – that is, the encounters between humans and demonic figures as a site of demonstration of embodied power of Jesus Christ – carefully crafted to accent the thaumaturgy of the power of the Pentecostal identity, continues to reproduce a notion of triumphalism in Nigerian Pentecostal circles.

While Bamiloye attributes the compelling message of *Agbara Nla* to the depth of cultural symbolism that gave it resonance with Africans who live in a spirit-filled world, I would argue that it was the era that made the message in *Agbara Nla* applicable on physical and spiritual levels. Here, I agree with religious studies scholar Simeon Ilesanmi who mapped the rapid growth of African Pentecostalism into a mainstream cultural practice and observed that, "as in the rest of the third world where Pentecostalism has flourished, it is neither the indigenous tradition per se nor a penchant for emotional spiritualism that explains the success of this movement, but rather the larger cultural and political milieu in which it arose."[50] For *Agbara Nla* and other productions by MZFMI that featured demonic encounters, the evangelizing story reverberated with the audience because of the political context in which the imaging of good and evil landed, and which also accentuated the Pentecostal desire for power as its identity. *Agbara Nla* was broadcast in 1993, a most significant year in the political history of Nigeria. That was the year Nigerians had also gone to the polls to elect a civilian president and finally end the years of autocratic military rule. Although the election was adjudged free and fair by local and international observers, it was annulled by the military government unwilling to yield power to civilian leaders. The election results have never been fully released officially, but the unofficial figures pointed in the direction of a winner: Chief Moshood Kashimawo Abiola, a billionaire philanthropist who won on a largely pan-Nigerian mandate. Nigerians, unwilling to accept the subterfuge against a popular mandate, poured into the streets to riot against the military authority. Those public demonstrations marked one of the bloodiest and most traumatic periods in the history of postwar Nigeria.[51] In that period, the urban spaces were marked

[50] Ilesanmi, "From Periphery to Center."
[51] Obadare, "Democratic Transition and Political Violence in Nigeria"; www .nytimes.com/1993/07/07/world/rioting-in-nigeria-kills-at-least-11.html; www

by fear and disempowerment, an uneven notion of power that people would seek to redress in their churches through the superior force of an ultimate power.

As a youngster in that era, I still have vivid recollections of the chaos of those times, the social uncertainties, and the anxieties of the sinister times that still lay ahead. I recall youth demonstrators setting up bonfires with used car tires, running from teargas set by the police and soldiers who sought to disband the protests, and relentlessly returning to the sites of demonstration to start another bonfire. They made an effigy of the then-military head of state, General Ibrahim Babangida, placed it in a coffin and took it to the local broadcasting television station where they set it on fire. It was a ritual my late uncle, one of the demonstrators, imagined would have a supernatural effect on the abusive military rulers of the period. In those polarized times where good and evil were considered starkly divided between the ruler and the ruled, people staged physical and spiritual showdowns they thought would restore the moral imperative of the triumph of light over darkness. None of their enactments of imprecation so as much as grazed the leaders who were seemingly shielded behind the impregnable force of totalitarian power they possessed. In addition to the riots and bloodshed were curfews, scarcity of essential household commodities, industrial actions – the aftershocks of the economic programs of the '90s such as Structural Adjustment Programs that left the country weakened – the breakdown of social and public facilities, corruption, and a palpable feeling of trepidation and despondence that overwhelmed the country.

Nigerians, finding themselves swirling amidst the vertiginous performances of power play from government officials whose distance from their oppressive realities added to the soldiers' mystique, poignantly prayed against the spiritual forces and the "principalities and powers" that threaten their lived conditions. The world was being upended along with the prefabricated values and ethos that formed its cornerstones, and the reigning idea of desirable moral justice in the political and economic crises was an apocalyptic vision of the oppressed citizens finding the superpowers to violently overthrow their sadistic leaders. That cathartic conclusion to the ongoing moral

.nytimes.com/1993/07/06/world/nigerian-protests-erupt-in-violence.html?auth=login-email

crisis in the polity was not going to come from a formal or legalistic instrument of justice, they realized, but from a source of power that transcended all the forms of power they knew.

The drama, *Agbara Nla*, came on TV in that political context where the military government's power loomed large in the imagination, and the collective sense of disempowerment was acute. The prophetic message of *Agbara Nla* was thus a timely one, and its visualization of a power tussle between the forces of light and darkness reverberated across the populace who saw – through their screens and in their minds – that there was indeed a form of power that was above all other powers, and could dislodge that of their political leaders. *Agbara Nla*, however, did not just dramatize the subsisting power that powered the ethical and political life in Nigeria to the audience. It also aroused visceral feelings of disempowerment and nudged people to seek empowerment in the *ultimate power*. It urged them to convert to this new way of life, to give up the traditional ways of life and the accompanying sociality as a means of achieving victory over the deprecating forces of evil.

The project of religious conversion typically becomes inevitable when a new sociopolitical order has established symbols of producing power with which everyone now reckons. Personal conversion happens either when, within the newly configured milieu, someone has had experiences of triumph over odd circumstances or when the new religious form promises better protection against some threatening forces.[52] Either way, the larger social changes make people more amenable to converting to a new faith. Whatever fantasies the new order promises, this religious ideology also promises to fill people with the ingenuity necessary to attain the many possibilities that have been triggered in their world. By destroying the evil powers that lurked in the rural areas/villages that represented traditions and origins, and from there go forward to banish the demons that existed in cities, *Agbara Nla* taught that the terror that evil powers wreak can be overcome by breaking the loop between the demons of one's origins and the ones that dominate the present. Through various symbolisms, the story links the vindictive power of evil to one's provenance and the social processes that formulated one's subjectivity. To exorcise the demons that haunt the city – modern life, that is – requires one to go back to one's

---

[52] Horton, "African Conversion."

primal African roots to displace the conventional sources of power with the power of Jesus's name and these reformulated roots will, by God's design, correct what is wrong with the present. By consistently costuming the Christian who confronts the devil in white attire, they even outlined the puritanical grounds through which these malignant forces could be confronted: an ethic of self-discipline that demanded Christians to purge themselves of any moral contaminants.

In the traumatic Nigerian '90s, disempowerment and the prescribed spiritual solutions drove many to the churches, especially the Pentecostal churches that were growing at an exponential rate and whose central message was screaming "power in the name of Jesus."[53] Political theorist and historian Olufemi Vaughan noted how much the hardship of the times led to mass conversions of people seeking renewal through the born-again experience. He said, "As the crisis of the Nigerian state deepened by the 1980s, mass conversion to Pentecostal churches from mainline Catholic and protestant churches, as well as African-initiated churches, centered on material and spiritual empowerment."[54] Literary scholar Niyi Akingbe, speaking of *Waiting for an Angel*, one of the literary accounts of the period, noted that the writer, Helon Habila, "defines the underlying theme of despair and despondency, which pervades the Nigerian political atmosphere which lasted from 1993 to 1998" and also "underscores the reign of terror orchestrated by successive military administrations in Nigeria, especially the military regimes of Ibrahim Babangida and Sani Abacha."[55] Writers of that period, like Habila, succinctly captured the deprivation and the stranglehold of fear that characterized life at the hands of a brutal, corrupt, and oppressive military government.[56]

---

[53] Marshall, "Power in the Name of Jesus."
[54] Vaughan, *Religion and the Making of Nigeria*, 140.
[55] Akingbe, "Saints and Sinners," 27.
[56] Akingbe notes *Waiting for an Angel* captures life in Nigeria at this period. He says that even the title of book, *Waiting for an Angel*, betrays the notion of a benign intervention from cosmic forces. "It looks more like a supplication offered to the divine in order to get rid of the military scourge plaguing Nigeria. . . .. The novel reiterates the anguish of people under military repression, waiting anxiously for supernatural intervention to break the dire social and political straits in which they find themselves" (30). While I agree that Nigerians waited for divine intervention, they did not passively wait for a change in their circumstance. They also actively battled in idioms of the spirit.

As people sought divine intervention in a political situation, the already permeable barriers between spiritual, cultural, and political spheres further dissolved to orient people to there being only one source of the ultimate (supernatural) power, and it was the only force effective against the usurpers currently at the helm and who needed to be displaced. Stories like *Agbara Nla* aided this flight toward churches because it dramatized the limitations of even the most brutal and repressive modes of power and liberated minds to see how their conversion could move them from being subalterns to becoming producers of the symbolic instruments of power. This is not to argue that a singular vision or cultural production created Pentecostalism, but that the story gave shape to curiosities and feelings that were part of a larger current of sensibility. It also did so at a crucial historical moment. The quest for empowerment drove many people to the churches to find answers to existential problems that the leaders of the state could not address.

The next significant date in Nigerian political history was 1998 when General Sani Abacha, the repressive military head of state who had held down the country, died in suspicious circumstances. The country could, suddenly, exhale. The media (which the military also fought hard to suppress then) had reported that Abacha was sick and dying in the presidential villa, Aso Rock. Abacha, a Muslim from northern Nigeria, had reportedly been bringing in Islamic marabouts from several regions of Africa and the Middle East, and those people were carrying out fetish activities at Aso Rock.[57] The public's idea of repressive political power was therefore not just that of indifferent institutions or soulless bureaucracy but was also shot through with supernatural elements.[58] Amidst the chaos, those who would engage the state found an outlet in idioms of spiritual warfare, and they did so both by negotiating and legitimizing the indigenous cosmological traditions – such as spectral figures and the supernatural means of their conquest – that present the spiritual as the alternative space of engaging the political.[59]

By what Nigerians generally interpret as an act of divine intervention, the dictator, Abacha died in June 1998, a Monday. He had been

[57] Obadare, "Pentecostal Presidency?"
[58] Marshall, "The Sovereignty of Miracles."
[59] Adogame, "Dealing with Local Satanic Technology."

sick, but his aides had gone to great lengths to hide the information from the public. Coincidentally, less than forty-eight hours before, at the Friday Holy Ghost service, the leader of the largest Pentecostal gathering in Nigeria, Pastor Enoch Adeboye of the Redeemed Christian Church of God (who was named as one of the fifty most powerful people in the world by *Newsweek* in 2008), told his church members that God was the beginning a new phase in Nigerian history. The Friday prophecy was a hint that it had settled in the spirit realm. At the news of his death, thousands of Nigerians poured out into the streets to celebrate their freedom from the clutches of oppressive political power. The bloodless coup of Abacha's death, they reasoned, could only have been sponsored by God. Shortly after his death too, political prisoners were freed all over the country and the march toward democratic governance began.[60] One of those who marched out of prison was Olusegun Obasanjo, a former military leader, who would become president the following year. Considering the role that faith in the God that Pentecostals propagated had played in keeping people alive through the turbulent '90s as they waited for divine intervention, it was not strange that they associated the death of Abacha and the subsequent historical events that freed Nigeria from the clutches of military power with Pastor Adeboye's prophetic message.[61] More than a coincidence, it became a confirmation that the ultimate power that Pentecostals embodied would triumph over evil in both social and political life.

The Fourth Republic in Nigeria started in 1999 with President Obasanjo, a southern Nigerian Christian who identified with Pentecostalism (much of which is domiciled in southern Nigeria, particularly the west). This association with the highest office in the land was a major factor that boosted the surge of the Pentecostal movement in Nigeria.[62] With the new era also came liberal modes of governance that guaranteed civil liberties, free markets, and new models of social prosperity for the populace. The year having marked a critical transitional phase for Nigeria Pentecostalism in many ways, also created a mood of sanguinity that converged in visions of boundless growth

---

[60] Abacha died June 8, 1998. The march toward civil rule began and culminated in "Democracy Day" on May 29, 1999.
[61] Pastor Adeboye still repeated this testimony at the annual convention in December 2018.
[62] Obadare, *"Pentecostal Presidency?* See also, Obadare, *Pentecostal Republic.*

and lack of limitations. The aspirational qualities of global Pentecostalism – the prosperity gospel theology, the vibrant use of media technology, appropriation of market techniques, and the fusion of the political and Christian religious spheres – that the Nigerian Pentecostal movement had been witnessing from the sidelines became fully attainable within their immediate society. Harvey Cox once said that Pentecostalism is "not a church or even a single religion at all, but a *mood*."[63] His observation is important to understanding how the wave of Pentecostal preachers could tap into the optimistic mood of the newly freed Nigeria in 1999, and through the ethics and practices of Pentecostalism, create a Pentecostal milieu that would define the sociopolitical culture. Relatively young – the age bracket of Mike Bamiloye when he acted Paul Esupofo – this generation was not only brimming with optimism at the new Nigeria that was about to unfold, but they also brought their professional expertise and entrepreneurial instincts into organizing the church. The newly elected Pentecostal president's public identification with his faith helped generate a prevailing ethos of Pentecostalism around the nation and boosted the power of pastors as the public face of the faith movement. With the massive resources the Pentecostal church could now mobilize as their church sizes exploded, they dominated the media and public culture to the point they also developed a symbiotic relationship with political power. From being the spectators of power, they become coproducers of it in the Nigerian polity. They became identified with power.

Since then, Nigeria's political history has been jointly underwritten by the Pentecostal moral and spiritual imagination, a massive reworking of the political topography from the time power was coterminous with military dictators whose clique of power was dominated by Muslims from northern Nigeria. Political actors in Nigeria's rebooted democratic society have latched on to Pentecostal idioms of power and corralled their vivid supernatural imagination into governance mechanisms.[64] The ways liberal democracy promotes policies that advance freedom for institutions such as the media, the economy, and social ethics, helped make the society amenable for collective and individual religious self-expression. This idea of freedom is not only

[63] Cox, *Fire from Heaven*, 45.
[64] Obadare, *Pentecostal Republic*. See also: Dowd, *Christianity, Islam and Liberal Democracy*.

abstract, it also has implications on bodies in the polity. Having been constricted by the forces of military power and abuse, these bodies are now freed to reshape social order with their vision of a moral citizenship that links self-mastery to the ability to influence the conduct of others.[65] In their reconceptualization of the moral order, they offered ethics and ideals through which people could envision and practically fashion a better life for themselves. As religious studies scholar Paul Gifford noticed, the Pentecostal faith movement is geared toward success. This orientation is quite conspicuous in their language – breakthrough, success, prosperity, abundance, victory – and these terms are mostly understood in terms of financial or material matters.[66] However, beyond the tendency to look to the supernatural for solutions, they also provided opportunities for upward mobility for their members through initiatives of economic enterprise and networking opportunities. These factors contributed to shaping the manifestation of Pentecostal power identity, such that they became one of the most influential groups in the country.

This growth from the margins to the mainstream of social culture and becoming the people of power is also highlighted by the similarities and differences in the rendering of the demonic encounters in the *Agbara Nla* and *Abejoye* series. While for *Agbara Nla*, Paul Esupofo faced a devil as an "other" presence that possessed the Christian body and needed to be urgently cast out to repair a fractured relationship with God, in *Abejoye*, Olayiotan is a "self-possessed" figure who could make a literal joke *of* and *with* the devil. The way conquest over evil is dramatized – either as a raw, spectacular and belabored contest that we see in *Agbara Nla* or a refined battle where the devil is commuted into metaphor and recedes into the imagination – are instructive gauges of the structures of feeling that inhere in the audience within the period. The notion of a comical moment with the devil, one tame enough to dance with, would perhaps have been unthinkable in the period that *Agbara Nla* was produced. Given the sociopolitical exigencies of the time, such an act would have been considered too frivolous and its effect counterproductive. The Pentecostal movement was relatively young, its fontanel was still pulsating with the thrilling prospects and uncertainties of a new birth. Thus, the narrative of devil as the

---

[65] Marshall, "God Is Not a Democrat."
[66] Gifford, "Persistence and Change in Contemporary African Religion."

quintessential depiction of the evil "other" had to be treated as an agonistic confrontation and a spiritual mandate that needed careful handling.

Enter *Abejoye*, the King Maker, the Already-Made King

The factors differentiating Olayiotan's demonic encounter from that of Paul Esupofo encapsulates the various social changes that have occurred in Nigeria, along with the evolution of the Pentecostal movement. One, there is the factor of aging demographic, particularly by the vanguards of the movement, along with associated issues of maturation, conservatism, slow-down, and inevitable biological decadence. The generation of young people who pioneered the movement are now advanced in years.[67] The actor playing the "old man" character in *Agbara Nla* was costumed to embody an idea(l) of patriarchal power through theatrical artifice while in *Abejoye* he played the role by just being himself. In *Agbara Nla*, Mike Bamiloye's act as an older man was an almost too obvious put on, a façade the low-budget film achieved with unsophisticated makeup and costumes. The audience had to – literally – suspend their disbelief for the attributes of old age in *Agbara Nla* to be convincing. By the time Bamiloye was acting the role of an old Christian patriarch in *Abejoye*, he no longer needed artifice to simulate aging. The very fact that he had truly aged in the eyes of the public/audience who had also aged with him gave Olayiotan's character even extra-cinematic credibility. From 1993 to 2020, Paul Esupofo had not only grown into Olayiotan, but also became a formular for confronting evil. Restaging of the earlier demonic encounter in *Abejoye* with striking similarities to *Agbara Nla* shows how a novel cinematic presentation can take a prescriptive turn and be less prone to arousing primal dread.

By the time *Abejoye* was released in 2020, Pentecostalism had become one of the most formidable forces in not only Nigeria but through Africa as well. Millions of people had become born again and joined a Pentecostal church, making the church a vast social network of people bonded by their spiritual and social relationships. The vanguards of the faith movement that had unabashedly proclaimed their agenda of creating a new sovereign order within

---

[67] Ojo, "The Church in the African State."

Nigeria to which even the state authority would defer were succeeding.[68] As anthropologist Jean Comaroff narrated of the Pentecostal imperative to override social and political spaces, much of what is at stake is not just about people at the grassroots level questioning the existing order of liberal democracy. Instead, they also aim to "counter the institutional arrangements that have nurtured the modernist worldview … canonized above all in the liberal nation-state as imagined community, a model that posits a neutral public domain, clearly separated from the realm of private commitments and belief."[69] Their practices of overwhelming the modern order that authorizes the civil law and market secularization has seen them striving to "unify the fragmented realms of plural cultural registers of liberal modern societies, thus to recover the profane reaches of everyday life as vehicles of divine purpose."[70]

In *Agbara Nla*, the demonic encounter was a means to stake a political claim within the debilitating Nigerian social order and demonstrate to beleaguered Christians that divine providence was on their side. The imagination of the devil was to project an end to a repressive military rule through the ultimate power of God. With the timeless word of God and the established tenets of spiritual warfare, they could use the devil figure to collapse the past, present, and the future into a counter-discourse of resistance against the hegemonic power that ruled their lives. Within the context of the brutal military government, this approach was just practical and strategic because important counter-discourses of overthrowing authority could be rendered to the public as part of a divine plan, and it could be taken for granted that their vision had long been embedded in His agenda. At the time of *Agbara Nla*, unlike Abejoye, their power identity, now also marked through the prosperity gospel, had not become a self-evident reality.

The prosperity gospel, an aspect of Pentecostal theology, is a doctrine of reciprocity between God and believers; people give their resources to God in faith and receive abundant blessings, usually in the form of money and other material goods. Also called the "health and wealth gospel," it is a spiritual contract that posits that faith in God

---

[68] Ihejirika, "Media and Fundamentalism in Nigeria."
[69] Comaroff, "Pentecostalism, Populism and the New Politics of Affect," 49.
[70] Ibid.

should be accompanied by financial and material health for believers.[71] Through the speech acts of prayer, tithes payment, positive confession, ritual enactment, and "seed-sowing," people key into divine promises of material well-being to enable them to survive the wounds of global capitalism. In a globalized economy where market forces are deemed autonomous, and the sites/forces of production are de-anchored from those of consumption, money becomes susceptible to the idea of the occult economy – the imagination that physical money can be conjured.[72] A monetary flow de-anchored from obvious means of productivity gives money a magical quality, and treats capitalism like the magic dust of social reformation, the messiah itself.[73]

The Pentecostal prosperity gospel can, to some extent, be credited with boosting a work ethic, engendering an optimistic outlook of upward social mobility, creating a wide network of social support from religious cohorts, and encouraging a transcendence over the structural imbalances that have kept Africa poor. The teachings have been popular, especially among the poor and the benighted who are urged to sow a part of their income to the Lord and expect an abundant blessing in return. People have shared testimonies of how they sacrificed their personal property such as entire monthly income, cars, inheritance, school fees, and so on only to receive a miraculous yield. Even those who do not get a spectacular reward still maintain their faith and ultimately expect some degree of return on their investment.[74] The theology altered the way they thought of impossible dreams of wealth, and the realistic means by which it could be acquired in post-military Nigeria. Prosperity gospel provided a conscious moral paradigm through which people could engage in consumption of modern goods without feelings of guilt or worry about sliding into sin.[75] By literally "demonizing" poverty, the preachers created an apprehensible spirit for its manifestation and transposed the imagery of the devil onto it. The specter of dread the devil evokes in people became synonymous with the wretchedness of poverty, and further drove people to seek the divine power to survive brutal conditions.

---

[71] Wariboko, "Pentecostal Paradigms of National Economic Prosperity in Africa." On the logic of this spiritual transaction, see: Wariboko, "Faith Has a Rate of Return."
[72] Comaroff & Comaroff, "Privatizing the Millennium."   [73] Ibid., 306–309.
[74] Wariboko, "Faith Has a Rate of Return."   [75] Lee, "Prosperity Theology."

The discourse of Pentecostal prosperity theology as engaged by different scholars such as David Maxwell, Ebenezer Obadare, Birgit Meyer, Simon Coleman, Amos Yong, Asonzeh Ukah, Naomi Haynes, Nimi Wariboko, Lovemore Togarasei, and Deji Aiyegboyin can be placed on a continuum. On one end of the spectrum, scholars are optimistic that the prosperity gospel, and its power to format cultural orientation toward capitalism, offers an ethic of empowerment that fosters upward mobility in African contexts where the public bureaucracies tasked with providing the social infrastructure for collective uplift are either inefficient or markedly absent.[76] Thus, churches provide educational, medical, economic, and social benefits to their members who invest the capital they receive into wealth-generating enterprises. In addition to the strong sense of identity formation the churches provide, they also energize the entrepreneurial instinct of those who want material success as proof of their immaterial faith.[77] On the other end of the spectrum are scholars who, having weighed the neoliberalist bent of the prosperity gospel and how it has made Pentecostal Christians unwitting propagators of society's demise through their encouragement of primitive accumulation and their reactionary attitude toward capitalist predation, dismiss its value for navigating a path to prosperity for Africans. Whether the prosperity gospel has generated the ethic necessary for galvanizing Africa to development or not, the business savviness of these faith enterprises is worth acknowledging. Their many successes as social reproducers reflect their pragmatism in assessing the spirit of their times, conducting market research, and employing tested business practices in the enterprise of church growth.

Pentecostals have never been a monolith, and the quest for power through economic means was not initially the defining trait of the faith movement. They initially aspired toward asceticism and were far more

[76] Ayegboyin, "A Rethinking of Prosperity Teaching in the New Pentecostal Churches in Nigeria"; Coleman, *The Globalisation of Charismatic Christianity*; Haynes, "Pentecostalism and the Morality of Money"; Maxwell, "'Delivered from the Spirit of Poverty?'"; Meyer, "Pentecostalism and Neo-liberal Capitalism"; Obadare, "'Raising Righteous Billionaires'"; Togarasei, "The Pentecostal Gospel of Prosperity in African Contexts of Poverty"; Ukah, "Those Who Trade with God Never Lose"; Wariboko, "Pentecostal Paradigms of National Economic Prosperity in Africa"; Yong, "A Typology of Prosperity Theology."
[77] Heuser, "Charting African Prosperity Gospel Economies," 8.

conscious of an afterlife.[78] They made a conscious choice to reject the way of the world and retreat into social enclaves where they would not be morally tainted by worldly influences.[79] When still a novel movement, they tried to flatten out divisive differences by subsuming divergent personalities under the all-encompassing Pentecostal identity.[80] With the economic squeeze and the crushing poverty that befell Nigeria during the turbulent years of the '80s and '90s, more people turned to God to meet their economic needs. Salvation was no longer about the soul, but urgent material needs as well. Over time, the capitalist imperative that underwrites the prosperity gospel yielded to the desire for the "finer things in life" such that even Pastor Enoch Adeboye, the General Overseer of about the largest congregation in Nigeria – and possibly Africa – recently lamented,

The most worrisome thing I see (about the future of Christ) among the younger ones is that majority are beginning to forget that Jesus is coming back again. In our younger days we were always expectant of the coming of the Lord. And in fact, we used to greet ourselves in that direction. We were always looking forward to when the Lord would come back. We also always prepared for the rapture and we ensured we did not do things that would make us miss rapture. But today people are more concerned about prosperity. They are beginning to forget that we have a home in heaven.[81]

The prosperity gospel indeed changed the moral temperature of the church. Those whom the early Pentecostals looked down upon as "ungodly" because of their attachment to worldly groups have become the ones to dominate the church. The bejeweled outsiders who were

---

[78] Marshall, *Political Spiritualities*, 76.
[79] Under the social and economic conditions of the Nigerian 1970s when the country was awash with "petro-dollars" and the corruption that typically attends extractive economies, most of those in the earlier wave of Pentecostals shunned flamboyance and worldliness, and practiced an ethic of self-denial. In appearance and in quotidian practices, they were expected to live a life that contrasted with the rest of the social culture and was driven only by faith. Some churches proscribed the television, saying it was the devil's box. They also spurned wealth in all its forms, preferring to focus on the imminent second coming of Jesus. Komolafe, "The Changing Face of Christianity"; Pierce, *Moral Economies of Corruption*.
[80] For instance, they called themselves "brothers" and "sisters," and stridently denied worldliness. Gaiya, *The Pentecostal Revolution in Nigeria*.
[81] www.vanguardngr.com/2020/04/my-worry-for-this-generation-of-christians-adeboye/

once candidates for hell because of their worldliness became proof of divine benevolence. Today,

Pentecostal churches now count members of the upper class, military officers, top civil servants, and political and business leaders among their fold. The major denominations among them have complex bureaucracies, celebrity pastors, and often function as (or at least claim to be) agents of national development and sociopolitical redemption. They are increasingly emboldened by their successes to view themselves as divinely sanctioned change-leaders ushering in a new Africa.[82]

The demographic of church membership is vast, cutting across generations and social classes. Thousands and thousands of churches of various cathedral sizes litter the entire southern Nigerian landscape, particularly in its urban centers where their advertising – huge electronic billboards with pastor's faces – hits one on the face. Pentecostal churches have built – and are still building – virtually all the infrastructure of social reproduction: huge church auditoriums, media houses, universities, popular entertainment facilities, politics, gymnasiums, malls, schools, prayer cities, financial institutions, housing estates, science laboratory, printing presses, and publishing businesses. They demonstrate a promiscuous attitude toward absorbing forms, practices, and bodies into their fold from the spheres deemed "secular." They treat spaces as dynamic and can site churches in cinema halls, nightclubs, and places similarly marked as "sinful" without being bogged down by the contradictions.[83] Dozens of megachurches have not only established churches in virtually every town and city across the thirty-six states of Nigeria, they also have multiple branches in other parts of the world from Africa to USA, UK, Europe, Australia, and even Asia. Pastors have become superstars, and their celebrity culture sometimes usurps artists on the popular culture scene. Politicians regularly corral pastors' theological influence to win elections and maintain their hold on power. Pastors have become a part of the power brokerage economy, and they have become invested in worldly politics to the point their partisanship leaves them vulnerable to public criticism. Faith in God's power to convict gets downplayed, and the coercive power of partisan politics is used to override personal decisions.

[82] Wariboko, "Pentecostalism in Africa."
[83] Adeboye, "'A Church in a Cinema Hall?'"

Many of the most elaborate architectural buildings in Nigeria are initiated by large churches that need to enter the cluttered, yet intensively competitive, religious market. All over the country, especially in the major Nigerian cities, churches large and small keep springing up to cater to the ever-expanding Pentecostal population. In Lagos, for instance, there is an ongoing church-building project with architecture that is a high-rise, towering at the same height – or even above – the headquarters of corporate business organizations. During the celebration of the opening of a cathedral that was said could accommodate up to 100,000 worshippers at a time in the FCT in 2018, one of the men of God invited to speak at the occasion, Archbishop John Osa-Oni, boasted about the progress of the Pentecostal denomination, "We were called the mushroom churches, but today we are the much much room church."[84]

As Pentecostalism vigorously preached material success and widened its congregation, it also ostentatiously performed wealth, particularly through the activities of the pastorate at the higher levels of the church hierarchy. Pastors of megachurches have raised enormous amounts of money for their ambitious projects, some of which came from morally tainted sources.[85] The pastors of the megachurches themselves have become icons of dazzling wealth who boasted of the rains of divine blessings on themselves and their households, construing themselves as legitimate proof of the viability of the prosperity gospel. Church members, deriving empathetic pleasure from watching their leaders embody so much economic power, use material acquisition as a spiritual "point of contact" for their own aspirations. There are examples of the scandal where Christians were arrested for defrauding the business organizations they worked for and the investigators found that churches had received part of the stolen wealth either through generous donations to the church or to the pastors.[86]

Paul Esupofo's demonic encounter reenacted in *Abejoye* also shows people uprooted from their local roots, who migrated to other territories to nurture and be nurtured by the unaccustomed earth of other lands. As Nigerian Pentecostals migrated and took their God with

[84] www.youtube.com/watch?v=801IOJ-uzTw
[85] For instance, two of the top bankers indicted in the financial institution scandals of 2008, Cecilia Ibru and Erastus Akingbola, were top-ranking members the Redeemed Christian Church of God.
[86] Faleye, "Religious Corruption."

them, they also formed a global diaspora of faith that, despite its particularistic differences, is like a spoken universal language that expresses the vision of Jesus Christ to gather his own as "one flock" under "one shepherd."[87] In his theological-historical analysis of Pentecostal transnational routes, sociologist Waldo Cesar uses biblical accounts of the Tower of Babel and the Day of Pentecost as narrative paradigms to track humanity's disunification from God and eventual reunification. In the respective biblical accounts of these two events, language is a motif of separation – when God separated people at the Tower of Babel by confusing their language – and reconciliation – when, on the Day of Pentecost, the disciples spoke in tongues and people of different countries heard them in their individual languages.[88] The unity that Pentecostalism has forged by transcending linguistic barriers across all nations, he says, makes it "the greatest expression of human communication."[89]

Pentecostals have not only created a global formation, they – like the folks at the Babel Tower – are using the powers of unifying language of the spirit to build "a city and the tower." On the day of the Pentecost, they spoke in tongues which were diverse but mutually intelligible, a symbolic interplay between differences, yet an identity built on sameness.[90] As Wariboko interpreted this event of Pentecost, ordinary folks were fired by the Holy Ghost and imbued with diverse gifts to go out and organize the infrastructure of the world; the relationality "marked by diversity, inclusiveness, invitation, equity, and new relationship-making power."[91] The "city and the tower" – synecdoche of empire-building with no prescribed limits – links Pentecostals from all over the world and inspires a global religious domination based on the interplay of a similar language yet different tongues.[92] This flexibility of principles leads to a self-justifying habit of overpromoting capitalist ideologies and the unembarrassed display of money, wealth, and splendor, as co-signifiers of spirituality. The headquarters of the Pentecostal global empire may not be domiciled in a singular spatial location as, for example, the Catholics have Vatican City, but the vision of a holy city is individually embodied by Pentecostals who have formed a vast network of interdependent

---

[87] John 10:16, NKJV.   [88] César, "From Babel to Pentecost."   [89] Ibid.
[90] Wariboko, *Methods of Ethical Analysis.*   [91] Ibid.
[92] Cesar, *From Babel to Pentecost*, 30.

local churches.[93] During this endless expansion to acquire an even broader stage on which to perform their power identity, Nigerian Pentecostalism acquired traveling companions that trimmed the sharp edges of its ideologies to be more accepting of the worldly as long as it expanded their sphere of authority and consolidated their hold on power.[94]

Given how pervasive Pentecostal practices are, and how much its powerful ethos dominates the Nigerian social sphere, the ghostly quality in the return of the demon figure in *Abejoye* felt rather routine. The concept of demonic encounters seemed easy: the devil was too tame, too voiceless, and even too familiar to the deliverance minister for its capacity for evil to be considered radical. So why did demonic encounter become a matter of amusement? From its earlier tentative position, Pentecostalism has built up a network of middle-class members whose rise amidst the strangulating economic conditions of the society in the country and in the new world has been tremendous. Such feat necessitated self-proclamation, and the faith movement, through its prosperity gospel, has become one of the biggest propagators of the conquering power of capitalism and the freedom of consumption. In a social context where domains of religion, economics, and politics have mapped onto each other, their feat of success impacted even their representation of demonic encounters. Rather than narrate novel stories that prime people for an imminent victory that will displace established political authorities who repress the destiny of children of God, their formulaic restaging of a deliverance scene is a narration of a victory that already happened and needs sustaining with appeals to the tropes that made them great. The identity of Pentecostals as a people of power was more assured and though the fear of the devil works still through their imagination, when demonic figures appear, they could also be treated as objects of amusement and as playthings.

---

[93] Wariboko, The Charismatic City and the Public Resurgence of Religion, 172–173.

[94] For a study on African religious/Pentecostal transnationalism see: Adeboye, "Transnational Pentecostalism in Africa"; Adogame, *Religion Crossing Boundaries*; Adogame, "Transnational migration and Pentecostalism in Europe"; Asamoah-Gyadu, "Spirit, Mission and Transnational Influence"; Knibbe, "'We Did Not Come Here as Tenants, but as Landlords'"; Maxwell, "Christianity without Frontiers."

Conclusion

This chapter has been a reflection on the power identity of Pentecostals through the stages of evolution within Nigerian social and political contexts, using the narrative elements of spiritual warfare in two television series across a span of almost three decades. These two accounts are similar, but their pinpointing different periods expresses the power identity through the politics of self-representation. Within the nation's troubled political sphere, they unleashed demonic characters through which they staged confrontations, expressed desires, and approximated their power as Pentecostal Christians. The consistency of narration from *Agbara Nla* to *Abejoye* shows how this sense of imaging self-identity has discursively solidified through years of performing power both in local and global contexts. The arc of Esupofo and Olayiotan's character development from the early '90s when Nigerians dwelled in an unstable polity to the 2020s reflects the trajectory of the Pentecostal identity.

This unceasing power identity performance does not remove the factors that accentuate the Pentecostal desire for power. The country's perennial economic woes and political upheavals even within the context of democratic rule heighten the desire for power among Pentecostal subjects. The pursuit of power propels the performance of power – to attain it, sustain it, and become identified by it. As people continue to face precarious conditions, they develop even more apocalyptic visions to process the structures of their reality and their self-understanding as people of power gets heightened. In the next chapter, I will be looking at the performance of power identity through an analysis of electoral contests in both Nigeria and the USA, and what it meant for the Pentecostal and evangelical Christian power bloc transnationally.

2 | "What Islamic Devils?!": Power Struggles, Race, and Christian Transnationalism

Pentecostalism's incursion into the political arena has been a well-documented part of the contests by Islam and Christianity, the dominant religions in Nigeria.[1] With an almost equal number of adherents distributed across the nation, the two forces counterbalance each other's excesses.[2] Their long histories within the country means they shaped the foundations of modern Nigeria, and the nation's structures have calibrated their relational terms as permanent mutual contestants.[3] By mutually acting as foils, both have situated themselves as political constituencies whose forces are equally interpenetrated by geospatial politics. Their reciprocal tensions and politics of encounter have shaped their trajectories.[4] Both Islam and Christianity, in a cycle of perennial contest for dominance, mutually appropriate each other's techniques of worship.[5] Driven by the conversion impulse, they both also confer religious leaders with political legitimacy (and vice versa) and ultimately blur the boundaries between faith and politics.

Pentecostalism would not have been as impactful as a mainstream practice if, as religious studies scholar Matthews Ojo submitted, it had not presented itself to Pentecostals "as an alternative centre of power to solving human needs."[6] But, over time, as the message imbricated into the normative order, its practices also intertwined with the hegemonic formation in society. As the Pentecostal movement raised a vast army of the Lord's redeemed, they inevitably attracted social and political actors who needed their cultivated legitimacy to extend spheres of power and authority. Political leaders, seeing a blossoming site filled

---

[1] Falola, *Violence in Nigeria*; Kenny, "Sharīa and Christianity in Nigeria"; Kukah, "Religion, Politics and Power in Northern Nigeria"; Rasmussen, "Christian-Muslim Relations in Africa."

[2] Adogame, "Politicization of Religion and Religionization of Politics in Nigeria."

[3] Vaughan, *Religion and the Making of Nigeria.*

[4] Akinade, "Cross Meets Crescent."

[5] Obadare, "The Muslim Response to the Pentecostal Surge in Nigeria."

[6] Ojo, "Pentecostalism and Charismatic Movements in Nigeria."

with people whose religious impulses could be readily corralled into political gains, moved in to appropriate the charismatic authority of pastors.[7] Astute Pentecostal leaders fraternized with politicians to realize the dominion theology they preached and prayed about in their churches. This symbiotic relationship where pastors consecrated government decisions and the government officials, in turn, conferred political legitimacy on pastors and inevitably ran them against the forces of Islam, another political faith practice equally invested in political power.

In Chapter 1, I indicated that both 1993 and 1998/9 are significant dates in the political history of postwar Nigeria. Here, my study in Pentecostal political theology notes that 2015 was equally significant because a rupture occurred in the political ecology Pentecostal leaders had steadily built over a sixteen-year period. After a Muslim candidate defeated a Christian president who was backed by many Pentecostal pastors in the 2015 elections, political alliances changed and the network of power they had enjoyed was disrupted. For all the much-vaunted theo-political influence of Pentecostal pastors and for which they have been canonized as "Africa's big man,"[8] and a shadow political institution,[9] the 2015 electoral outcome showed the limits of their influence. The election marked a time when Pentecostal power and influence was vigorously contested along with the general election. The "Christian" presidential candidate lost the election to a Muslim, and that meant a redistribution of political power among the new cadre of winners. Having lost the direct access to the highest political authority, they switched to the other mode of performing power—the marginal and oppressed.

For those who had openly supported the Christian candidate, the electoral loss also meant the rollback of some of the gains they had made as a dominant social group in the country. Considering that the politics of spirituality in Nigeria is also intertwined with ethnic identity, the loss of democratic influence that followed the loss of the election was double-layered for those who committed to a side based on religious and

---

[7] This political elites' appropriation of a social order built through religious ethos is not quite new. In colonial era, the British took a similar turn with Islam and in northern Nigeria to extend their rights to rule the colonized country. Here, I defer to Wariboko's exploration of religious relations in Nigeria and how their politics engendered state formation processes. Wariboko, *Dynamics of Muslim Worlds*.

[8] McCauley, "Africa's New Big Man Rule?" Also see Adelakun, "Pastocracy."

[9] McCauley, "Pentecostalism as an Informal Political Institution."

ethnic identities. The years of implanting their Pentecostal values into the
social ecosystem suffered a setback. One of the ways they reoriented
their desire for power was support for Donald Trump, the forty-fifth US
"Christian" president. He was seen as a centripetal figure of Christian
institutional forbearance, the one around whom people could anchor
their political spirituality and identity politics pending reascendance to
political power in their own country. Their turn to Trump is significant
for exploring how power identity seeks out other means to maintain its
dominance even while inhabiting the position of the embattled. One of
the ways they have gone about this has been to look outside their
national shores for the dominant power.

There is a growing genre of literature that investigates political theology in the age of Trump, a president whose alliance with US evangelicals negates the doctrine of the constitutional separation of church and
state. These studies locate the Christian support for Trump as an imperative of white nationalism. One of such accounts is Katherine Stewart's
investigative study of the Christian Religious Right in the USA, *The
Power Worshippers.* Her study reveals a political movement that comprises a network of interests converge around the political vision of
reinstating America's Christian origins. She describes the movement as
"Christian nationalism" to capture the overlapping sentiments of politics and religion that drive those involved. According to her, Christian
nationalism is a political ideology that,

promotes the myth that the American republic was founded as a Christian
nation. It asserts that legitimate government rests not on the consent of the
governed but on adherence to the doctrines of a specific religion, ethnic and
cultural heritage. It demands that our laws based not on the reasoned
deliberation of our democratic institutions but on particular, idiosyncratic
interpretations of the Bible. Its defining fear is that the nation has strayed
from that once made it great. Christian Nationalism looks backward on
a fictionalized history of America's allegedly Christian founding. It looks
forward to a future in which its version of the Christian religion and its
adherents, along with their political allies, enjoy positions of exceptional
privilege and power in government and in law.[10]

This group's ambition of domination, of course, predates Trump and
like Nigerian Pentecostals, what they too want is power. If power is the
ability to make things happen, people who seek to take over power in

[10] Stewart, *The Power Worshippers.*

the name of religion also understand the necessity of (re-)arranging the world order in the image of their faith. Achieving this means effective organizing, and liaisons with other power brokers to ensure their representatives are plugged into strategic public positions to influence the social ethos. These efforts do not stay within their national borders, rather they spill over into other places where their influence extends through their missionary activities, media houses, and outreach programs.[11] Through these networks, they spread not just the message of Christ but a conservative agenda, an instance which resulted in the harsh "kill the gay" law in Uganda.[12] With modern media technology, the circulation of their conservative ideas has become much easier.

Following Stewart, I call this relationship between evangelical Christian nationalists in the USA and Nigerian Pentecostals "Christian transnationalism" and it describes a shared devotion to keep America Christian as it supposedly was at its founding, and for Christians in both countries to continuously enjoy privileged positions and power. Donald Trump is a node that connects this mutual desire. The public sphere where both meet consists of a carved out moral space – the Internet – that, in generating an ethos of support for their candidate, also abjures complex nuances of identity politics in their respective countries and center conversations around Christian political power. For Nigerian Pentecostal Christians, having someone who represents them in power is crucial to maintaining their power identity. If nothing else, a "Christian" president triumphing, albeit in another

[11] In episode four of *The Family*, an American web television miniseries that examines a conservative Christian group – known as the Family or the Fellowship – with prominent influence on American politics, one of their members talked about traversing Africa to evangelize as representative of Christianity and American government. Rep. Mark Siljander (R-MI) met with Libyan's dictator, Muammar Ghaddafi. Senator James Inhofe (R-Oklahoma) also talked about meeting Nigeria's brutal dictator, Sani Abacha, in 1997, and telling him that Jesus loved him. With the soft power of Christianity, these evangelical representatives eased the way for political relations and subsequent influence on those African leaders. Also, see Marishane's article on religious right and US foreign policy; "Prayer, Profit and Power."
[12] Kapya Kaoma has written about the ways US evangelical right-wingers ideologically mentored Ugandans to write the bill. See, for instance, www.pri.org/stories/2013-11-15/how-american-evangelicals-made-life-unbearable-gays-uganda; www.theatlantic.com/international/archive/2013/12/uganda-passes-law-punishes-homosexuality-life-imprisonment/356365/

country, alleviates the shame of being tied down by their nation's leadership failures, activates the fantasy of being a chosen people of God, and overall, nurtures their identity of power.

Trump's claims of fulfilling a vision of Christian domination defies his country's secularism and liberalism to offer them a representation of their faith in the highest political office in the world. One writer explains the Christian investment in US politics saying,

America is the leading supporter of Christian missions in the world today. While the American government may not invest a dollar in missions, the Evangelical community in America does. In fact they invest massively in mission outreaches to various communities and countries in Africa and whatever affects them will ultimately affect us. If the liberal ideologies of the Democratic Party take over America today, that nation would be sold to unrighteousness and the words of scriptures would be fulfilled on them: righteousness exalts a nation and sin is a reproach to its people (Proverbs 14:34). It is righteousness that brought America to where she is today and sin will bring her down. If America goes down, mission support to African countries will deplete also and this will affect outreaches to unreached areas here. So America's politics is our own politics also.[13]

Such sentiments demonstrate a vicarious realization of power identity through Trump.

In forthcoming sections, I will track the historical patterns of Nigerian politics at key historical junctures to show how the politics of the Nigerian Pentecostal Republic is not contained within provincial national borders. With globalized modern technology having facilitated congregating across previously impenetrable borders, Pentecostals' performance of their religious politics far more readily crosses the Atlantic. The face of Christianity might have long changed from that of the white European to encompass the humans of other worlds,[14] but there are also non-whites in other parts of the world protective of maintaining Christianity's whiteness due to the efficacies of its accrued power. In their engagement, they look beyond whiteness as color to engage with it as a trope that corresponds with political and spiritual power.

At this point, a caveat is necessary. Not all Pentecostals/Christians or people of southern Nigerian heritage are Trump supporters. There are always significant differences in the politics of faith and the allure of

---

[13] Deji Yesufu, http://mouthpiece.com.ng/evangelicals-support-of-donald-trump/
[14] Sanneh & Carpenter, *The Changing Face of Christianity.*

political personality. However, it is a fact that Trump has a following in Nigeria, and it is connected to the ethnic and religious politics of the 2015 election. Nigerians supporting Trump is particularly ironical because while majority of native black Americans perceive Trump and his white followers as irredentists, some black Africans adore him and this perplexes many Western commentators who think his demeaning comments toward them should have discouraged their partisanship. What these Western writers miss is that Trump is also a beneficiary of Nigerian Pentecostals' resentment against former president Barack Obama. These Christian classes have not only historically identified with the American evangelical establishment, but also jointly saw Obama's liberalism – for instance, his support for same-sex marriage (and the subsequent Supreme Court victory for the LGBTQ groups that advocated their right to marry), bathroom culture wars, and what they perceived as his pandering to the Muslim countries and communities in the USA – as a threat to Christianity, whiteness, and the civilizing force they have always associated with these identity categories. These Nigerians are empathetic members of the Republican Party in the USA, and anyone who visits the comment pages of social media sites of media like CNN; the social media pages of the White House and Donald Trump; right-wing media, Breitbart and others, will typically find them echoing the denunciation of the evils of "liberals," Democrats, and the "fake news" of mainstream media. On the 2020 Election Day, some of them held a rally for Trump in Nigeria. An elated Trump tweeted the video saying, "A parade for me in Nigeria, a great honor!"[15]

To clearly narrate the formation of these dynamics, I go back a little to chart the Nigerian political terrain, and how sentiments and sensibilities build up along other identity axes such as Pentecostalism. I start with a quotation by one of the pastors of the biggest churches in Nigeria, Bishop David Oyedepo, the presiding pastor of Living Faith Church (aka the Winners' Chapel). It is an excerpt from a previous sermon and prayer charge on Islam and Boko Haram terrorism held months before the crucial 2015 election. He said,

All the northern forces that are sponsoring these uprising and killings, I decree the curse of God upon them.

[15] https://punchng.com/us-election-trump-hails-parade-in-nigeria-says-great-honour/

Come on, pray in the spirit everybody! Pray in the spirit, open fire, call down the Holy Ghost fire to descend on the camp of the enemy! Enough is Enough!

What demonic devils! What Islamic demons!

If Nigeria waits for the church to rise, Nigeria will disappear as a nation.

I was even told from report that they were targeting this church. I said what? Even if I was asleep, if you see anybody here kill him! Kill him and spill his blood on the ground. I am saying that to you! What nonsense! What devil! You think our God is an idol? I declare their collaborators cursed. I decree their sponsors cursed!

Must the north continue to rule? What devils!

God has anointed me to lead a revolution against the Islamic jihadists and as the Lord liveth and as the anointing of Jeru-Baal that's on me, we declare them extinct in the name of Jesus! Amen!

You catch anyone that looks like them, kill him! There is no reporting to anybody. Kill him! Pull off his neck! And we spill his blood on the ground. What nonsense!

Every agent of destruction in Government today, call fire down on their head, call fire down on their head.

Everyone sponsoring evil against the nation, let your fire fall on him!

They said why Christians should say they could defend themselves.

Hold it! What stupid statement.

Why shouldn't Christians say they could defend themselves? So, they should watch for you to put a knife to their necks? You think we are dummies?

Don't mistake only those in politics as in power.

The anointed in the Lord are the ones in power. By divine ordination, don't mistake that. There was a king in the land, but Elijah was determining the events of the nation.

If I say it will not rain here for three years, it will not drop.

What nonsense![16]

Islam as the Devil Synonym, and the Politics of Deliverance

Despite the shifts in Pentecostals' fortunes, diabolization never goes away. The specter of imminent demonic attack is regularly conjured to wage spiritual battles, enact practices that contest power, and confirm power identity. Demonic specters are a teleo-affective use of language

---

[16] www.premiumtimesng.com/news/top-news/220482-living-faith-church-reacts-video-showing-founder-oyedepo-urging-members-kill.html

and imagery that fuels bipolar narratives and enforces borders when religious faith ventures into other spheres such as politics or popular culture. The image of the devil figure, now universalized by religious and nonreligious actors, is a timeless resort for Christians who want to confront an existential threat within an era and legitimize a favorable social order.[17] The naming of the demon itself is accusative, rhetoric that activates a persecution complex by instantly framing a polarizing identity of good "us" vs. bad "them."[18] What might evolve with time is the dramatization of exorcism from the social body or the Christian's physical body. The drama of the eventual expulsion of the devil tells us what fear haunts the people at present and the kinds of rituals they are amenable to collectively carry out to expel the agents metaphorized as demonic from their union. Demons are "forged in the crucible of collective weaknesses, misshapen by national ambivalence toward the political system . . . readily projected toward external sources which are then conjured as evil and defined as public enemy."[19] The rhetoric of demonization is thus an important indicator of the resentment building in the society and the level of instigation of violence possible with the people.[20]

The aforementioned sermon by Oyedepo on Muslims in Nigeria as devils and demons vividly illustrates the politics of demonization. It demonstrates the flexible uses to which the demonic can be rendered in a context where majority religious authorities are fighting for the control of state power. Diabolizing Islam, as both political theorist Ruth Marshall and religious studies scholar Matthews Ojo show us, is not entirely new in Nigeria's political history. In her study of Nigerian Pentecostalism, Marshall copiously demonstrates how the fear of the demon of an "Islamized government" has always haunted the nation, and "both the Born-Agains and Muslim reformers conjure the devil in the name of each other."[21] Oyedepo's describing political contenders as "Islamic devils" that ought to be defeated was similar mobilization agenda. The church assembly is about the most political

---

[17] Kotsko, *The Prince of This World.*
[18] Normand, *Demonization in International Politics.*
[19] Ivie & Giner, "Hunting the Devil."
[20] Dawson, "Black Power in 1996 and the Demonization of African Americans"; Smiley & Fakunle, "From 'Brute' to 'Thug.'"
[21] Marshall, *Political Spiritualities*; Ojo, "Pentecostal Movements, Islam and the Contest for Public Space in Northern Nigeria." Also see Ogbu Kalu's narration of these intertwined histories: Kalu, *Power, Poverty, and Prayer.*

space for this kind of manipulation because that is where pastors can "provide interpretative maps for understanding cause, effect, and possibility in the world."[22] Given the context of Boko Haram terrorism Nigeria was facing – bombs going off in some parts of the country and killing people – the sermon alerts his congregation to the precarity of Christian life in the Nigerian political order. When replayed in the context of the 2015 election, it was an urge to weaponize their ballots.

For the Nigerian context, personifying a rival other as the devil is rather significant because belief in the dark, foreboding, and possessive transcendental force of evil is not merely metaphoric but familiar and instinctive to the church audience that regularly congregates to pray against its activities. Due to the experiential nature of Pentecostal belief, temporal events acquire a sacred import and secular history is rendered through the registers of spirituality and the radical evil of demonic activity.[23] As Pentecostals negotiate the contradictory impulses to love their neighbors as themselves and also survive antagonistic social conditions, they are caught in the throes of eternal vigilance of their neighbors' true nature.[24] Within the social context of Nigeria where religious differentiation could become a matter of life and death, the theology of loving and being at peace with one's neighbor clashes with the reality of survival. Therefore, the Nigerian believer, "forever scans her neighbors for a detailed reading of their true spiritual state."[25] Labeling them as demons is the judgment of the x-ray: they are a radical, resident evil due for destruction. With a name and a silhouette in the minds of the congregation, the enemy is rendered "visible," "monstrous," and a "full-fledged resistance of the mind, spirit, and body," is enabled.[26]

The auditorium where he preached that sermon, Faith Tabernacle, sits a huge congregation of 50,000.[27] In the middle of the church is an expansive altar on which Oyedepo walked back and forth as he addressed his congregation, priming their feelings with reminders of the country's historical injustices. The church, now on their feet, segued to the prayer session where Oyedepo's voice over the lavalier microphone – sometimes throaty and sometimes raised to a high pitch as he exhorts the congregation with a metaphorization of Islam

[22] McClendon & Riedl. *From Pews to Politics.*   [23] Bloch, *Visionary Republic.*
[24] Wariboko, *Nigerian Pentecostalism.*   [25] Ibid. 267.
[26] Portier-Young, *Apocalypse against Empire.*
[27] http://news.bbc.co.uk/2/hi/africa/542154.stm

as demonic – called for violence against Islamic terrorists. He roused their psychic energies toward action. Oyedepo, a well-known preacher of dominion theology, interspersed his political commentary in the prayer session with tongue-speaking and prophetic declarations, a code-switching that suggests crossing natural and supernatural realms as he spoke to the church. The bishop's characteristic animated manner of speaking to the church, plus the urgency of the situation he was describing, and in the context of prayer, combined to prime the congregation to be amenable to the rendering of Islam and terrorism as thoroughly inhuman enemies who must be destroyed.

Prayer, especially the one of spiritual warfare that Oyedepo enjoins his audience to unleash, makes militants out of otherwise loving Christians.[28] It is,

an exercise by which Pentecostals vigorously summon spiritual powers from the Holy Spirit to "violently" attack every enemy and obstacle blocking their progress or causing any form of suffering in their lives. It is executed with the dedication of warfare, creating an enactment or performance of the struggle for higher levels of human flourishing ... Spiritual warfare is the discourse that in praying about something also prays on the fact that it is praying about the ongoing prayer itself. Spiritual warfare manifests prayer and, at the same time, itself.[29]

An intensely psychic and physical activity, spiritual warfare prayer works on the minds and the body of the congregant. In the intensely focused moment of spiritual exertion where the vivid image of God vanquishing the forces of evil is conjured by a massive congregation such as the one Oyedepo superintends, people's convictions are aligned with a stated or underlined political agenda. Prayers are spiritual means of accessing power; the sheer physicality makes the body a channel to both draw and exercise power.

More than a corporeal activity, the components of the message is also significant. He frames the narrative as an urgent contest for the future from the grip of totalizing Islam. The message went viral in 2015, before the general elections in which the stakes of victory had been raised so high it subsumed all other issues of social development under the binary of Christian vs. Muslim, and northern vs. southern Nigeria. The sense of

---

[28] Marshall, "Destroying Arguments and Captivating Thoughts."
[29] Wariboko, "Pentecostalism in Africa."

urgency that underwrote the message was not only in objective terms, but messianic as well. The Pentecostal conception of messianic time, based on the idea of how much time they have left before the second coming of the messiah, infuses their activities with a sense of urgency as they approach end-time.[30]

The sermon combined messianic time with objective time, and made general elections urgent, one in which the fate of Christians would be decided. By asking, "Must the north continue to rule?" he dredged up lingering sentiment about the history of northern Islamic hegemony and their dominance of spheres of power before Pentecostals became a competitor. Using biblical registers, he could describe Islam as a monstrosity in ways that would instinctively tell his listeners that they were dealing with an opponent with an exceptional capacity for destruction. He instigated them to see their prayers as a call for justice denied through the instruments of juridical power and calling for graphic violence inscribes this vividly. Asking them to pray was also urging them to see how much the moral responsibility to save the country from the grip of Satan rests on their spiritual and civic participation.

Framing political issues around demonic paradigms was not without basis in material reality. He was also speaking to extant reality and potently politicizing it so that his congregation could make sense of the oppressive powers whose confounding brutality and lust for power, seemed to have transcended human capabilities. By 2015, Nigeria had been badly depressed by insecurity. The devastating forces of Boko Haram terrorists were routinely carrying out terrible violence, bombing churches (and later, mosques too) and other public places. They ransacked villages, murdered people, and went as far as capturing Nigerian territories for themselves and planting their flags on them. It did not help the country that the national security crisis happened under the watch of president Goodluck Jonathan, whose administration lacked the efficiency to curtail the crisis and chalked down its helplessness to an insidious Islamic agenda by those who had lost power in the previous election, 2011, and who swore to make the country "ungovernable" for him.[31] Oyedepo's message resonated

---

[30] Marshall, *Political Spiritualities.*

[31] For a study on Boko Haram, please see: Adenrele, "Boko Haram Insurgency in Nigeria as a Symptom of Poverty and Political Alienation"; Akinola, "Boko Haram Insurgency in Nigeria"; Awortu, "Boko Haram Insurgency and the Underdevelopment of Nigeria"; Bappah, "Nigeria's Military Failure against the

ahead of a critical national election where the political forces of Christianity and Islam were aligned against each other, and the victory could determine who owned the soul of the nation.

As I outlined in the Introduction, due to the evil the autocrats wreaked on both the polity and the body of its inhabitants, particularly during the repressive years of the military that comprised on northern Muslim leaders, people forged imaginative links between political power, evil forces, and Islam. As most of the religious violence in Nigeria happened in the northern part of Nigeria (and with near-zero consequences for the perpetrators), the idea of Islam as a form of malevolence supported by official power is engraved in the mind of the Christian public. With their rule and domination over Nigeria's politics for a long time, Muslims have formed an almost impenetrable fraternity around their intersecting ethnic and religious identities such that political power became metonymized with "northern Muslim."

When the last military dictator, Sani Abacha, died in 1998, one of his political captives, Olusegun Obasanjo, a former military ruler, was released from jail. He left prison publicly proclaiming to have become a born-again Christian. He won the presidential election the following year. The myth of his trajectory from prison to palace was similar to that of Joseph in the Bible. His handlers correlated this coincidence of Bible narratives and unfolding biography to create a "theocratic class" around Obasanjo; they packaged him as a "Pentecostal president."[32] As president, Obasanjo dutifully performed rituals such as building up the chapel in Aso Rock (the presidential villa) and naming pastors as his spiritual advisers.[33] Obasanjo also publicly associated with organizations like the Christian Association of Nigeria, Pentecostal Fellowship of Nigeria, and made several pilgrimages to the "Redemption Camp" of the Redeemed Christian Church of God, one of the largest regular gathering of Christians in the world.[34] By publicly reckoning with Pentecostal

Boko Haram Insurgency"; Comolli, *Boko Haram*; Gilbert, "Prolongation of Boko Haram Insurgency in Nigeria"; Okoli, Chukwuma & Iortyer, "Terrorism and Humanitarian Crisis in Nigeria"; Weeraratne, "Theorizing the Expansion of the Boko Haram Insurgency in Nigeria."
[32] Obadare, "Pentecostal Presidency?"
[33] https://allafrica.com/stories/201011220110.html
[34] Ukah, "Pentecostalism, Religious Expansion and the City."

pastors and their congregation in the eight years of his presidency, he helped Pentecostals to also inscribe their ethos into the political sphere and roll back the many years that Islam had done the same while in the seat of power. Christianity, or specifically, Pentecostal culture, became the defining paradigm for the nation's "vision for moral leadership, a form of public influence that is shaped by ethics and faith while also being powerful and respected."[35] Having inhabited the presidential villa, Pentecostal culture also percolated to other public spaces where its values could create meanings that rule social life. By centering famous Pentecostal preachers in his governance, he also created the conditions that made it possible for Pentecostal culture to demarcate the boundaries of politically symbolic activities and frame the contours of collective subjectivity. With such glorification, the rituals of their faith practices became the loom through which their habits, values, visions, ideas, ideals, and ethics were woven into the fabric of daily life. The Muslims, concerned they would be upstaged in public life, quickly moved to counterbalance the rising Pentecostal influence. In 1999, one after the other, governors of the states in the northern regions of the country launched Sharia law in where they held sway.[36]

By 2003, Obasanjo's presidential term was rounding off. He followed the unwritten law of alternation in Nigerian politics that, for instance, a southern Christian would be succeeded by a northern Muslim. Obasanjo campaigned vigorously for Umaru Yar'Adua, the candidate who not only fulfilled these criteria but with whose family dynasty he also had a relationship. The incumbency factor helped Obasanjo muscle Yar'Adua into power through an election fraught with massive irregularities. With the ascendance of Yar'Adua, the Muslims were back in power, although it was not to last. Yar'Adua, it turned out, had a terminal illness. Elsewhere, a president with such a debilitating condition would have walked away from the office to give his country a chance to move on without him. However, in Nigeria, relinquishing power was to deprive a geopolitical zone and a religious bloc of their turn in public office. The crass level of shenanigans that Yar'Adua's inner caucus resorted to keep his dying body in the office at all costs showed the ridiculous extent political actors in Nigeria would

---

[35] Lindsay, *Faith in the Halls of Power.*
[36] Kalu, "Sharia and Islam in Nigerian Pentecostal Rhetoric, 1970–2003"; Kalu, "Safiyya and Adamah."

go to retain power. As Yar'Adua's handlers fought to preserve his presidency, others began to look forward to a possible conclusion to a bizarre tale. Their eyes rested on the vice president, a Christian from southern Nigeria, whose name, ironically, was "Goodluck Jonathan."

The name "Goodluck" encoded the myth of Jonathan's political trajectory. He was a deputy governor in oil-rich Bayelsa state in southern Nigeria when the governor, Diepreye Alamayeseigha, was removed from office for corruption, thus paving the way for him to become governor. In 2003, this unassuming character, self-effacing to the point of self-negation, was selected as a nonthreatening counterpart to Yar'Adua, who was equally lacking in charisma. Jonathan was handpicked because power brokers thought he would not usurp the president.[37] The arrangement worked well enough until fate – and good luck – decided otherwise. Yar'Adua died in 2010, and Jonathan became the president. This development upset the pattern of presidency alternating between northern and southern regions of Nigeria.

Now thrust into an arena he would probably never have dared to enter on his own strength, Jonathan became a figure of Biblical myths: the archetypal David the shepherd boy whom God chose as king ahead of his older and more experienced brothers. The myth of the name "Goodluck" (and his wife's name was Patience) proved irresistible for mythmakers and Christian religious leaders who touted the miracle of his rise from being a lowly deputy governor in a backwater state in southern Nigeria to occupying the most powerful office in the land. His ascent became stuff of legends and church sermons. Beyond the realm of myths, however, was also the management of political realities. Jonathan came into power by chance. He had neither clout nor godfathers, and his unassertive demeanor did not help. To survive the treacherous waters of Nigerian politics, Jonathan turned to one constituency whose visibility in the public sphere, economic strength, and moral backing could become a viable source of support: Pentecostal leaders.

To a lesser degree, Jonathan also had to hold on to an ethnic identity to survive. He was known to be Ijaw from the south-south region of

---

[37] In a sense, Jonathan was also what Wariboko called a "counterfoil choice," one where the custodian of a society includes in a set of choices to delimit possibilities and manage collective identity. By showing someone a negative, they enhance the motive for choosing what they have deemed as the "positive" choice. Wariboko, "Counterfoil Choices in the Kalabari Life Cycle."

Nigeria, the fourth largest ethnic group (but which gets swallowed up
by the triune dominant ones: Hausa/Fulani, Igbo, and Yoruba), so his
handlers conferred an honorary Igbo identity on him by calling him
"Azikwe" after Nnamdi Azikwe, the African nationalist who was Igbo.
They gave him the name to expand his ethnic identity to cover more
regions in southern Nigeria.[38] For southeasterners (mostly Christians)
who adopted Jonathan as "Igbo," the politics of identity is also layered
with ethnic sentiments that encompass survivalism and memory-
making in post–civil war Nigeria. Jonathan took the template of
a religionized political identity even further by building his public
identity around being Pentecostal. As the 2011 election approached
and he signified his intention to run, he cultivated a more acute
Pentecostal identity. Like Obasanjo before him, he visited the
"Redemption Camp" where he not only requested prayers so he
could govern with divine wisdom, but for the first time in the history
of Nigeria, a president knelt before the pastor for those prayers. The
image of President Jonathan, humbled before God and a man of God,
splashed on the front pages of almost every national newspaper the
following day. For a multicultural nation where, for some, kneeling is
part of a tradition of respect to an authority figure and for others,
kneeling before a fellow human is virtually forbidden, his act generated
some furor. However, the differences were moderated by a shared
Christian identity and the biblical frame of reference that kneeling is
a symbolic act of humility, self-surrender before divine authority, and
consecration. Thus he became the "anointed candidate," the one God
had chosen to be president.[39] Although there were other contributing

---

[38]   His middle name was also Ebele, a name borne by the Igbos of southeastern
       Nigeria. The mistake of assuming that because he had a name that was common
       among Igbos, that he had to be Igbo, is one of the ways ethnic identity gets
       weaponized in Nigeria for the sake of power.
[39]   In the Bible, to be "anointed" was to be doused on the head with oil as a ritual of
       consecration by God either for priesthood or kingship, but the term has crept
       into Nigeria's political lexicon. Appropriated from Pentecostals' use of it to
       describe divine consecration, "anointed" is now the go-to terminology for
       describing a political candidate favored by power brokers to hold a public
       position. Interestingly, the term has become so normative that scholars deploy it
       in academic texts without either contextualizing it or even acknowledging the
       irony. Fawole, "Voting without Choosing"; Mudasiru, "Ethnicity and the
       Voting Pattern in Nigeria's 2015 General Elections"; Omenma, Onu &
       Omenma, "Factors Limiting Nomination of Women Candidates for Elections in
       Nigeria"; Omotola, "Godfathers and the 2007 Nigerian General Elections";

factors, such as the power of incumbency, Jonathan handily won the election and would go on to become another "Pentecostal president" after Obasanjo.

Once in office, Jonathan sought ways to establish himself as a hero of a national myth, to develop a second body – *a la* Ernst Kantorowicz – that would fuse his physical body into the ethical realm of national life.[40] To achieve this transcendence entailed suffusing the nation with Christian symbolism especially as propagated by Pentecostals. As the myths are already available in the social imagination, Jonathan needed only to repurpose them to the body politic. For instance, in September 2011, months after he had won his first election and had been sworn in, he attended an interdenominational church service in the nation's capital where he marked the fifty-first independence anniversary. By then, he was already being criticized for his slow approach to government, and confidence in the man that would bring good luck to the country was fast eroding. Jonathan responded to critics of his methods saying,

You have been praying for us but others will not even want us to move an inch, especially those of us who are politicians. But one prayer I will continue to request because if you listen to Nigerians or read their statements, some Nigerians still want the President of this country to be a lion or a tiger, somebody that has that kind of strength and force and agility to make things happen the way they think. Some others will want the President to operate like an army general or my Chief of Army Staff commanding his troop. Incidentally, I am not a lion, I am not also a general. Somebody will want the president to operate like the Kings of Syria, Babylon, Egypt, the pharaoh, all the powerful people that you read about in the Bible. They want the president to operate that way, the characters of the Goliath, unfortunately I am not one of those.

But God knows why I am here even though I don't have any of those attributes, or those kinds of characters I have used as an example. But through your prayers God placed me here. The only thing I ask you to do for me and that is the prayer I pray every time, is for God to use me to change this country. I don't need to be a lion, I don't need to be Nebuchadnezzar, I don't need to operate like the Pharaoh of Egypt, I don't need to be an army general but I can change this country without those traits . . . . Somebody was

Sule, Mohd Sani & Mat, "Godfatherism and Political Party Financing in Nigeria."
[40] Kantorowicz, *The King's Two Bodies*.

asking, is Nigeria on an auto pilot? Meaning a plane without a pilot and I say Nigeria is being piloted by God himself.

It is not going to be easy because ... there are Goliaths everywhere; very terrible Goliaths; the ones that can even kill their father and mother and even their children in order to stop government. So, we have these terrible Goliaths that are trying to frustrate us but surely with God we will conquer them ... every Goliath has an exposed forehead. God will expose their foreheads to the stone of David.[41]

Jonathan's public performance of faith was over-the-top and he reportedly made more high-profile visits to churches than hospitals and schools; he became the president who made churches his site of policy enunciation.[42] At some point, it was announced that he would lead 30,000 pilgrims to Israel for holy pilgrimage, the first Nigerian president to visit the Christian holy land.[43] On the trip, photographs of him and other political officials who accompanied him praying at several sacred sites appeared in several newspapers and blogs. *Christianity Today*, the American evangelical flagship magazine founded by Billy Graham, noted that he undertook the pilgrimage to pray for peace between Christians and Muslims in his country, sign an agreement with Israeli leaders on international flight schedules, among other matters to be discussed.[44] To also appease his Christian constituents who were repulsed by the debates about same-sex marriage debates taking place in the USA, he signed the notorious Nigerian "gay bill," composed of laws so harsh that they are hard to implement properly.

While the "anointed candidate" narrative might have propelled Jonathan to office, it did not help him when the challenges of public office arose. During his tenure, Nigeria's economic fortunes from the boom in global oil prices – Nigeria's major export – did not translate to tangible gains for the majority.[45] Much of the gain was misappropriated by the elite political class that surrounded Jonathan, people whose incorrigible tendency toward corruption made it impossible for whatever policy conceived at the federal level to percolate to the people.

---

[41] www.vanguardngr.com/2011/09/we-ll-conquer-goliaths-jonathan/
[42] Ukah, "The Midwife or the Handmaid?"
[43] www.algemeiner.com/2013/10/15/nigerian-president-to-lead-30000-christian-pilgrims-to-israel/
[44] www.christianitytoday.com/news/2013/october/nigeria-president-israel-pilgrimage-jonathan-goodluck.html
[45] Adetula, "Nigeria's Rebased Economy and Its Role in Regional and Global Politics"; Nwanosike et al., "Economic Development Dynamics in Nigeria."

While most Nigerians remained as poor as ever, political actors, including known Pentecostal pastors, became richer and flaunted their wealth. It was an era in which the prosperity gospel became self-confirming. While pastors claimed the wealth with which they procured their private jets came from heaven above, people were not blind to how their association with politicians favored them. Pastors allegedly used their high-profile connections to political power for their ends. As Jonathan's administration became enmeshed in several high-profile corruption scandals and allegations of financial mismanagement,[46] pastors' conduct and relationship with him ultimately sped up their loss of credibility. They tanked their power to influence the public by once again anointing his candidature for a second term.

Again, there were other contributing factors to the angst against Jonathan. One of the major ones was the Boko Haram national crisis under his watch. Although the problem predated Jonathan's presidency, the situation peaked during his tenure. By the time the Chibok girls' kidnapping happened in 2014, and the incident became global news especially after Michelle Obama helped propagate the news with her photograph bearing the "bring back our girls" placard, Jonathan's failings became stuff for global headlines. His opponents weaponized every one of those foreign media reports against him. By the 2015 elections, when Oyedepo was openly riling up his congregation by urging them to pray against "Islamic devils" and their penchant for perpetuating themselves in power, the political terrain had changed so much that the political weapons of warfare wielded by Pentecostal pastors were not as effective as before. While the problem of Boko Haram might have been seen as part of an Islamic agenda by those who cannot survive without political power, the failure to quell it – as well as other economic failures and the problem of corruption – was also placed at the feet of the Christian president. The political agenda of demonization of Islam around the elections – a campaign run by pastors who had parleyed with politicians – had become indistinguishable from the devil they sought to exorcize, and was not quite as effective.

Again, a caveat: While there is a degree of opposition to Nigerian Pentecostal leadership's angling to be a part of the inner machinery of the government and the corrupt exchanges that are perpetrated there, these ecclesiastical authorities are still highly respected by their

---

[46]   Ojo, "Looting the Looters."

members. They are Christianity's ringside tickets to the arena where the dividends of democracy are distributed. As the "men of God," they embody the idea of the "man of the people" – in the way provincial representatives in the executive and the legislative arms of government never can – because they represent a constituency of people who identify by their faith in a supreme being. That puts the pastorate well above politicians who are supposed to represent all and sundry, and that also contributes to making pastors a sacred vehicle for the moral refurbishment of a debilitated polity. Even their fraternization with elite politicians and corrupt bigwigs is considered to have spiritual efficacy, a viable means of expanding God's kingdom in a world full of the threatening other.

When it turned out that Jonathan's opponent in the 2015 election was going to be Muhammadu Buhari, a Muslim from northern Nigeria and a former military dictator (1983–5) who had thrice run for the presidency (including in 2011 when Jonathan defeated him), the campaign for the Christian president became an urgent one that urged people to vote to stave off an impending "Islamization agenda."[47] Buhari was perceived to be an Islamic bigot once reported to have told fellow Muslims in northern Nigeria to never vote for a non-Muslim (one of the several reasons he had never been popular outside his northern enclave). He was also seen as a northern Muslim revanchist who would complete the Islamization agenda begun by two former Nigerian military dictators, also Muslims from northern Nigeria, Generals Ibrahim Babangida and Sani Abacha.[48] The autocratic leadership of the duo of Babangida and Abacha, and their unapologetic pandering to northern Muslim interests, had long propagated sentiments of cynicism, distrust, and disaffection against Buhari and the religious/ethnic ideologies he embodied.[49]

The anti-Buhari campaign took on a transnational dimension as well. The Islamists' threats and terrorism were taking place in Nigeria and also in the traditional Christian stronghold like the

---

[47] Onapajo, "Politics and the Pulpit."
[48] Babangida upgraded Nigeria's status in the Organization of Islamic Countries from "observer" to full membership in 1986 while Abacha, in 1997, made Nigeria a member of the D-8 Organization for Muslim Co-operation. Faseke, "Nigeria and the Organization of Islamic Cooperation"; Obinna, "Violence in the Name of God."
[49] Falola, *Violence in Nigeria.*

USA.[50] Nigerians plugged into right-wing narratives about Obama being a secret Muslim who was yielding to Islamists in the Middle East. When Obama invoked the Leahy Law to refuse to sell ammunition to Nigeria to prosecute the Boko Haram war, they imagined he wanted Islam to thrive in Nigeria at the expense of Christianity. They also echoed the grudges of American Christians who claimed they were losing the moral grounds of their faith because of the legalization of same-sex marriage, gender-inclusive bathroom wars, legal battles about baking cakes for gay weddings, the accusations that people were no longer free to say "Merry Christmas," and overall, that the tyrannical reign of political correctness being used to censure dissenting opinion. These perceptions oversimplified the complex ideological issues at stake in American culture wars. Still, these Nigerians bought wholly into the distress of American evangelicals who complained that the Christian ethos, integral to the founding of America, was being erased.

Nigerian Churches not only resounded the campaign against the said looming "Islamization agenda," they became some of the strongest political evangelists as the election date drew closer. One pastor, Bosun Emmanuel, a member of Christian Association of Nigeria, made and distributed tapes where he had narrated how countries like Turkey and Syria used to be Christian territories but are now dominated by Muslims due to lack of vigilance by the Christians who once occupied these places.[51] His conclusion was that a similar fate awaited Nigerians if Buhari was allowed to win. The scare-mongering about a looming Christian displacement on the political scene met with a lot of pushback from Buhari's supporters who were, by now, no longer just northerners but southerners and Christians (including Pentecostals) who said they could no longer stomach Jonathan's incompetence.[52] Buhari's support gradually extended to cover the southwest, a region that had roughly an equal number of Christians

---

[50] For instance, the terrorist attack in San Bernadino in 2015; Chattanooga in 2015; Boston bombing in 2013; Fort Hood attacks in 2009; Little Rock killing in 2009.
[51] www.youtube.com/watch?v=5FhYpKBKusQ
[52] www.pmnewsnigeria.com/2015/04/18/pastor-bosun-buharis-jihad-and-christianity-in-nigeria/; www.vanguardngr.com/2014/11/pastor-bosun-emmanuel-political-red-herring/

and Muslims, and also concentrated almost all the mega Pentecostal churches in its territory. While a quantifiable number of Christians in the southwest stayed with Jonathan, an appreciable number of Muslims devolved toward Buhari partly because of religious sentiment. Among the many fracture lines the election exploited and deepened was the religious divide in southern Nigeria, and the ethnic divide with northern Nigeria. Most religious leaders did not declare their religious interests upfront, but by directly or subtly encouraging their members to vote for a candidate, they indicated their partisanship alliances. The southwest region was also where the swing votes were going to come from, and, therefore, it was targeted heavily for religious manipulation by various interested groups. The masterstroke came when Buhari selected as his running mate, Yemi Osinbajo, a pastor with RCCG, and also a lawyer and a professor. Thus, Buhari undercut the specter of "Islamization agenda" that had hung over his imminent presidency. He gradually became acceptable to Christian constituencies and some of their leaders who began to endorse him.[53] By the time President Goodluck Jonathan announced to the country that he would be visiting a different church every Sunday to the election, it was too late. He had lost a chunk of the Christian/southwestern votes to his opponent who chose a pastor as his vice-presidential candidate.

A few days before the election, Obama made a video urging Nigeria to vote wisely in their elections and shun violence. Even though he did not commit to any candidate in the video, his intervention was interpreted as using his moral authority to subtly urge Nigerians to change their incumbent government.[54] Therefore, when Jonathan lost the elections, the first time in Nigerian history where the incumbent was unseated, Obama took part of the blame for foisting a northern Muslim on Nigerians.[55] Buhari, now the new president, turned out to be equally incompetent in fighting the corruption he promised to tackle. His cardinal campaign agenda – to combat insecurity, refurbish the

---

[53] www.christianitytoday.com/news/2015/april/christian-case-for-nigeria-new-muslim-president-buhari.html

[54] www.politico.com/story/2015/02/nigeria-presidential-election-goodluck-jonathan-muhammadu-buhari-115190; www.theguardian.com/uk-news/2018/mar/21/cambridge-analyticas-ruthless-bid-to-sway-the-vote-in-nigeria; www.premiumtimesng.com/news/159014-governor-nyako-accuses-jonathan-administration-genocide-northern-nigeria.html

[55] www.pulse.ng/news/local/fani-kayode-ex-minister-writes-on-john-kerrys-unadulterated-garbage/fbrp3rd

economy, and reduce corruption – barely scratched the surface of Nigeria's problems. Under his watch, Nigeria became the country with the highest number of poor globally. A nepotistic leader, Buhari ran a divisive government, and accusations of an Islamic agenda picked up again as Buhari appointed his northern Muslim kin to "juicy" public positions.[56] Despite his posturing about being an ex-general who understood the tactics of war, he did not have an answer for Boko Haram either. The violence and massacres continued, and the public resigned to the fact that the perennial war against terrorism was merely an excuse for the corrupt political elite to siphon funds out of public pocket. The anger and disappointment of Jonathan's supporters at their loss extended to Obama, who they believed must have despised Nigerians so much that he imposed an incompetent Buhari on them.

When the Nigerian economy started tanking and Nigerians became massively impoverished for reasons that included both the dynamics of global economic forces and sheer ineptitude on Buhari's part, Jonathan supporters became Trump supporters in Nigeria and ascribed part of the blame of the nation's misfortune to Obama's meddlesomeness and supercilious attitude toward Africa.[57] Had he not jinxed the country with his subtle support for Buhari, they reasoned, they would be better off.[58] When another round of insecurity problems arose in the form of herdsmen believed to be of Fulani ethnicity engaged in ethnic cleansing

---

[56] In Nigerian parlance, a "juicy" public office is a bureaucracy that controls large finances and, as such, gives room for financial mismanagement and corruption.

[57] Obama was also disliked for the way he was perceived to have treated Africa with disdain. As the US president, he visited Ghana (and not Nigeria) and much of his speech was to lecture African leaders in a manner they consider berating. His "gay agenda," constantly raising the issue of LGBTQ rights, was also irritating to them because they found it infantilizing.

[58] There were also other minor contributing issues such as the role that former Obama campaign manager, David Axelrod, and his political consulting firm played in changing Buhari's image from that of a ruthless dictator to an appealing one. https://qz.com/368219/how-nigeria-challenger-buhari-went-from-ruthless-dictator-to-weak-leader/; www.buzzfeednews.com/article/rosie gray/firm-founded-by-david-axelrod-worked-in-nigerian-election-as Also, in August 2016, when Obama's secretary of State, John Kerry, visited Nigeria, he pointedly ignored Christians and southerners. Instead, he met with President Buhari and the governors of the states in the northern regions. The meeting was hosted by the Sultan, the topmost Muslim political leader. The Christian described his meeting with a section of the country, many of them Muslims, as discriminatory and divisive: www.newsweek.com/nigeria-christian-group-rails-against-john-kerry-divisive-visit-493796

of rural communities, it was perceived to be part of the foretold Islamization agenda.[59]

When Trump emerged on the scene and proposed "a Muslim ban," a policy that would restrict Muslims from some countries from entering the USA, his Nigerian followers were as excited as their American counterparts. Trump dredged up their resentment against the liberal values "browning" America, and which had culminated in the legalization of same-sex marriage. The eight years of the Obama government had given rise to nostalgia for a country where the religion of Americanism – a composite identity that subsumes all other categories and whose patriotic ideals are tested on loyalty to whiteness, Christianity, patriarchy, capitalism, and conservative ideologies – would recover from its seemingly waning influence. This longing for a return of Christian nationalism – defined as a cultural framework that encapsulates the "myths, tradition, symbols, narratives and value systems … that idealizes and advocates a fusion of Christianity with American civic life … assumptions of nativism, white supremacy, patriarchy, and heteronormativity along with divine sanction for authoritarian control and militarism … ethnic as it is religious"[60] – that gripped Americans also resonated in other places that had cultural and spiritualties to the USA. Like these Christian nationalists, other Christians elsewhere who subscribe to the "founding myth" – the tale and tradition invented in the late nineteenth, early twentieth century that America was founded as a Christian country and has grown precisely because of its Christian identity – find themselves equally invested in the future of the Christian faith in the USA.[61] When in January 2016, Trump complained in a campaign speech that Christianity was "under tremendous siege," Christians were not pulling their weight enough, and if he were elected president, he

---

[59] Just like several Nigerian ethnic groups, Fulanis are not a monolith and they have Christians among them but such nuances are easily eroded in the oversimplification of politics where the elites among them like Buhari become symbolic devils. Also, the case of Libya – the aftermath of the Arab Spring and the US invasion that led to the death of Muammar Ghaddafi – bred another round of resentment. Often the story of the US invasion of Libya gets sequestered from the context of the Arab Spring and becomes emblematized as another instance of Obama's malevolence against African stability.

[60] Whitehead & Perry. *Taking America Back for God.*

[61] Hall, *Did America Have a Christian Founding*; Seidel, "The Founding Myth."

would represent Christians better and "Christianity will have power," they were all listening intently.[62]

"Don't Mistake Only Those in Politics as in Power!": Christian Transnationalism and the Pentecostal Republic

When historians sketch American political history along the axis of evangelical influence, they tend to think of these issues as self-contained within the USA. The rise of Trump supporters in Nigeria and a few other places in Africa challenges this assumption. Nigerian Christians too, particularly those whose ethnic identities intersect their politico-religious affiliation, constitute a following for Trump. This Pentecostal Christian transnationalism partly goes back to the alliances Nigerian churches and American Christians forged as far back as the 1970s when white American Pentecostal preachers started coming to Africa to evangelize.[63] While the relationship has largely waned since Nigerian Pentecostalism came into its own, Nigerians still take the outreach of their American counterparts as well-meaning. They are invested in America remaining "Christian" because the moral force of US evangelicals impacts Christianity in Africa. Christian congregations on the continent could – and would – continue to draw oxygen from the USA as long as Christianity thrives there.[64] Oyedepo's words provides a clear insight into this mindset of vicarious empowerment by those for whom power is an identity: *it is not only those in politics that are in power*. Not everyone has to occupy a political position to be part of the network of power. Some will be in power through their faith, and as faith is a social identity, their performing their faith will be potently political.[65]

One Nigerian-based church leader, citing the scriptures, told me they support Trump because God uses the basest tools to fulfill his agenda so he could confound people already assured of their methods. God does not look for perfect people, he said. If God did, what would result would be a triumph of secular competence over divine agenda. He said Trump was God's way of using the "undesirable element" to achieve

[62] www.nytimes.com/2020/08/09/us/evangelicals-trump-christianity.html?smid=fb-share
[63] Corten & Marshall-Fratani. *Between Babel and Pentecost.*
[64] Deji Yesufu, http://mouthpiece.com.ng/evangelicals-support-of-donald-trump/
[65] Wald & Calhoun-Brown, *Religion and Politics in the United States.*

His perfect plan on earth. That way, the invisible hand of God at work would be more obvious. To choose someone more refined would undermine the glory of conquest that was supposed to go to God solely. Those like this pastor who were on the Trump train during electioneering because they saw a potential victory for Christianity shrugged off his excesses and even chalked it down to part of divine agenda. The morning after Trump won the election, one of Nigeria's well-known pastors, the Senior Pastor of The Covenant Nation and Convener of *The Platform Nigeria*, Poju Oyemade tweeted, "I have read it in scriptures but now I have seen it; a united church in prayer governs world affairs. Evangelicals were united for Trump."[66] It was, to them, a Christian victory, a resurgence of their earnest beliefs on a much bigger and shinier stage.

Since Trump won, the people of the Nigerian Pentecostal republic who repatriated moral citizenship to the USA have taken it upon themselves to be the defenders of his presidency in the same manner they would have done for a Christian president at home. For instance, they are the ones – going by their distinct Nigerian (sur)names – most likely to be found in the comments section of the social media pages of news network such as CNN declaring their blackness before registering their support for Trump. Some would preface their comments with, "I am black, but I support Trump because ..." My reading of these supporters' conscious and contingent identification with blackness is that they are partly familiar with the American discourse of race and also aware of Trump's low popularity among native blacks in his own country. Therefore, their foregrounding their comments with their racial identity is to make Trump transcend the provinciality of white identity politics and give him legitimacy that spreads across races and nations.

Like American evangelicals, Nigerian Christians saw Trump as a repudiation of every demon that Obama had come to symbolize – multiculturalism and accommodation of Islam, the triumph of liberal values over conservative Christianity, the forfeiture of ground for whiteness and its closely allied Christian identity. To them, liberalism is a rearrangement of the moral order and they owe it to themselves to restructure the world to sustain free expression of the Christian faith as they have always known it. The invading forces of liberalism – Islam,

[66] https://twitter.com/pastorpoju/status/796295987010617344

secularism, multiculturalism, socialism, abortion, homosexuality, anti-family values – are all threats to Christianity. If allowed without pushback, it would culminate in a dystopic world where their faith and power identity would be relegated to the background. The Nigerian Christian demographic who wanted Trump to beat Hillary Clinton also wanted it because it would be a defeat of Obama himself, an erasure of his legacy, and pushback against what they saw as forces of Islamism exploiting western liberalism to inscribe their ethics on dedicated western/Christian soil. They were concerned about Islam in Nigeria, and also in western societies which they identify as Christian civilizations. Most of those I interviewed were also convinced that Trump was appointed by God to reverse *Roe v. Wade* and cancel gay marriage in the USA. One of them said to me, "Obama really set back Christianity in America by approving gay marriage and because of his love for Muslims. God has appointed Trump to correct all of it."[67]

Trump won the heart of these Nigerians because they want their Christian values to remain etched in the public sphere, particularly those from south-south and southeast regions of Nigeria where Jonathan came from, and who also consider the loss of the presidency as part of a historical agenda of diminishing them. For the southeast region comprising Igbos particularly, the loss hit hard, and it also formed the basis for renewed agitation to separate from Nigeria. Buhari got to office in 2015, and he did not move to heal the wounds that resulted from that election. His divisiveness spurred people from the southeast to explore the option of breaking away from Nigeria like they tried to do in the 1960s. This time, they were led by Nnamdi Kanu, who started the Indigenous People of Biafra Movement (IPOB). Kanu was charged with treason and detained by the Nigerian government even after a court had granted him bail. While in jail, he wrote a letter to Trump (shortly after he won the election in 2016) asking him to intervene in their self-determination cause and "liberate enslaved nations" in Africa.[68]

Kanu and his supporters saw Brexit – which Trump supported – as proof of his moral investment in the self-determination of a people, and they thought he would extend the courtesy to them as well.[69] Although

---

[67] Personal interview.
[68] https://dailypost.ng/2016/11/11/us-election-nnamdi-kanu-writes-open-letter-trump/
[69] www.voanews.com/africa/nigerias-biafra-separatists-see-hope-trump

Trump has never spoken about Biafra or even about his foreign policy to any African country specifically, they continue to invoke Trump's name in their activities.[70] By engineering such illusions of international support for their cause, they hold their supporters together and also stir their people to support Trump as both a potential helper of their cause, and a guarantor of the endurance of Christianity which most of the people from that region of Nigeria practice. An evangelist from southeastern Nigeria that I sampled for this research told me that he has written more than 200 prayer points for Trump, and he posts them on a WhatsApp and Facebook prayer fora that comprises of Nigerians both living in Nigeria and in the USA. He said to me,

Trump has interests in protecting Christians from all over the world, particularly in Nigeria. I am of the Igbo tribe, the tribe that fought the Civil War from 1967–1970. Ever since then, we have been under oppression. Right now, the Fulanis, the leaders of this country, the militant and the Boko Haram, have stationed themselves in all the eastern parts of Igbo land and they are ready that the moment Donald Trump loses the election, they will come out and kill all the Christians. Donald Trump has warned the Nigerian president against killing Christians and that is why they are on a break now. That is why many people from this part of the country have a burden to pray for Trump. Every Sunday evening, many believers gather from 4–7pmn to pray for him. Sometimes we speak in tongues for two hours.[71]

To all the Christian supporters of Trump in Nigeria, regardless of their ethnic group, Jonathan was not the only one who lost the election: the Christianity that he represented lost too. That displacement of the ethical order that a Christian president embodies worries them, and they cling to what Trump does as the hope that their faith did not lose out entirely. The things Trump has been doing became a confirmation that God had selected him for the moral restoration of the USA. For

---

[70] For example, when Trump had a rally in Iowa in February 2020, IPOB shared a picture of Kanu sitting at the venue with a cap on which had been inscribed, "Make American Great Again." Then they commended the leadership of the US Republican Party in Iowa for extending a VIP invitation to Kanu to attend the event, noting that he sat in "the VIP section of the arena reserved for the top echelon of the Republican Party in the state including the Iowa State Governor Kim Reynolds whom he met briefly." www.vanguardngr.com/2020/02/ipob-commends-us-over-kanus-vip-invitation-to-trumps-rally-says-leader-not-a-terrorist/

[71] Personal interview.

instance, after Trump declared Jerusalem the capital of Israel, some of these Christians saw the development as the hastening of biblical prophecy and celebrated it as such. Mike Bamiloye (see previous chapter) shared on his Facebook page, a commentary that I reproduce below unedited.

> DOES ANYONE TAKE NOTICE OF THE TRENDING WORLD NEWS?
> JERUSALEM WAS DECLARED CAPITAL OF ISRAEL, BY DONALD TRUMP.
> THE WHOLE OF ARAB NATIONS ARE NOW BOILING IN PROTEST ....
> THE ARABS ARE CLAIMING THE OWNERSHIP OF THE CITY OF JERUSALEM.

We are in a time when we need to pay more attention to Current news: Trump approved Jerusalem as the capital of Israel today, December 6, 2017.

Note: Both Israel and Palestine claim Jerusalem to be their Capital.

Truth: Jerusalem has been the Capital of the Jews from the time of King David in the Bible, until around Ad 35 to 70, when all Jews were forced to flee from Jerusalem to other countries.

What to Look out for in this Period:

There is going to be more increase of intifada, war of Muslim countries against the Jews and against America.

The Jews need to build the Last Temple Prophesied in the Bible ...

The Temple whose building material has already been prepared could only be built in Jerusalem, the exact place of the Dome of the Rock, which the Muslims see as the only SURVIVING Share (shrine) of the Muslims in the Middle East.

Anything could happen between now and the end of Trump's Presidency.

12 Major Events to Watch out For After This Meeting:

1. Moving Israel's Capital To Jerusalem.
2. Building of the Last Temple in Jerusalem.
3. Rapture of the Church
4. The Great Tribulation
5. The Physical Manifestation of the AntiChrist
6. The 2 Prophets and Their Ministry.
7. The War of Armageddon.
8. The 1000 years millennial reign of Christ with the saints
9. Final Judgement of the dead and the living ... total destruction of this sinful world and Satan & his kingdom
10. Emergence of the new heaven and the new earth

11. Believers being with God forever enjoying the presence and the glory of God forever
12. Believers Walking the streets of Gold . . . eat the fruit of the tree of life . . . while sinners (unsaved) spend eternity in hell fire with gnashing of teeth forever and ever . . ..

(Please note that these events are not written in strict sequential order ie order of occurrence)
There is no time to waste so Let me start with you . . ..
Beloved, you have heard it all. Win souls and turn them from destruction. Search yourself, examine your life and walk in line with the scriptures. See if there are areas in your life where you have gone astray, make amends and follow the word.
The end is at the door! Therefore, please share, it could save a life. God bless you![72]

In the Nigerian Pentecostal performance of this transnational solidarity with a supposedly Christian president, African Americans sometimes become the battering ram of bigoted sentiments. The Nigerian Christians who spend a lot of time on the media pages of right-wing websites and news blogs that support conservative values eventually absorb and echo racist white people who claim black people vote for the Democratic Party – rather than the Republican Party that freed the slaves – so they could get everything free. They parrot some of these racist narratives in their support for Trump because they have only a superficial knowledge of the complex dynamics of race in America. Again, this is where the incoherence of logic and paradox of partisanship comes in: even though some of the these Christians in Nigeria and the USA frequently hold up the Republican Party as pro-black because Abraham Lincoln, a Republican, supposedly freed the slaves, they also jump over that inconvenient part of history where the racial composition of both Democratic and Republican party changed because of the signing of the Civil Rights Act by President Lyndon Johnson. Some of my respondents said the Republican Party is better for black people in the USA because, "Were they not the ones that freed the slaves? Where were the Democrats to free the slaves? How come they are voting Democratic Party now?" These convenient elisions of history have

---

[72] www.facebook.com/MIKEBAMILOYE/posts/10154880867671831, accessed July 9, 2020. At the time, the posts had 1.4k reactions, 2.7k shares, and 327 comments. Most of his followers on the page acquiesced with this position.

been a useful weapon to tout in their defense of their "Christian president" against the countervailing forces of Islam, liberalism, secularism, and the Democrats whom they perceived as anti-Christianity. They faithfully display their partisan support on social media, either their private spaces or others' spaces, performing their Pentecostal citizenship within the limits of the possibilities available to them. By contributing to the idea that any attempts to hold this president responsible for any moral or political infraction – the impeachment episode, for instance, was deemed a liberal cum "mainstream" news network agenda against God's chosen president – they uphold a social ecology that presumes the infallibility of a politician, and which ultimately creates an atmosphere for abuse of power.

After months of studying how Nigerians display their partisanship on Facebook, I also noticed that when media houses like CNN share news reports that are not favorable to Trump on their social media pages, they join other Trump supporters to vehemently attack news sites as "fake news." Some of these commenters get a lot of "likes" and "loves" as they participate in the transnational politics of Christianity on news media pages. When I click on the profile of such a person on the social media pages of the news networks they comment on and scan their pages, most of the time, their posts are pretty consistent in their pro-Trump and anti-Buhari (their home president) sentiment. They criticize their home president and complain about the political systems of the country that produced such an incompetent leader. Often, I click "follow" on their profile page to keep tabs on their public comments over time. As a rule, I do not contribute to the discussions on their page. I merely observe their public narration of self through their posts, and these do not always have to do with politics although their religious sentiments come up frequently. After a while, I find that they have accrued other followers whose profile pages say or show they live in the USA. These Nigerians and the Americans mostly do not seem to have mutual friends, so there is a high likelihood that they became "friends" and followers the same way I did: by following the comments of those Nigerians on globally accessible news pages to become their social media followers. When I run through the profile pages of those in the USA too, I find they are mostly white people whose pages are splashed with pro-Christian, pro-Trump, pro-guns, pro-capitalism, anti-abortion, anti-socialism, anti-immigrants, anti-liberal, anti-mainstream news, anti-Democrats and, during the COVID-19 pandemic, anti-mask rhetoric. These Americans, as I observe in their interactions with Nigerians, regularly show up on posts that have to do with Trump (especially during the impeachment saga), Democrats vs. Republicans, and Christianity (no, they do not interfere in issues of local politics when these Nigerians criticize their leaders). Their contribution to discussions usually ranges from bashing Obama and Hillary and their fellow "globalists," liberals and liberalism, and even praising God for Trump who now guarantees Christianity for them.

On this world's largest playground (the Internet, that is), where they have found one another, the dynamics of their interactions makes it hard to track where the pro-Christianity sentiment stops and where the tendency toward clout-chasing – especially one that aligns strange white people looking for like-minded black people to reassure themselves of their racial liberalism – stops. Nevertheless, they jointly play politics of debating to ultimately generate an atmosphere favorable to Trump. American Christians who seek out these Nigerians seem to appreciate their stumbling on the right kind of black people who "get it," who are not trying to immigrate to America , and whose solidarity for Trump satiates their own desire for transnational alliance as well. This sentiment particularly served them well during the impeachment saga when these Nigerians were some of the loudest voices in support of Trump. They prayed for him and denounced the Democrats in caustic language for daring to work against divine agenda.

Even when confronted with the possibility that Trump, now as president, could not single-handedly revoke same-sex marriage and abortion laws without recourse to established instruments of jurisprudence, my respondents did not waver in their faith. They remained adamant that he would set America back on a path of righteousness. If he had enough power and time – and, according to someone, "If only the liberals will just let him be!" – he would achieve the divine plan. Not much else mattered than him winning back the ground that Christianity supposedly lost in the Obama years. When Trump overlooked the Leahy law and sold weapons to Buhari to prosecute the Boko Haram war, it only confirmed Obama's malevolence rather than Trump's lack of moral concern with internal violence in Nigeria. They get ecstatic when images of pastors standing with Trump in the White House are circulated. They excitedly share media reports of Trump attending anti-abortion rallies, his grandiloquent acts of signing superfluous laws that would "return" prayer to schools, and so on. They consider these moves an affirmation of Christian resurgence in "God's own country." Interestingly, some privately think abortion should be a personal decision, but they also publicly support revoking *Roe v. Wade* to provide a valid moral basis for their Trump support. Not all, however, were simply deluded by religionized politics. Some say they are quite aware Trump is neither born-again nor even a model of Christian ethics, but as long as his presidency services the Christian cause, and keeps Islamic violence at bay in Nigeria and the USA, that is enough for them. To some degree, their inflexibility on issues of, for instance, returning prayers to school, is practical politics. African Christians' experiences have taught them such consensual politics and privatized Christianity is a strategic error.[73] To be open and liberal is to risk their faith and social ethos being subsumed by the forces of secularism.

Ayelujara: Power Identity and Globalization

The Yoruba word for "Internet" is *ayelujara*. Like many local words for modern artifacts and gadgets, it describes people's encounters with modern realities and their grasp of its essence. Ayelujara considers the world as a unit where things seep into each other from the holes bored into its components. It is an image that is useful for thinking of the present globalized era, the internet technology as a part of the organization of the present world order, and how politics crosses the bounds of the nation-state to seep out at another end in ecstatic bursts of partisan support. This ongoing network of anxieties manages to set aside the exotic differences of race and nationality, the complicated and nuanced history of global anti-blackness, and the political realities of white nationalism invested in the idolized figure of Trump. As their ongoing histories, desires, and other similar proclivities seep out and are mutually absorbed, they become embodied performances through which they each influence cultural ecology and local politics. Thus, the performance of power identity forges connections that sustain the ethos of their power identity.

This support for a Christian president across the transnational divide feeds into two streams of sensibilities: one, it gives Nigerian Pentecostals still pained from losing power an anchor, a moral bearing,

---

[73] Sanneh, *Whose Religion Is Christianity?*

to stabilize despite their devastating loss of territory at home and central politics in 2015 until 2023. This stretch of time is because Buhari also won a second term in 2019 despite the efforts of Christians who supported his opponent (Atiku Abubakar, also a Muslim northerner but whose putative cosmopolitanism and strategic alliance with southern Christians could have overturned Buhari's government).[74] Support for a US president whose public conduct can be insalubrious grounds its moral and ethical validation in policies such as anti-abortion, LGBTQ issues, and Christian values, and projects it on partisan and primal politics. The Internet has been particularly invaluable in forging these links, because it has provided a meeting room and deliberative spaces for people who would otherwise not have met. In the two forthcoming chapters, I will explore more of the roles internet technology has played in evolving the power configuration of Pentecostal leadership and what that development has meant for the people who see pastors, especially given the public role they play, as a repository of their power identity.

Now ubiquitous, the Internet brings Christians together from across the world to feed off each other's strength and jointly mobilize against all the forces that stand against their faith – liberalism, Islam, and any other factors that impede the expansion and continuous realization of Christianity along with the identity complexes, be it race in the USA or ethnic validation in Nigeria. While people manage to live in peace with their neighbor, Islam and its potential for numbing violence is never far from their minds. The many histories of Islamic violence directly link to Nigeria's political history where Muslim leaders and powerbrokers allow these acts of impunity to go unpunished. For Nigerians who have been imperiled by Islamic violence in all its forms, the assurance that an external moral figure protects Christians is invaluable. Also, such a leader's close identification with power means they retain their power identity even when their local national Christian representative is not in power. There is perhaps also the understanding that Christianity will be anchored in the global south in the years to come, and they are already preempting that.[75] Nigeria, given its expansive population of putative 200 million people and still growing, will play a major role in this relocation of Christianity's empire to the global

---

[74] www.thecable.ng/oyedepo-why-i-accompanied-atiku-to-obasanjos-residence
[75] Jenkins, *The Next Christendom: The Coming of Global Christianity.*

south. In some ways, both sides are looking into a mirror, seeing the moral and human resources both represent for Christianity, construing each other as the future mecca of global faith, and building a global identity of power.

Second, as I stated earlier, political Islam is imagined as demonic, and this is a politically potent aesthetic that depicts evil in its most monstrous form imaginable. By using a religious-related image that claws into the past and portends the future, a preacher like Oyedepo could adequately divine a vivid image of a malevolent power with an exceptional capacity for ruinous mischief. Through the horror its visage evokes, destructive political powers can be rendered as implacable and nothing short of annihilation or suppression would do. Those Nigerians invested in seeing America remain Christian fear that the liberalism that has already embraced Islam and homosexuality will diminish Christianity. For them, the threat of the devil is not a metaphor, it is reality. At some point though, it is pertinent to ask, as Achille Mbembe did, when "the demonic through which people divine the terror of their condition and state their desire for redemption becomes an indication of the dark politics of vengeance, suicide, and the ecstasy of score settling?"[76] Pastors who whip up demonic specters have personal interests in characterizing Islam as demonic. The demons work for their identity-building agenda, and that is why their liturgical activities need to be read against the wider grain of contemporary politics.

Another reason demonization works in cultural contexts where its myth is powerful is that it also helps instigate people to be willing to go as far as possible to exorcise the demons possessing the physical body and also manifest evils in the social body. They build, channel, and exercise their power identity through prayers of spiritual warfare with which they try to expel the devil. Beyond attacking demonic forces in prayers, people sometimes demonstrate flexibility in their identity politics to the point that the anti-blackness of white nationalism does not bother them. One of my respondents told me that he had no problems with white nationalism; after all, black and African people have had their own versions of nationalism. "Why can't there be a white nationalism? Why discriminate against white people?" Another one said that he could empathize with the anti-immigrant rhetoric of Trump

---

[76] Spivak, "Religion, Politics, Theology."

supporters because "too many black and brown people in America will
just stain their country and destroy everything white people there have
achieved."[77] This shocking reductionism of history and the unaware-
ness of the complexity of the racial identity politics that makes a black/
African person consider fellow black (and brown) people as a blemish
on "the clean edifice of white supremacy"[78] is troubling for those who
live in a culture where race is an everyday reality. However, for these
people who relativize racial relations with their own ethnic identity
struggles, racial nationalism is only practical politics; that is, they insist
America has the right to maintain control over its means of meaning-
production by closing in on itself. By pushing back against liberal
secular forces, they believe it would coherently fuse its myths into one
that bespeaks the power and enduring authority of Christianity. To be
an open-ended society where inconstant factors are being relentlessly
introduced through immigration is to open the door to ideologies that
militate against Christianity even if they have to resort to anti-
blackness.

Definitely not the sole reason, but protecting Christianity is a key
factor in the joint "possessive investment in whiteness"[79] through
Nigerians and (white) American evangelical Christians who network
their support for Trump, the emperor of a political order that stabilizes
what could have been a drift in identity performance. For Nigerians
particularly, proximity to whiteness in forms of identifying with the
Republican Party, Christianity, and actual white people means they
could also be pliant tools in the hands of murky racialized politics. For
instance, when the Trump administration announced an immigrant
visa ban on Nigerians, his biggest supporters on the decision were
these Nigerians. For those who reacted with joy at the development,
the ban was schadenfreude – it would only affect the elites who are the
ones who could travel abroad anyway – while some others were appre-
ciative of the development because it fed into the narrative they wanted
to see happen: that Buhari the Muslim president was so incompetent,
Nigerians were banned from the USA while he was president. Even
when CNN analyst, Fareed Zakaria made a report on the visa ban
saying that Nigerians were the perfect kind of immigrants that Trump
should want in the USA for their level of educational expertise and

---

[77] Private interviews.   [78] Gilroy, *Against Race*.
[79] Lipsitz, *The Possessive Investment in Whiteness*.

work ethic, this set of people remained insistent that Trump did the right thing. On the CNN news pages on Facebook, they were the ones vehemently arguing that Zakaria's position was not borne out of love for Nigeria but simply a demonstration of the network's anti-Trump stance.

In wrapping up this chapter, I want to restate note that the politics of Christian transnationalism is the fallout of an era in Nigerian politics marked by religious and political grudges and also a reflection of how ideologies of culture wars transcend the bounds of nation-state in recent times. Facilitated by modern technological opportunities, these people mine global discourses of race for political exigencies through contingent racial identification politics that provides "black" support for Trump. Justification of white nationalist politics demonstrates a blindness to how racial politics has featured in global formations of power. For them, they are working to preserve a global Christian identity that feeds triumphantly on power and domination on the world stage. In the networking tactics that help sustain their power identity, they tend to downplay the complexity of race and racial situations in the USA. As long as the USA exists in their imagination as a global headquarters of Christianity, they will invest their energies in protecting it from secularizing forces. Respective Christians in Brazil and South Korea might not have much in common with Nigerian Pentecostals, but they understand and jointly relate to the universal symbolism of American evangelicalism. Because the Nigerian Pentecostals are joined by faith with others everywhere else through the USA, its president is treated as deserving of their (black) fealty. They offer it even when he denigrates their countries. As far as they are concerned, he is warding off the demons of Islamism, multiculturalism, secularism, socialism, and any other -isms that threaten their moral vision of both the USA and Nigeria, and his actions stabilize the threats to their power identity.

3 | "Touch Not Mine Anointed": #MeToo, #ChurchToo, and the Power of "See Finish"

When, in 2013, four years before the global #MeToo movement, a young woman named Ese Walter made a damning revelation – in a blog post about having had sex with a pastor – she perhaps did not envisage how far her willingness to damn the social censure that was sure to follow would go in shaking up the patriarchal structures of power that defined Nigeria. A parishioner at one of Nigeria's mega-churches, Commonwealth of Zion Assembly (COZA, aka The Wealthy Place), Walter alleged that the married Senior Pastor, Biodun Fatoyinbo, had groomed her over two years with personalized attention and favor-seeking, culminating in a week-long sexual affair in London. She wrote that after much private trauma and vain attempts to make it right with her conscience, she decided to publicly tell her story to free herself of the guilt and shame of the incident. It was not typical for a woman to make such a public confession of sex with a married man in a society like Nigeria where issues of sex galvanizes puritan instincts. The fact that the male involved was a well-known pastor made it an even more salacious scandal. When the pastor in question responded to the allegations, he merely promised that he would give a "robust reply" to the accusations in due course. That response never came. Finding no means to either get his side of the story or make him accountable, people eventually moved on. Walter's story, though an account of abuse of trust, power, and privilege by a man of God she had held to higher standards, never moved beyond the level of jokes and gossip about pastors' hypocrisy.

By the time *The New York Times* 2017 exposé on Hollywood producer Harvey Weinstein propelled women all over the world to share their stories of sexual abuse and violence on Twitter with the hashtag "MeToo," a lot more had changed in public attitudes toward how allegations of sexual abuse against men in power were received. In different countries, women told stories of sexual assaults. By doing so en masse, they gave one another the moral cover needed to deflect the shame of individuals admitting assault. As those stories cracked the walls of silence, more women in different countries felt freer to speak up. In Nigeria, six years after Walter first spoke up and two years after #MeToo exploded, a celebrity photographer, Busola Dakolo, launched allegations of rape against the same Pastor Fatoyinbo. Now thirty-four years old, she alleged he raped her twice when she was seventeen and living in Ilorin, Kwara State, the town where COZA church started before moving the headquarters to the nation's capital. Shortly afterward, another woman also came forward to make a similar claim of rape against the pastor. She said the family had hired her to be their children's nanny abroad, but she ended up sexually assaulted by the pastor.[1]

By the time this batch of revelations came, the women were stepping into a coursing stream whose sands had been ruffled by Walter and the #MeToo campaign. Just like Walter's case, these fresh accusations too were – as far as anyone could recall – almost unprecedented in Nigeria where issues of sex and abuse are typically hushed for fear of being subject to public ridicule.[2] Dakolo's allegation led to mass outrage on social media, and right away, people began to organize mass protests at the church headquarters in their Abuja and the Lagos branches. The Sunday after the video of the Dakolo allegations was published online, protesters stormed the church demanding the pastor stepped down. These church protests took place during Sunday services. They were attended by both Christians and non-Christians (including a Muslim woman who stood out starkly because of her hijab). The #MeToo protest at the church in Nigeria was thus an important development of making church organizations confront their responsibility to address sexual assaults. The controversy of the Dakolo allegation resulted in pastor Fatoyinbo canceling upcoming church programs and stepping down from his position temporarily.

While the protests took place at the church, something similar happened simultaneously in virtual spaces where many people carried on

---

[1] The woman who made the accusation requested anonymity from the media organization she told her story to, and although her identity was uncovered by a journalist, I omit her name here.

[2] An instance of such a story that did not get hushed was the case of a Canada-based woman, Stephanie Otobo, who sued Kaduna pastor Apostle Johnson Suleman of Omega Fire Ministries. She claimed she had an affair with the pastor, he promised to marry her, and then reneged.

commentary on the intractability of the Nigerian rape culture, and why it had come to a head. They – those on the ground and those online – not only correlated the problem of rape with the various power structures in the society that enforced the mechanism of social control, they also implicated the church (and even more broadly, organized religion) in the cycles of abuse endemic in the country. Looking through the various placards the demonstrators carried that read #*METOO*; #*CHURCHTOO*; *YOUR PASTOR IS NOT YOUR GOD*; *NO TO RAPE IN THE CHURCH*; *GOD CAN FORGIVE YOU BEHIND BARS*; *THIS IS NOT ABOUT RELIGION, THIS IS ABOUT HUMANITY*; *THOU SHALL NOT RAPE*; *DON'T USE GOD'S NAME TO SHELTER A RAPIST*; AND *WE ARE ALL THE LORD'S ANOINTED*, the protests felt like a collectively shared angst and simmering resentment against religious authorities who have remained untouched by accusations of transgressions. The reference on the placard to the "Lord's Anointed" is an allusion to an immunity clause that pastors and their defenders have typically referred to deflect accountability for moral infractions. Based on a verse from Psalm 105, the text refers to the migration of the Israelites through different lands and God's protection of them from potential attack. Verses 14 and 15 say God reproved kings for their sake and said, "Touch not mine anointed and do my prophets no harm." However, those who prooftext this verse typically extract the first few words and use them to give even an errant pastor a moral canopy to hide from the shame of their actions.

To read the uniqueness of the event – protesters ripping apart the myth of the Lord's anointed servant as "untouchable" and demanding he stepped down – as a reproduction or a consequence of the global influence of the #MeToo movement is all too easy. Not all social actions that erupt in countries outside the USA are owed to similar movements in metropolitan places of the world, even when they borrow the vocabulary and dramatics of such movements. While the global #MeToo moment might have boosted the relative weight now given to women's stories of sexual abuse, there were other nuances from that moment that demonstrated how people process the power identity of religious figures. From some of the text on the protest placards and the simultaneous dialogues that occurred on social media while the protests were happening on the church grounds, there was a sense that the issues that rankled people went much further than just the immediate accusations of rape. The allegation was the trigger, but there was an already existing dissatisfaction with the institutionalization of the untouchability of pastors who had attained a certain level of social influence. In this chapter, I am going to read that moment as one of "see finish," a moment where the performance of power had made him knowable to the point that the intelligibility facilitated censurability.

The protests, underlined by festering displeasure and the desire to reconfigure the authority and immense power that pastors have wielded almost unchallenged, had to happen. The global #MeToo campaign might have been one of those times an advocacy campaign ignited in the USA becomes a transnational affair and even provides a framework for which others fashion their own advocacy,[3] but classifying it as a knockoff also misses important nuances. In Ogbu Kalu's historical analysis of Pentecostal development through the years, he noted that the influential position that Pentecostal pastors occupy did not occur till around the 1980s when "fascination with media technology and the hypnotic allure of prosperity gospel quietly reshaped the Pentecostal attitude toward status, elitism, and the big man syndrome." The pastor, considered to be divinely anointed, became the "powerful man of God." He took over "the local image and idiom of the big man, no longer to be suspected but seen in its traditional sense."[4] The contemporary pastor's image as the modern "big man" that replaced the traditional "big man" owed to the fact of his anointing. He became a powerful leader of the people and "as God was praised, so was his visible viceroy on earth."[5] This earthly representative who is taken as a "superhero," Kalu noted, derived from indigenous traditions that perceive an authority figure such as a witchdoctor as chosen by the gods. In essence, the anointed pastor is the modern figuration of that local witch doctor who used to exist in traditional societies.[6]

If the perception of the anointing over a pastor's life is what gives the pastor his moral weight, the protesters' contention that everyone is equally anointed by the same God banalizes the uniqueness of such authority and power. Stating that there is nothing sufficiently exceptional about the anointing of God to put a pastor in a protected class – within a realm where he cannot be touched by social censure – is

---

[3] Adelakun, "Black Lives Matter! Nigerian Lives Matter!"
[4] Kalu, *African Pentecostalism*, 114.   [5] Ibid.   [6] Ibid.

also making a case for a new ethical agenda that grants equal privilege
to everyone regardless of their social or spiritual status. From
a theological point of view, this contention is a call for the reinstitution
of the moral order that the death of Jesus Christ once established. The
Bible records that right after the death of Jesus, the veil of the temple
was torn in two, from the top to the bottom.[7] The veil was the curtain
that separated the place – the holy of holies – which only the priest
accessed in order to mediate between God and man; and it was a space
from which ordinary congregants were barred admission. The ripping
of the temple cloth, the physical and symbolic barrier between God and
humans, was thus a significant event in the history of the relationship
between humankind and God. It granted humans direct access to God.
When these protesters argued against the singularity of the anointing,
they were enacting a similar demystification of the special honors
pastor have into the velvet-roped circles of power.

    This radical move to democratize the anointing is a crucial one. By
virtue of being born again, Christians are God's anointed. Divine
anointing produces the power that helps one overcome all negative
situations in life,[8] and it also affirms one's humanity and sense of self-
determination. However, in a culture where both social and supernatural relationships are denominated by power, pastor-congregation
relationships too quickly mimic the hierarchical structures prevalent
in the secular order such that even within the body of Christ, the equity
of Christian brotherhood yields to power – the urge to use it, and the
will to dominate. Just as modern technology of the 1970s was integral
to the construction of the pastoral figure and his empowerment
through the anointing,[9] so has also new media technology been to the
ongoing *de-construction* of the exceptionality of that anointing.
I regard the stripping down of the inimitability of the anointing as
part of the fallout of "see finish," which in the Nigerian pidgin vernacular means the contempt that arises out of the hyper-exposure of
one's body and everything that mystifies it to the gaze of the public.

    My reading of the #ChurchToo #MeToo event was that it could also
have happened because the characters involved were familiar to all, not
just as public figures but also because of their self-narration through
images. In the case of the accuser, Busola, she was not only

---

[7] Matthew 27: 50–51a.   [8] Akintunde, "Holy Dilemma," 154.
[9] Kalu, *African Pentecostalism*.

a photographer, a career that entailed putting one's reflection out there for public eyes, she also fit into the mold of social respectability. She was the wife of a well-known singer; she was a mother – all publicly available information which she also shares on her social media through photos and commentary. With those social credentials prefacing her accusations, many people took her seriously because they reasoned that a woman who had so much going for her was highly unlikely to stake all she had to make a frivolous accusation. Even in the press release where the pastor himself denied the accusation of rape, he too noted the relevance of her social position to the charge she made: "Looking at her status and that of her husband, I am dumbfounded by why she would say such a thing."[10]

On the other hand, the pastor too was quite familiar to many people, but not necessarily through his sermons or spiritual activities. A prosperity gospel preacher and an avid user of social media, he had put up images of himself with luxury goods that went viral many times. He must have understood that anyone who can control images would also control the body politic, and such control in the age of social media involved dumping a series of photos that featured him performing economic power into the public domain. Every now and then, a blogger would pick up several of his pictures from his social media pages to profile him as "best-dressed pastor" or to note that he is "rocking a Gucci supreme tote bag" that costs this much, or to compare him with another pastor to find out which of them is classier, or to generally describe his flamboyant lifestyle.[11] He was frequently described as "Gucci pastor," and the gossip about him was usually accompanied by images of him as a conspicuous consumer.

With the glut of technological devices and internet connection facilities linking previously discrete worlds, we carry our faith and even our pastors around with us at all times more than ever. The ability to see

[10] https://punchng.com/coza-pastor-fatoyinbo-denies-rape-allegation-threatens-to-sue/

[11] www.gistmania.com/talk/topic,365651.0.html; https://echonaija.com.ng/bio din-fatoyinbo-coza-rocks-n1m-gucci-supreme-tote-bag/; https://ke.opera.news/ ke/en/entertainment/3c3f4eaba5a781ec65b2e32e2df63d61?news_entry_id=t7 d61232a200627en_ke; http://bluenews.com.ng/god-mercy-coza-pastor-goes-worldly-flaunts-bag-worth-1-million-naira; www.google.com/url?sa=i&url= https%3A%2F%2Fwww.tori.ng%2Fnews%2F126197%2Fphotos-of-the-flamboyant-lifestyle-of-pastor-biodu.html&psig=AOvVaw08ZmEijgXP43LEx y_J-8nB&ust=1595616221007000&source=images&cd=vfe&ved=0CA0Qjh xqFwoTCMDR3ueD5OoCFQAAAAAdAAAAABAy

their images over and over through the looking glass of our phone screens, to carry them around in our digital devices like our private possessions, turn them off or tune them out when our phone screens go into a lock mode, and even talk to them at a close range, can result in a depth of familiarity that makes viewers consider themselves eminent judges of their character. The viewer, having known them enough through their self-narration on social media, can associate certain virtues or vices to them even while having never met them physically. The point is not whether such an evaluation of their character is true or fair, but the shaping of reality through the power of perception. By the time such person accused of a crime or someone testifies about their good conduct, it resonates deeply with the audience who thinks they already know them because they have watched them perform aspects of their lives on social media.

Even before the advent of social media, Pentecostal pastors have iconized their images by repeatedly placing their photos on a range of church publicity items from electronic billboards to devotional objects.[12] In Nigerian urban space particularly, imposing billboards carrying blown-up photos of pastors (and their wives) dominate the public spaces, sometimes swallowing up other urban markers.[13] Pastors have always known that it was not enough to embody power as God's anointed. They also needed to be hypervisible and subsume their enlarged presence into the signs and symbols that define urban habitus. If political hegemony in modern times has depended on the ability to control images,[14] then religious authority also recognized the need to assert power by making and circulating images of leadership figures as a fetish. For instance, pastors testify – and churches have encouraged congregations to do the same – that their photographs in their congregants' homes have healed the sick, and even chased away armed robbers and kidnappers.[15] This veneration of their own images is a strategic means of imbuing their disembodied self with auric power, or to put an embodied self in a selfie. Visual symbols are a veritable

---

[12] Ukah, "Roadside Pentecostalism."   [13] Ajibade, "'Lady No Be So.'"
[14] Conze, Prehn & Wildt, "Photography and Dictatorships in the Twentieth Century."
[15] www.lindaikejisblog.com/2019/12/bishop-oyedepo-shares-testimony-of-his-photo-speaking-in-tongues-and-saving-kidnap-victims-uti-nwachukwu-beverly-osu-and-daddyy-freeze-react-video-2.html

instrument in the art of constructing power and transmitting it into everyday life,[16] and adding mythos of what even pastors' illustrations can achieve with supernatural power helps maintain their position within the large web of social relations. By saturating public space with their images, either massively enlarged unto life-size electronic billboards or even printed on small souvenirs, they try to impose multiple simulations of their disembodied selves into the public sphere as means of making themselves part of the ethical ordering of the body politic. Through symbolizations of their anointing compulsively imaged before the public, memories and structures of our worlds are articulated through the frame of social references they provide. Their images become part of the instruments of facilitating cohesion to the plural meanings that are endemic to modern society and urban heterogeneity. All of these have existed before the age of social media where images began to go viral, and people could see a person until they get to the point of "see finish."

In forthcoming sections, I will explore how Pentecostal pastoral power was typically performed on church altars as a stage, and how epochs of media technological advancement caused those altars to be repatriated to social media networks where the performance of the digital self now required even catchier visual symbolizations. To implant themselves in public consciousness, powerful people in political culture have always depended on the aesthetics of power. Throughout history, these have been effected with accoutrements and props relevant to the public at that point in time and therefore resonate strongly with them. For instance, from military uniforms laden with shiny medals to animal skins draped on imperious shoulders, autocratic leaders construct ideas of power and might in the images they supply to the public sphere.[17] On the power of "controlling images," Black feminist scholar Patricia Hill Collins describes how images can be symbolically used to maintain the power structures that subjugate a marginal population.[18] The key word here is "control," because just as images can be used to manipulate a population into compliance, influential figures also use their personal reflections to affirm their power and influence. Religious leaders too, representing a constituency that wants to be socially dominant, have used the same imaging techniques to

[16] Morgan, *Visual Piety*, 5.   [17] York, *Dictator Style*.
[18] Collins, *Black Feminist Thought*.

achieve and maintain the perception of their power as the Lord's anointed. The public already understands the idea of the anointing because it is preached to them in church and also enacted with actual olive oil during ordination services or ritualized liturgical practices.[19] In the case of this pastor, Fatoyinbo, however, in addition to the perception of non-physical anointing as a pastor, he also added to his public image the visible trappings of late capitalism and consumerism – designer labels, sports cars, tailored suits, shiny objects, and so on. These images, taken from his social media page and circulated across various social media networks, made him go viral many times.

Just like military regalia helped dictators construct an image of power, prosperity gospel preachers too understood the importance of modeling power through their sartorial choices and other material goods. While there were spiritual and physical threats of violence militating against the children of God, poverty was also an existential issue they battled with daily. In a social context like Nigeria where poverty was rife and carried over across generations, the prosperity gospel knew to speak to the social situation that imperiled daily life by demonizing poverty. By that, I mean that the instinctively understood operations of demonic forces were commuted into metaphors and were used to explain people's social condition. Rather than poverty being a consequence of larger structural and political forces, it took on the idioms of spiritualism – the spirit of poverty, the spirit of lack and want, the spirit of unemployment, the spirit of generational poverty, the spirit of hunger and deprivation, etc. By turning poverty into a horror that could be overcome by personal spiritual striving, poor people were blamed for their own poverty.[20] Ultimately, demonized poverty induces fear in people; the fear of being despised and denigrated as that abject monstrous figure that is unworthy of occupying certain places with other humans and should be legitimately exorcised.

In demonizing poverty, prosperity gospel preachers reiterate that Christ had already been done the spiritual work necessary to free people from the clutches of poverty and sickness on the cross, and anyone still trapped in those conditions of deprivations was there out of choice. People take such blame from their pastors seriously, and they

[19] Asamoah-Gyadu, "Anointing through the Screen"; Asaju, "Noise, Fire and Flame," 95.
[20] Vengeyi, "'Zimbabwean Poverty Is Man-Made!'"

begin to see themselves and their social condition as blotches on God's perfection. One woman in a prosperity gospel preaching church shared a testimony of how fervently she prayed for a financial breakthrough, saying she would look at her material condition in relation to the wealth the pastor preached and which even other wealthy congregants had, and then pray to God that she would not be turned into an object of insult against the God of her church's pastor.[21] The unsettling image of being poor, or being possessed by the spirit of poverty, while at the same time being surrounded by lavish promises of divine prosperity pushes people to be more resolute in confronting their social condition. The demonization of poverty places responsibility on their own efforts such that their resolve to overcome poverty by any means necessary is shored up. They are driven to pray even more fiercely and more urgently. Where their human ability to transcend poverty runs up against incapacitating structural factors, the demonization of poverty also helps people create a moral justification to sidestep their religious values and do whatever helps to make them rich.

As demonized poverty breeds urgency in people to see an estranged version of themselves through a magisterial lens that also casts them as a problem, it also further correlates with other production forces such as late capitalism and neoliberalism. From the earlier period when the idea of wealth and consumption dogged Pentecostal organizations,[22] people now mostly see money as about the only remaining visible symbol of spirituality. Money is "the supreme good" and those that possess it are considered good and godly persons too.[23] Those whose lives do not typify financial power are treated as living antithetically to the truth of divine blessing. Within a neoliberal order that takes its rationalizing logic from religious culture, those of lower social class are treated like Satan who chose to rebel against God and whose casting into hellfire is therefore justified. Framed in such legalistic terms, the message of prosperity gospel preachers does not blame larger systemic forces for the precarity of human lives, but rather makes it principally about individual righteousness. Those who fall by the wayside, like Satan himself, are simply living lives that are consequent of their wayward or imprudent choices.[24] Those who manage to claw out of

---

[21] This came from testimony I listened to while attending church service.
[22] Meyer, "Pentecostalism and Neo-liberal Capitalism."
[23] www.marxists.org/archive/marx/works/1844/manuscripts/power.htm
[24] Kotsko, *Neoliberalism's Demons.*

those conditions are those who made the right choices to be free from the spirit of lack and want, and who are now free to consume voraciously to assert the side of the divide to which they belong.

Prosperity gospel also helps the creation and condemnation of devils by shaping a sacralized "self" that will symbolize the good/light/God with the power – the immense wealth, that is – to vanquish poverty-causing devils. God, of course, does not appear materially but His viceroys on earth, the pastor, could take His place and have us look at them as if we were looking *up* to God. Looking itself is part of our religious formation process, and the practice of it is an expression of belief.[25] Pastors spectacularize themselves and make their embodied self the visual focal point and point of contact to divine power. Thus, the duty of the anointed pastor of prosperity gospel as a model on the runway of social culture performing the highest ideal of what people's lives should look like – rich, comfortable, happy, relaxed, happily married, healthy bodies – is legitimized for the church audience. That is how the pastor as a Pentecostal subject uses those markers to attain and sustain power identity. It is to this idealized image that congregants sow their seeds – tithes and other special offerings – as a point of contact toward escaping from demonic poverty, the hellfires of their perilous social conditions, and establishment of their own power identity. It was this image that had virally circulated on social media, the one people had seen and "see finish," before the pastor was hit with accusations of moral turpitude.

Pastoral Performances and the Power of Looking

As a consecrated space, altars were traditionally the stage where ritualized religious activities took place. They are typically distinct from the rest of the church, and the architectural style and ornamentation intensify the belief that the space is endowed with holiness and power. There is a mostly elevated dais where the officiating priest, clothed in religious regalia, solemnly carries out their officiating function before the audience sitting some distance across from the altar. The architecture of church altars varies across historical eras and church denominations, but they were mainly attached to the wall while the areas bordering them consisted of various relics, elaborate art pieces, and sacramental

---

[25] Morgan, *Visual Piety*, 3.

items, all of which converge to infuse the space with a sense of sacred-ness. Like the proscenium theatre stage, they offered close to maximum visibility for the man of God from all parts of the church.

However, with the Pentecostal mode of worship came a reconstitution of the altar space to suit the character of church rites. From the classic notion of a shrine laden with sacred relics that bestows sacred authority on the priest, Pentecostalism invented a modern space aesthesized with artifacts of modernity and the artistry of trained set designers. Their worship space got rid of the traditional architecture such as stone pillars around the altar space, artifacts, and even opaque and fixed pulpits. In their place – particularly in the megachurches – came booming speakers, large projector screens and flatscreen TV, moveable glass pulpits (or less opaque ones), artificial flowers (used for decoration), colorful drapes, and twinkle lights. Much of the sense of the sacred that the orthodox churches used to effect through the items they place on the altar gave way, but that sense of sacred power endowing the altar has remained quite strong in the Pentecostal church through other means. The profundity of the messages and the ability of religious messages to make meaning no longer relied on relics and sculpture but on the presence of the Lord, the pastor's anointing, his pulpit-craft (that is, his charisma as a performer), and the excitable responses of the audience. The idea of sacred in this re-figuration of the altar no longer derived from museum sculpture pieces laid out on the altar but the human figure in whose living and moving body all the symbolic articles of the sacred now converge. In Pentecostal hierarchy, this was the pastor.

With the altar now mostly free of constraints, pastors got more demonstrative in their preaching. Like the altars and space in orthodox churches, the spatial arrangement of Pentecostal churches is also designed around maximum viewership of pastors as they walk to and fro along the length of the altar, preaching and praying. The thrills of their energetic preaching and vocal pyrotechnics stimulate the earnest-ness of worship among the congregants who actively engage with the sight of their pastor on stage. Those pastors who have an extended altar space in their big churches also run across its entire length. They jump. They gesticulate. They also shout. When they speak, they modulate their tones as required. They mimic other voices. They crack jokes. They move from the altar directly into the congregation space. They look people in the eyes. They sing and dance more freely. In place of the pastor's natural voice permeating the church, there are now cordless and lavalier microphones to carry their voices through in the church as they strut around. Also, because most pastors wear suits, they also move much more freely without their expressivity constrained by elaborate costumes. For those whose spiritual gifts include deliverance, they exorcize demons around the altar. Some lay hands on people around the altar space. For churches with well-known pastors and who receive special guests – such as politicians and captains of industry – part of the expansive altar (or some close distance to it) also serves as a seating place for these guests. The reconstitution of the altar space where the Pentecostal pastor performs has been helpful to establish power in the supernatural, moral, and even political senses, because watching the pastor perform at the altar has greatly contributed to the understanding of those forms of power. The church in itself is a place of power because it is the house of God, the place where His spirit descends to fellowship with His children. For churches where politicians fellowship with the congregation, seeing pastors being solicited by the political class converges the moral and supernatural power embodied by the pastor with political power. As active spectators, the congregation discerns through looking, how the activities taking place on the altar establish the connections between these forms of power.

Now surrounded by the accoutrements of modernity, when the pastor is at the altar, he is twice seen: first, as a real-life person and second, as a hyper-magnified image projected through supersized screens. The sizes vary according to the wealth and size of the church, and some churches now have an entire wall of the altar space backgrounded by a screen that enormously magnifies the pastor's image to tower before the congregation. As televangelism made closer scrutiny possible, pastors realized they must not only speak the word, but they must look the part as well. Close-up shots on their magnified appearance meant their proclamation of the goodness of God had to be made self-evident. When people see their bodies projected on those massive screens, they must look as flawless as possible. Their appearance must be compelling and true to the gospel they preach. More than the screens that enhance the pastoral figure visualization, the spatial arrangement of cavernous auditoriums typically mimics that of theatre houses, where the audience sits in the dark looking up at the lighted and elevated stage opposite them. At some point, the lights might be turned on inside those churches. With the blinding illumination, all the shadows are exorcised and worshippers are exposed to the glare of divine revelation.

Even when there is no ongoing action on stage, or between one session of the program to another, the audience is continually stimulated through enormous screens and projectors. They feature a kaleidoscope of virtual psychedelia that teasingly lightens the church arena. The hypnotizing art onscreen alternates with warm multicolored disco lights turned on and off at calculated points during the service, and combine to intensify the church experience. And even though the church service can already be visually overwhelming, this is combined with audio effect thunderous enough to make the church's very grounds vibrate under the feet of thousands of worshippers. Although the visual and aural stimuli are already intense, fog machines emit colored smoke when the church rapturously shouts, "Halleluyah!" The combined immersive experience of immediacy, liveness, haptic technologies, and a maniac charge that feels no different from standard theatre and its instrumentation of the sensuous.

The altar is that affective space where deft combination of graphics and design itself invites a critical study in the subfield of scenography – the creation of the visuality in the space the stage occupies – in theatre and performance studies.[26] The altar is an aesthetically fashioned space that, by virtue of its consecration, becomes ritualized by believers, "who ... motivated by the belief that the Altar is a locus of divine power, stake their claim on a better life"[27] and whose excitable practices can turn it into "sites of superfluous emotionalism."[28] For Pentecostal worshippers, the altar space soaks in the divine power that descends during the worship service. It is not unusual for believers to make a frantic rush to the altar at the close of the service to "tap" into the anointing that had permeated the space. According to theatre artist Chukwuma Okoye,

The space surrounding (the altar) is particularly saturated, thereby making it once-removed from the general church geography and twice-removed from the everyday. This holiest space is the stage which holds the altar, and is effectively more circumscribed than the conventional theatre stage:

[26] Collins & Nisbet, *Theatre and Performance Design*, xxiii.
[27] Osinulu, "The Road to Redemption," 7.   [28] Crawley, "Let's Get It On!"

geographically, it is usually elevated, aesthetically, it is more decorated, spiritually, it hosts a more concentrated presence of the Holy Ghost, strategically, it constitutes the visual focus for everyone who is not on it, and manually, it is policed by security personnel in dark suits who forcefully discourage unwarranted invasion.[29]

In some churches, when the congregation is touched by the message and its ministration, even while the service is ongoing, they drop money, jewelry, or other treasured items in the altar's offering baskets or on the altar itself.[30] They plant their offerings as seeds to manifest in their lives the truth and the power of the message they were hearing from the altar.

The evolution of the altar as a space for the pastor to display his charisma and artistic virtuosity owes its success to the development of technologies that made those devices possible. The changes are also a function of the focus on prosperity gospel teachings that demanded that the church space and worship services reflect the promises of transformation that the sermons of abundance and happiness guarantees to the congregation. Generally, any physical changes to the church's design, ideas of ornamentation, and furnishing styles are "intimately connected to religious, social, and cultural transformations,"[31] taking place within the society. At the same time, those physical changes also reflect an evolution in both theology and liturgy, the church's attempts at enhancement of congregational participation in the sermons, and the innovativeness necessary to compete with other churches. For Pentecostalism to have fully accommodated prosperity gospel, churches also had to gradually change their worship modes from somber affairs of mostly prayer and sermons that reflected the strict holiness and asceticism of the early stages of the Pentecostal revival to more sensational forms that thrill as much as they convince with their spectacles. Other additions to church style also came in the form of popular dances and songs, live drama, and even stand-up comedy performances.

As the prosperity gospel got popular and drove people to church, the festive atmosphere needed for it to be credible with their congregation required more tweaking.[32] The church, in preaching the gospel in

---

[29] Okoye, "Technologies of Faith Performance."
[30] I witnessed this during services at a church I attended as a member for years.
[31] Kilde, *When Church Became Theatre.*
[32] Bowler & Reagan, "Bigger, Better, Louder."

which God is able to do exceedingly abundantly above people's imagination, also replicates the exuberance and spectacle of excess in the expression of joyful worship. Prosperity gospel celebrates capitalist consumerism, and thus its liturgy too had to accommodate a celebratory atmosphere complete with a dazzling choreography of acoustics, visual displays, and a sensation(alism) that turned the average Pentecostal church into a sensorium where people could luxuriate in the excess of happiness and pleasure they were trusting God to make happen in their personal lives. Pastoral appearance too had to correspond with the message of abundance. It was not enough to look healthy and wealthy at a basic level; they had to look superlatively glamorous and convincingly play the part of the kingdom businessman whose duty was to convince people that God was indeed good and could give them a better life. The pastor's body, oiled to perfection, emitted symbols of prosperity and wellness, a testimony to the self-evidential truth of their gospel. The altar space and the pastor's acting skills were aestheticized too, choreographed to be telegenic, that is, to fit into the visual character of the television medium or the various projection screens that dot the altar. All worked together as an advertisement of the transforming power of faith.

While the altar is the stage where the pastor exhibits his artistic virtuosity, the stage is also occasionally shared with the audience. New converts occupy the altar during the "altar call" where they give their lives to Jesus Christ, and the conversion journey begins. Also, newcomers are sometimes invited to the altar to get a handshake with the pastor who welcomes them to the fold. Other activities also take place in the altar space, such as testimony time – that time during church service when congregation members also get a chance to perform through their personal stories of conquest that they have crafted and rehearsed to deliver before the congregation – though in some churches, the practice of people coming physically to the altar to share their testimonies has evolved to projecting just their images. For instance, I noticed that in some churches, the photograph of the testifier smiling brightly is projected on the massive screen onstage and captioned with a brief summary of their narration. Although a pastor also reads out the testimony, all attention is focused on the image that looms on the massive screen.[33]

---

[33] This is also a technique to cut down time as some church members spend a significant amount of time relating their well-rehearsed testimonies, often

Despite active congregational participation and the congregation's responsiveness throughout the service, the pastor is still the star of every church service. He is the bearer of the message of prosperity and abundant life for all. His duty to "sell" the redeeming hope in God to the congregation relies on demonstration as much as it does on the inspiration of the message. With trained vocalists who effortlessly move from chanting God's praise in indigenous oral forms to the Bible, music jazzed up to high amplitude and played by a choir trained to deftly combine African talking drums with electric guitars, the congregation sings and dances in joyful celebration before God. As the Pentecostal worship service is a combination of catharsis, recreation, devotion, display, piety, and play, people immerse themselves in the activities that precede the sermon.[34] When they have been well-primed, the pastor gets on the altar and begins to relay his message with words and gestures. The foreknowledge of the anointing of God on him, the passion with which he addresses the church, the techniques he deploys to get the congregation to participate, and the precarious social conditions that drove them to church all combine to affectively move them. The transforming power they came to solicit God for is produced in the minds of the congregation during worship services. At the end of the sermon, when asked to pray, they do so with ardor – a potent blend of kinetics, emotions, and symbolic expressions.[35] It does not stop there.

Beyond moving people to pray or worship animatedly, the joyful excitement stimulated during church activities makes the phantasm of power and the power of phantasm isomorphic. The pastor's body, already a locus of various forms of power can – especially in those intense moments of spiritual laboring – generate erotic charges. Such development is not merely incidental, but a consequence of a conscious structuring of church experience to be sensational and sensuous enough to induce the erotic.[36] As sociologist Ebenzer Obadare noted in his study of Pentecostal pastors, the virtuosity of pastoral performance under the influence of the spirit while being watched by

going beyond the allotted time. Alternatively, this could have been devised to prevent people from saying things that could embarrass the church; that often happens.
[34] Wariboko, "West African Pentecostalism."
[35] Asamoah-Gyadu, *Contemporary Pentecostal Christianity*; Wariboko, "African Pentecostalism."
[36] Meyer, "Aesthetics of Persuasion."

a multitude can also be powerful and hypnotizing. The power does not just come from the immediacy of that experience but is also a function of a social atmosphere already saturated with talks about sex and the pastor himself who is, "nonetheless drawn into a drama of self-fashioning in which dressing, mode of preaching, aesthetics, personal 'tone', automobile ... a vast personal entire repertory, is sexually charged."[37] Like Obadare, religious studies scholar Kevin O' Neill's research on Christian eroticism in postwar Guatemala locates the eroticism in politics. O'Neill explores the conscious ways that Pentecostal churches deploy eroticism to speak to a younger generation whose conversion trajectory – unlike that of an older generation that tells stories of rupture – can be politicized through the erotic. While both Obadare and O'Neill's arguments on Pentecostal eroticism move on the spectrum of depolitization and repoliticization of the body, I see the efforts as far more introverted. That feeling of ecstasy that people experience while worshipping is not only useful for politics of the public sphere, but to intimately bond the congregation with their pastors.

The erotic sensation in the context of religious worship is also a consequence of the openness with which the liturgy event is approached. Spiritual activities require a full opening up of the self to invalidate the supposed borders between the supernatural and the natural realms, and the worshipper comes ready to indulge the entire gamut of their senses while at worship. In those moments of passionate worship within the bounded space of the church when people observed their pastors at a close range, the pastor's performance on the altar fosters intimacy with the congregation because they are sharing themselves with the church both physically and spiritually. When the pastor stands on the altar in church from a god-like height where the expectant congregation looks up to him with their denuding gaze on his body, the phantasmal engineering of the human imagination transmutes the image of the God the Father onto the male pastor, His earthly viceroy. The biopsychic activation of the divine, especially in moments of religious worship, is simultaneously erotic. The sensual stimulation of the religious comes from the same libidinal sources that power sexual acts.[38] The church administrators, well understanding how such

---

[37] Obadare, "The Charismatic Porn-Star."   [38] Mbembe, *On the Postcolony*.

moments of triggered passions can be transgressive, try to impose some level of order and control on worship activities because,

> Together, worship and worshippers' bodies become a site for the production of ecstasy, jouissance, and bliss. For some believers, the pleasures come from the excitement of the body and its senses; and for others, they are from pure contemplation of the divine or possible encounter with the Holy Spirit. *The former pleasure, though it is given space in worship, is also surveilled so that it does not exceed its limits.*[39]

The last sentence (emphasis mine) hits on something quite important: the notion of control in Pentecostal activities. Despite the boisterousness of worship and the emphasis of visual stimulation by pastors who needed to make the exuberance of prosperity gospel a visceral experience, there is some measure of control to the whole architecture of worship from where pastors also derive their moral power. They control the symbols and also regulate the range of feelings.[40] In the next section, I demonstrate how the variables that have helped pastors to put their bodies on the altar before the gaze of an audience while still moderating the symbols went out of the bounds of their surveillance when staged on the social media. Unlike the church altar where the congregation could look at their bodies in live performance on the altar but could not "see finish," social media multiplied the pastor's digital body so often that people could begin to see through the pastor's mystique.

---

[39] Wariboko, *West African Pentecostalism*, 6.
[40] Despite all the appearance of glam, the splendorous bombardment of stimulation, and the suggestion of the expansiveness of the altar as an arena where the play and imagination of the sacred would not be constrained, the discipline and control of the economy of pleasure during the service is also effected with a rather mundane item that in itself emblematizes modernity's control of the infiniteness of time: a clock (see John David North). In one of the church sites that I studied, the intricate metal beams that form the church ceiling, far above the head of the congregation had been rigged a computer monitor with a digital clock that counted down for everyone on the stage who ministered. As I observed, when the time set for each performer was up, no matter what they were doing and how much the audience was enjoying their act, the clock hushed them off the stage with clear instructions that come up on the screen. The only time the clock enforcement of time regulation was suspended was when the pastor was preaching. He could go over time, but the clock did not count against him.

Pastoral Performances in the Age of Instagram

During my fieldwork with social media departments of some Pentecostal churches, one of my observations was how churches not only used social networks as an electronic extension of the church but also strategically as a digital altar to exhibit the pastor as an objectified figure discharging embodied supernatural power. Churches have learned that by going on social media networks, they would invariably attract a "mixed multitude."[41] That is, a congregation of people who are not necessarily on their pages for purposes of worship and might not even be Christian. Now they have had to face up to the reality that with the technology of social media, all kinds of crowds, even the "mixed multitude" should be welcome because they keep the church's social media handle animated. In the age of the Internet, the reality is that "the body of Christ exceeds the limits of Christian membership. In the era of globalization and the emergence of the global commons, the worldwide body of Christ has become one immense, cosmopolitan city or *world city.*"[42] The church's media personnel, through their work, extended how pastors performed power to people who could now congregate on the Internet. The seat of pastoral authority, performance, and influence from the altar were simulated on social media networks using glossy images as a creative resource to engineer and reinforce ideas of the pastor as the big man of the big God. To this end, churches center their pastor in their display of church-making activities. Most of them now have a social media handle, and the pastor has one named after him as well (and for some of the churches, the pastor's handle has more followers than the church organization itself).[43] With those digital altars, the followers of Jesus Christ have seamlessly morphed into the pastor's Twitter/Instagram followers and to type "amen" to pastor's images and the accompanying caption of prayer

---

[41] This term came from Exodus 12:38. The Bible mentioned that when the Israelites left the enslavement of Egypt, some Egyptians went with them. As foreigners, they were the "mixed multitude," the polluting outsider to God's nation.

[42] Wariboko, *The Charismatic City and the Public Resurgence of Religion*, 169.

[43] As Rosalind Hackett observed in *The New Virtual (Inter) Face of African Pentecostalism*, pastors are the lead characters in their church's narrative on its website. Church websites are built around them such that they are both a *"portal"* providing access to the scope of their organization, and an *"endpoint,"* and this is because "all roads lead to him as the centre of operations."

is now a form of active spiritual participation in itself. This evolution did not happen providentially. Within a digital milieu where the vitality of the church correlates with its social media presence, religious leaders have reshaped ideas of access, interaction, participation, and religious creativity to meet up with the swirling demands of many contexts generated by interfaces of humans and algorithms.[44] Churches work hard to insert themselves into digital spheres where their messages, most now commuted into images and accompanied with minimal text, sail on the vast sea of other free-floating images. With that insertion and institutionalization of themselves into cyber-world structures also came a deluge of public interactions with churches through their social media pages that necessitated the setting up of a social media department with a workforce that managed the virtual church. Those social media workers therefore not only work to sustain the domain of the church from a physical space to the borderless possibilities of the cyber sphere, they also have to respond to reactions to pastors' messages, and they sometimes have had to push back against criticisms and attacks on their churches and pastors.

For their various social media pages, these churches have retained official professional photographers for their church services. The photographers take many photos during service, which they quickly sieve through sometimes even while the church service is still ongoing. The officials of the church's media department select the most animated of the images, mostly those that show the pastors in moments of spiritual labor where they were either preaching, praying, or even snagging moments of intimate pleasure such as dancing during praise/worship sessions. The choices of pastors' bodies on the pulpit stage, crisscrossing the material and transcendental realms while they minister before the church, are invaluable for demonstrating the pastor's spiritual charisma and artistic virtuosity. The church staff also selects images of the pastor's wife too either when she is ministering, or even sitting down and watching service proceedings with a look of deep concentration etched on her face. If they had a guest preacher, the same yardsticks of choosing images that illustrate attentiveness and response are mostly applied. The selection criteria also apply to the regular church members. The social media department chooses their images for the most vibrant expressions of responsiveness. They opt for those poses

[44] See, for instance, Drescher, *Tweet if You [Heart] Jesus.*

where the church members are either enthusiastically responding to the pastor's messages or praying or have their hands lifted to the heavens or even dancing. Those high-resolution photos of the pastors and congregation are primarily selected for how much they flatter those captured within them as they perform worship and how they can convince viewers on those social media pages about the potency of the message emanating from the man of God.

When the choice images of pastors and congregation are contrivedly linked together in a series uploaded on their social media pages, it comes across as a linear connection between two sides – the performer and audience, the pastor and the congregation. Although the nature of photographic images ostensibly mute or freeze their subjects as mere visual objects, the images of pastors shared on these sites must "capture" them in the act of performing spiritual power – generating and distributing it. They must be "in action" to retain the perception of their power in the minds of onlookers who see them as a projection of spiritual power that is produced during acts of worship. The images of the congregation too must depict (mostly) individual responses to the images of the pastor performing on the altar, to strengthen ideas about his performative power and the hold of his charisma on them. The selection of individuals who are worshipping in the church, sometimes with their eyes closed and their hands raised to the heavens or even shedding tears or with exultant looks on their faces as they sang and danced, gives more credibility to the message the social media department want to project. A photo series of singular individuals feel more personal and authentic than photos of a mass of people unless in the instances where people have formed a dance circle during the services. When these officials share images of a crowd, it is to show that their church is either large or growing. They want to show that they have the numbers, they are becoming popular, and that this is happening because the pastor's message is true and attracting followers. So, on one hand, they share images of the pastor in their spiritual labor and, on the other hand, those of the congregation in moments of receptivity. These carefully selected images – pastors and the congregation conjoined within a call-and-response format – become a handcrafted encounter between the pastor and congregation. After the social media department has uploaded the images during or after the services, they track the public reaction. They note which photos compel viewers' fingers to the "like" and "love" buttons and then double down on sharing more of those types of images. Throughout the week, they also share more of the pastors' photos to which they have appended excerpts from sermons on their various social media handles across the networks – Facebook, Twitter, Instagram, and so on.[45] They also make them into publicity materials to announce coming services.

All of these are, of course, possible because of the ubiquity of the technological devices enabling access to social networks. Social media presented pastors with new digital altars and they try to simulate the erotic economy of worship they had mastered on physical altars for a broader audience presently reaching them across wireless connections. If God has always revealed Himself to humans through visions, the social media further enabled pastors to spruce up the imaging of God's working power through the photos they share as complements to the gospel message. Modern communication technology expanded the range of narrative/textual possibilities and brought the opportunity for them to expand the sphere of their acts in mediated formats that use still images and short videos.[46] For pastors, it also means they can use their self-representation to visualize the image of God, restructure modes of relating to Him as worshippers, and simulate new aesthetics of persuasion.

Still, thanks to this same digital technology that has allowed anointed men of God to wield images and visual symbols in the production of power, the ownership and control of images are now far more democratized. Unlike live performances, we can now see pastors at a much closer range than from the separating distance of raised altars in the church. Unlike during the days of TV broadcasts where we saw their images fleetingly, we see it more closely, for longer, and we even touch it intimately. They encourage people to touch the TV screens portraying their images to receive healings, anointing, and blessings. Also, unlike the era of paper photography, their images are now more portable. We can call up images at will on our smartphones. With social media and networking sites such as Instagram and the proliferation of

---

[45] Where necessary, this team also defends the pastors. They create profiles through which they respond to issues concerning pastors during social media conversations or arguments.

[46] Baruh, "Mediated Voyeurism and the Guilty Pleasure of Consuming Reality Television"; Codone, "Megachurch Pastor Twitter Activity"; Hutchings, "The Dis/Embodied Church: Worship, New Media and the Body"; White, Tella, & Ampofo. "A Missional Study of the Use of Social Media (Facebook) by Some Ghanaian Pentecostal Pastors."

mobile phones, the endless human fascination with its own double finally finds an outlet. Each one of us, allowed a Narcissus's mirror, creates portable souvenirs of our own selves and reproduces them on other people's timelines. The techno-cultural changes engendered by the social media created a revolving door between the showmanship on the stage of the altar and on social networks, with one major addition now though: the diverse audience could also respond in real time and from remote locations. With such endless possibilities, pastors now face the reality of a world where the new wave of interactivity that allows them to assert their presence also, by the hyper-exposure the social media promotes, corrodes the world where myths obscured their human foibles and flaws.

After Ese Walter's accusations had fizzled out without an official response from the pastor, people moved on. However, the pastor, Fatoyinbo, continued to float on social media, even along with his choice of words, "robust response" which became an insider joke among Nigerians. The term "robust response" now emblematizes a promise of public accountability not intended to be kept. Apart from bloggers who frequently wrote about the pastor's sense of style and love for expensive stuff, he also actively promoted himself with images showing off his designer gear, sport cars, power bikes, gold-plated décor, and other signifiers of wealth. For a preacher whose church was also called "The Wealthy Place," he took care to look the part. His well-posed images with the luxury items went viral, cutting through the noise and endless uproarious chatter that characterize the Internet. He and his posh stuff grabbed the public eye, summoning a wide voyeuristic audience who wanted to ogle the lush green pastures of their pastors' personal lives on Instagram. Several images of him with his Porsche (with plate number GRACE 1–1) parked inside the church compound would be used as church publicity material. The flyer would show the image of a pastor standing tall inside the church compound. The Porsche would be visible in the background, and on the lower part of the poster would be written the church website address. The logo would be displayed, while another section would feature an announcement of the artiste who would give a church concert.[47] That flyer itself would say a lot already, but bloggers would pick the image

---

[47] The choir name is "Avalanche," a description that has ironic undertones for a church that premises excessiveness in all its public appearances.

and announce how they had run the model through the manufacturer's website and had found the price.

As one of his profile images – which several articles used to promote their news stories and gossip about him – he shared a picture of himself posing and checking himself out in what looked like a mirror, his frame tilted outwards to the viewer at about a 45 degrees angle. The pose and the angle show a man taking a picture that he is aware is destined for social media; hence he was already conscious of us watching him watch us. The image, feeding our voyeuristic instincts with an objectified version of himself, urges us to imbibe on the visage of the man of God. While the viewer cannot see the pastor's double in the mirror he seemed to be looking into, we see the photo on Instagram through the lenses of our mobile devices anyway. Sensing that he must be looking into a mirror as we look at him, we also conjure a visual echo of him in that looking glass. This doubling of the double means that the more we stare at the man of God, the more his image and likeness is multiplied in our eyes and in our minds. In the background of that same photo were various indoor décor items that let off a golden sheen, both accessorizing him and conveying his love for dazzling displays. He has at least one other photograph taken in that same spot and using the same pose too. With carefully selected spots in his private spaces and his church, he would frequently put his accessorized and aestheticized body on display, making multiple viewers crane their necks and gaze at the totems of upward mobility he had put on that body.[48] While sweltering in the heat of the #ChurchToo campaign, the media reported him to have thanked the church members for their support of him, "their best-dressed pastor in town."[49] Spontaneously coming in a moment of his vulnerability, this admission confirmed that his peacocking was a purposeful strategy to attract viewership to his body. However, staring at those viral pictures of him in flashy apparel could also be denuding because people could see him so often and at close range

---

[48] The pastor is one of the very few Africans who has been profiled on Instagram accounts such as *preachersnsneakers* and *prophetsnwatches*. These accounts post photographs of celebrity church leaders wearing a pricy clothing item such as shoes and watches. They find the price online, and place it right next to the preacher's photo. Fatoyinbo is one of those featured who wears very expensive items.

[49] www.thecable.ng/extra-im-the-best-dressed-pastor-in-town-says-fatoyinbo

that their admiring gaze could graduate to scrutiny or a deconstruction.[50]

The fate of art in the age of mechanical reproduction is that a circulated and viral image of a pastor would be too banal to conjure the erotic sensations that happen within the confines of a church worship service. The images from the digital altar might be shared and admired. It might even be accompanied by Bible verses and even depict men of God at prayer while a congregation listens or fervently prays along with them, but it does not compel the thrilling erotic charges that occur in live worship where actual bodies mingle. The viral circulation of images of powerful religious figures overshares the mystique of their body, and the authenticating force of eroticism that people feel in live worship is replaced by the "digital disincarnation" of the pastoral body.[51] As I noted earlier, pastors too try to mystify their photos such that the image does not become cheapened by overcirculation. For instance, during the 2019 annual convention of Winners' Chapel, *Shiloh*, Bishop Oyedepo told the story of a woman who had been kidnapped and held in a forest along with some others who were "tied down like slaves." The Bishop narrated that as the kidnappers were coming to take the woman's baby from her, she reacted by flinging her bag at them. A Shiloh publicity flyer that had his photo on it inside her bag fell out and he – the Bishop, that is – began to speak in tongues from the flyer. He said the kidnappers all fell down, paralyzed by the power of God. The woman and her fellow captives escaped from their den. Of course, the story was severely ridiculed by social media denizens, but it is still important to note pastors tell these stories about their photos to assert their power and control even outside the bounds of their church. With their photos mushroomed on all kinds of banal materials and sequestered from the contexts that imbue it with cult value, they deliberately stir libidinous urges by telling stories with visualizable details (for instance, saying people were "tied down like slaves"). The Bishop even advanced the plot of his narration by evoking shared understanding of a mother's protective urges that was so strong it compelled divine power. By introducing their photos – the simulacra

---

[50] As Gerardo Marti and Gladys Ganiel noted in their study of the "deconstructed church," to deconstruct is to resist institutionalization by regular questioning of practices and beliefs.

[51] Challies, *The Next Story*, 100.

of themselves that transcended space and time – into those sites of contestation between and good and evil, pastors become superheroes.

Within the church space, their spiritual laboring could foster intimacy to fuse the congregation, myths, and sensibilities enough for them to build relationships and even maintain control over them. Outside that space, the odds could not be as easily coordinated. For some people, the images of Porsche that advertised the pastor and his church might seem as rather too tacky and antithetical to the humility expected of Christians, but the people for whom the poverty had been demonized saw the financial prosperity he illustrated as aspirational. In a culture where people are either quite poor or where their middle-class status is planked on economic and political vagaries, wealth – particularly one sacralized with the name of Jesus – is a universal solvent. The images might lack the aura and intimacy that joint worship fosters, but the social media display was still a realistic exaggeration of their private imagination of their most idealized self. They would be drawn to his church while hoping the bestowed blessing of the gospel he celebrated before their eyes would be tautological. To this set of people, his worldly goods represented the triumph of God over the spirit of poverty. The rape accusations, to them, were a satanic attack against divine conquest and they were more driven to protect him against what they saw as persecution.

At the time the issues of Busola Dakolo's allegations raged, I viewed one of the church's online promotional videos that narrated their history from their lowly days to now occupying prime estate in Abuja, the Federal Capital Territory. They showed off the church exterior, a well-designed architectural piece that stood out among rather tepid architecture in many Nigerian urban spaces. The video has been posted four years earlier but with the new development of the rape accusations, people searched out the church and those online archival materials attracted more views and comments. One of the commenters, Seyi Olatunji wrote, "Haaaha, keep going. The devil is finished, Jesus won. More grace to you sir." Another person, Chris Israel, added "Wow!!! This man of God carries grace. No wonder there is a demand for his life and soul in hell. The Lord will see him through. May mercy and the blood prevail over guilt and judgement! Pastor Biodun, grace and mercy will speak for u!" Someone else named lovelyceleb Okoye wondered what the truth was. She asked, "I lack words, I don't know which is true? Could this man doing this much for God at the same time be destroying the lives of young ladies???" J mime Ministry responded to her, "Who does that? ... Who invest this much in the things of God and destroys it ... The devil is only against the church of God."[52] To these people, personal virtue might well be discernible from images. The sexual assault scandals the pastor faced only made him a more compelling Christian subject. His wealth as a child of God made him fit into the biblical tropes of the persecuted who deserved protection from an unrelenting world.

For others who went out to protest at the church and asked the pastor to step down, insisting that everyone was equally anointed, seeing a pastor whose fetish was consumer goods rankled. One photo after the other, they had seen enough of him to get to the point of see finish, the endpoint where the oversharing and overviewing wore off the mystique of the images. Social relations now somewhat leveled, they questioned the concept of the anointing as it was traditionally understood. His glaring obsession with being seen as the wealthy pastor of the wealthy made him so familiar with people that they thought they could see through him; oversharing himself had structured new visual literacies of his power performance. When people reach the disenchanting point of see finish, they also make synesthetic connections between seemingly disparate stimuli. Familiar things begin to disclose themselves through a flash of insight. In those moments, we creatively intuit new meanings into old and existing symbols. For those who had seen the pastor exhibit himself and his love for clothes, cars, designer gear, and expensive goods, the various accusations against him conflated the lasciviousness of his material consumption habit with his perceived sexual appetites. Once considered exclusive, the anointing was now seen to have served the tawdry habit of conspicuous consumption and the celebrity culture of Instagram. If even anointed men of God on social media have to force a redirection of eyes toward themselves to snag the lean spaces of popularity like regular Instagram celebrities, then what magic is there to the anointing? Without an attendant ennobling humility and a distinctive behavior, the anointing felt like something anyone could claim regardless of their social or spiritual status. It was like the moment people saw through the holy of holies at the death of Jesus on the cross, and the priestly class lost all their claim to elite social privileges. If the anointing that has always

[52] www.youtube.com/watch?v=mTcSy8iSx2o

been taken to be an exclusive preserve of men called of God could be oriented toward the compulsive consumerism of the Instagram Age, then why cannot everyone claim it? Why should people who demonstrate worldly taste have it both ways by living like social media celebrities and yet avoid a similar level of scrutiny? With that questioning attitude, protesters marched to the church with several of their placards reading, "We are all the Lord's Anointed."

Crowd-Sourcing Justice in the Court of Public Opinion

At the time of this writing, the rape saga with Busola Dakolo and the pastor has more or less reached an impasse. The #MeToo #ChurchToo protests that led the pastor to step down from his position turned out to be the easy part. The case was officially reported to the police but the Nigerian Police generally lacks the institutional autonomy and resources necessary for an adequate rape investigation, especially one involving high profile figures. Some months after her allegation became a hullabaloo, Busola Dakolo cried out that she was being intimidated by the police who were supposed to investigate the case.[53] When the story of police intimidation of her family was reported in the media, the nation's first lady, Mrs. Aisha Buhari, intervened on her behalf by tweeting on her personal page, "ATTENTION: INSPECTOR GENERAL OF POLICE #SayNoToRape #JusticeForRapeVictims #SayNoToIntimidation."[54] The police, embarrassed at the negative attention, pulled back and stated that all they wanted from the couple was to serve them official invitation letters to appear at the police station to aid investigations.[55] Church union organizations such as Pentecostal Fellowship of Nigeria and Christian Association of Nigeria distanced themselves from the issue.[56] When Pastor Adeboye, the patriarch of Nigerian Pentecostalism, was pressured to intervene, he did not issue a formal statement. Instead, he gave a sermon where he said,

[53] See story here: www.theguardian.com/global-development/2019/aug/06/nigeria-metoo-moment-accuser-busola-dakolo

[54] http://saharareporters.com/2019/07/20/%E2%80%98saynotointimidation%E2%80%99-aisha-buhari-responds-saharareporters-story-police-invasion-dakolo

[55] https://punchng.com/why-we-invited-dakolo-wife-after-aisha-buharis-tweet-police/

[56] www.premiumtimesng.com/news/headlines/337880-coza-can-speaks-on-rape-allegation-against-fatoyinbo.html

I feel compelled to say some things to those that are young and up and coming ministers. What I want to say is from the Bible: There is nothing hid that shall not come to the open or made manifest. Mark 4:22. Sooner or later, your sins will find you out if you continue in sin under the guise of grace. Numbers 32:23. Abstain from every appearance of evil. 1 Thessalonians 5:22. When you find yourself facing youthful lust, flee; don't say you're highly anointed or something, ask Samson. You may say I'm old fashioned, I agree. I'll never have a private secretary who's a woman. When a woman accuses you of something, nobody will listen to you whether you're right or wrong; be wise! I'm old fashioned, but I'm still surviving since I was ordained; it's better to be old fashioned & live than modern and die.[57]

His intervention was greeted with groans by people who thought he had reduced complex issues into vague sermonization and barely veiled victim-blaming. Without strong support from either juridical or the paternal figures of moral institutions, the symbolic victory of a pastor stepping down from the pulpit after he was accused was soon followed by normative reality. The pastor himself returned to the altar after a month and preached a message titled "Sudden Victories." Part of the crowd that had gathered to demand his resignation was disillusioned by the turn of events. Some others had moved on, lured away from the story of assault into the endless loops of breaking news cycles that characterize social media. There was another buzz when the pastor was arrested, but it was momentary. He was later released on bail.[58]

Part of the fieldwork for this book took place during the #ChurchToo campaign. In my survey with people on the issue, the questions that frequently came up were: Since the objective truth of these accusations is unknowable and the prospect of recompense is nearly impossible, what do these women want by risking everything to tell the stories of abuse by pastors? Why do they insist on rupturing the social and moral order, damage their social status, bring the Christian faith into disrepute, and all of these without a guarantee of any reasonable outcome? These concerns are not out of sync with the Nigerian social and political realities. Unlike the USA where the #MeToo movement led to a few investigations that made some privileged men like Harvey Weinstein lose their powerful positions and go to jail, the

57 www.premiumtimesng.com/news/top-news/339180-adeboye-speaks-on-rape-scandal-gives-advice-to-pastors.html
58 https://punchng.com/coza-rape-allegation-fatoyinbo-remains-in-police-custody-as-he-seeks-bail-perfection/

Nigerian #MeToo #ChurchToo campaigners soon found that the institutional forces that should hold sexual abusers accountable are far too
deeply invested in maintaining the status quo. They share an identity of
power, and creating the conditions that would make it possible to
challenge moral corruption in the issues of sex could also lead to
holding those politicians accountable for their stewardship. Similar to
how tribal identity politics allows a politician's infraction to be overlooked in the political sphere because such people hold power in trust
for their community, religious leaders are forgiven because they represent constituencies of gender and religion. The power they personify,
culturally and morally, in a fragmented society with many fault lines as
Nigeria, is seen as far too much for society to throw away because of
sexual abuse.

For Busola Dakolo, months after she filed a civil suit against the
pastor, her case was dismissed by a judge whose verdict did not stop at
noting that the statute of limitations on the case had passed. The judge
also added that the case even amounts to an act of injustice. Justice
Oathman Musa was reported in the media to have said that the case
was "an abuse of judicial process . . . empty and purely sentimental . . .
the matter amounts to injustice and was aimed more at cruelty than
obtaining justice." The judge claimed Busola Dakola wasted the court's
time, awarded a N1 m fine against her, and said the fine should even
have been ten times more.[59] What, to me, should have been an opportunity for the judge to speak to the intractability of the Nigerian legal
system and the ways its structures impede justice for rape victims was
turned into an avenue for further ridiculing an alleged victim. Rather
than the judge speaking about the issue so flippantly and handing out
punishment, it would have been far more helpful if the judge weighed
the bigger moral implications of the case for the country and challenged
the legal system on ways to tackle rape allegations. While the past
might be an imperfect tense, the tensions of the present still need
perfecting for the sake of the future. A year after she first made the
allegations, Busola Dakolo gave the public an update. She said the
police concluded their investigation, "handed over its report to the
Ministry of Justice in Abuja for onward prosecution of Biodun
Fatoyinbo. He clearly has a case to answer. But there has been silence

---

[59] https://punchng.com/court-fines-busola-dakolo-n1m-dismisses-case-against-
fatoyinbo/

from the ministry. Silence. A loud silence! We have written a letter but for over a month we have no response."[60] At the time of updating this in year 2020, the case was still stuck with everyone waiting for the Ministry of Justice to at least respond to her claims but nothing has come out of it yet, not even an official statement.

Ideally, what should have followed the #MeToo #ChurchToo moment in Nigeria is an intervention that transmutes the campaign from a social movement to a legal one. In the absence of that desirable turn of events, the court of public opinion remains the only option for those who have an allegation that the law courts cannot accommodate. It is an extra-legal recourse for those who claim sexual assault but whose cases do not (and cannot) find their feet on the grounds established by existing formal jurisprudent procedures. The law, supposedly a neutral adjudicator, typically offers a "sovereign judgment, predictable procedures, and dependence of tradition."[61] While they promise a dispassionate mediation in issues of sexual abuse, these factors can also impede justice with their formalisms. Trials are conducted based on admissible evidence, usually tangible, and considered relevant to the case. However, in real life, not many accusations can meet such lofty standards. Reality is far more complicated, and there are serious issues of gender, class, and social ethics that prevent people from collecting the evidence necessary to pursue a case in court. In such circumstances where people are not guaranteed a right to a fair hearing by the courts, they sidestep judicial processes by taking their case to a shadow forum like social media where the public holds court. With social media networks, they at least force a reckoning.

The ad hoc court of public opinion, emblematized by the Latin phrase *vox populi, vox Dei* – that is, the voice of the people is the voice of God – is one space where all evidence is admissible, and its self-appointed adjudicators have endless room to intervene in the ongoing case. In the court of public opinion, people with varying amounts of knowledge and expertise attack sensational issues with a hastiness that can overly simplify complexities and nuances because they want an answer right away. Although their senatorial attitudes can complicate problems, the court of public opinion is also the sphere where public

[60] www.pulse.ng/entertainment/celebrities/busola-dakolo-shares-update-on-case-against-coza-pastor-biodun-fatoyinbo/qtsezlc
[61] Burgess, "Between the Desire for Law and the Law of Desire."

debates are first launched and which eventually impact collective ethics and rewrite formal legal systems. Taking the notion of "God," not as a remote divine being with sole oversight over the affairs of men but as the overriding moral force that determines collective societal ethics, the voice of the people could transmute into the will of the divine if their emotions are consciously streamlined into an ethical agenda. In that case, accusations like that of Busola Dakolo and even Ese Walter are not a waste of either their social status or the energies of the public. What they do is to pull the trigger. Over time, the body of old traditions and oppressive behavior will drop.

The voice of the people is the voice of God, not because God descends from heaven to help humans reshape their behavior but because people build up their social consciousness to cohere with an ideal that is so good that it can be considered godly. It is the people who instigate the actions that rupture ongoing societal traditions and lay the socio-ethical foundations in tandem with the progressive spirit of the times. Part of the success of the #MeToo movement in the USA in enforcing some degree of reckoning was the force of public sentiment and organized economic actions. Having received the case in the court of public opinion, proponents generated a critical mass that was threatened political and economic organizations and forced them to make decisions about sexual abuses. The Nigerian social structures, however, does not accommodate such economic boycotts on a massive scale. For one, relatively fewer Nigerians have sufficient disposable income for people to vote with their pockets and thumbs – that is, to bring economic pressure on corporate organizations and political parties so they could use their institutional power to take some actions against alleged sexual predators. The country also does not have sufficient social, political, and economic coordination to organize a successful boycott of any goods and services as a form of moral advocacy. However, the force could be built up through constant pushing and pushbacks, enough to generate the ethical awareness necessary for reforms to happen. As Busola Dakolo herself said, "Awareness is victory. But we are pushing to another even great(er) victory: Justice."[62]

---

[62] www.pulse.ng/entertainment/celebrities/busola-dakolo-shares-update-on-case-against-coza-pastor-biodun-fatoyinbo/qtsezlc

In developing countries, the intricacies of power and abuse can be foggy and still need a lot more intellectual untangling before certain issues even get a start. For Nigeria, after the initial frenzy of the #MeToo #ChurchToo campaign died down, some campaigners, though realizing the enormity of the challenge of managing the momentum they had generated, remain undaunted. The feminist and social justice imperatives that drove them to campaign also had to acknowledge that the various underlying structural issues of the Nigerian legal system could not be addressed by a mere intonation of a globally generated chant. The voices of women accusing powerful men of sexual abuse might, at present, be unable to withstand the noisome pestilence of embedded patriarchy. Still, society's ethical ears can be primed to listen to alleged victims and respond meaningfully.

Despite the dismissal of the civil suit filed by Busola Dakolo and the sense of rage and despair felt by a lot of people who wanted to see the story through, neither the #MeToo #ChurchToo protests nor the momentum they generated were futile. It might seem that without at least one case pursued to a rational conclusion, the possibility of ever holding powerful people to account is too remote. However, the fact that the women spoke up and found support in sections of society also indexes some progress. While they were expectedly ridiculed by many people who considered them as seducers and Jezebel spirits who wanted to pull down the pillars of God's house, they also found massive support among people who saw them differently. The women were not victims the public was too mentally distant to relate with; what the supporters saw were actual people with a life that mirrored theirs. They were familiar with Busola Dakolo, particularly because they had seen her up close through her images and self-accounts on her social media pages. As I noted when Ese Walter made the first allegation and as it happened when Busola Dakolo made hers too, people turned to the women's respective social media accounts in their quest for the truth. They would drag out their pictures from their profile and try to discern their character through those images. Images of the women in clothes considered revealing became the basis of judging their character. The social media judges did the same thing for the pastor too. They judged him based on photos through which he had curated his public image over the years. A photograph of him in silk shirt and sitting in a chair with an ornately designed backrest, his glasses on his smiling face while looking away from the camera (as if he was looking around him in amused puzzle-ment) provoked hard-hitting commentary that a social media intellec-tual made of him. In that photo, his hands were stretched as if to say, "what is the fuss all about?" and it was an apt choice for a commentary on the obliviousness of patriarchal power.[63] There was also a particular photograph of him on the church altar, preaching. On the virtual screen that covered the entire wall behind him had been projected the text of the Bible which read, "Now the works of the flesh are evident, which are: adultery, fornication, uncleanness, lewdness, (NKJV) Galatians 5:19."[64] Outside the context of his preaching in the church and in the newly created context of the rape allegations, the pastor's photo preaching against the evident works of the flesh pro-voked knowing laughter in both those who circulated the image and those who received it. Those photographs, even though remixed to match recent events, became the basis for discerning virtues. Even those already familiar with them go back repeatedly to look until they see through the parties. People's reflections became the oracle with which the public scried an elusive truth.

The women's accounts may have titillated the public with a narration of alleged sexual encounters with pastors, but they also summon the court of public opinion to dialogue on the broader social issues of sexual abuse and the concomitant lack of legal structures to deal with it. The accusers' accounts are – and literally too – fleshed-out narrations staged before the public. Nuance might have been sacrificed to the outrage, but the accusations and argu-ments are useful to build ethical precedence. In talking about it, people stimulate empathy in the audience and instigate social and transformational changes by finding a (re)training ground for the collective moral imagination. The exchange and interaction compel rethinking social norms, commit emotions and intellect to question how larger factors weigh on individual choice, and, overall, make it possible to generate the conditions in which actual changes can be enacted.

---

[63] See that photo on this news media site: www.sunnewsonline.com/alleged-rape-pastor-fatoyinbo-responds-says-i-never-raped-even-as-unbeliever/
[64] Find that photo here: www.stelladimokokorkus.com/2019/07/pastor-biodun-fatoyinbo-takes-leave-of.html

Visuality and Power Identity

It is significant that the Pentecostal hierarchy was undercut by women who breached society's silencing norms to make accusations of sexual impropriety. To confront a pastor whose public appearance has been about constructing a notion of power through visuality was no mean task. That the campaign gained traction at all and even had the buy-in of a segment of the society that went as far as to protest at the church testifies to changes in the cultural perception of those who had serially performed power and now embodied it. This contestation of their moral authority met with severe pushback from conservative members of the faith movement who consider the dis-assembly of the power identity of the people who make up the face of the movement would come back to them as followers. Yet, the back and forth has been good for the society because it brought out issues that would have otherwise remained hidden.

On the rare occasions that women alleged sexual assault and abuse against a powerful male in the country, they found very mixed responses. However, these collective responses have not been the same, but a comparison would at least show positive development for two reasons: One is that a woman has broken through conformity and enforced silence and might thereby inspire another woman to do so too. Two, because it also means the society's ethics are changing. When the anointed men of God, also the men of power in the society, are confronted with accusations, the spate of events that follow reveals the various flaws inbuilt into the social and juridical systems. Because the protests that followed Bukola Dakolo's allegations invoked the language of the #MeToo movement, it too easily suggests that force with which the movement that started in the USA blew across various cultural spheres and through global media channels impacted Nigerians. While the global #MeToo movement was undoubtedly impactful, local motivation also propelled the event and this might still have occurred even if the #MeToo movement had not been ignited in the USA.

In this case, underlying factors were derived from how the pastor (and the woman) used images to narrate themselves prior to the latest allegations. By the time the allegations came, both were quite familiar to the public and this was the basis for the mental processing of the accusations. One's image in the public sphere is quite a powerful tool for shaping social narratives. However, for a prosperity gospel preacher, photos demonstrative of that gospel are important to imprint on the public consciousness more powerfully. Already, within the churches, worship practices and church design have been modified to make the pastor the star attraction. Printed and virtual images, I have noted, have been vital to churches achieving their goal of making pastors look powerful. With the prosperity gospel, pastors' use of images to celebrate consumerism in the name of Jesus got more advanced. The semiotic organization of the texts and photos make pastors the advertiser, the product, and even the means of production. Through clothing choices, the background of the photos, and even poses in the photos, prosperity gospel uses pastors to sell the truth of the possibilities of redemption to beleaguered people through capitalist and neoliberal consumption. People look and look at the images of the pastor on his digital altar until they think they see all there is to him. When they have reached the point of "see finish," they begin scrutinizing his habits, tastes, conduct, virtue, and even anointing. While some others might remain enraptured by the images of pastor in Gucci-labeled outfit and sports cars, others see it as a banalization of the anointing. In insisting that everyone is anointed, they are ripping the temple cloth from top to bottom and resisting the institutionalization of moral covering for powerful men of God before they are duly investigated.

As much as it desirable that cases such as rape allegations against a pastor would be reasonably concluded, that could not have been at the first push. Like earlier instances – such as where a social campaign Black Lives Matter launched in the USA had given resonance to a local one – there is a limit to what can be instantly achieved because issues fall on the hard ground of cultural sentiments, religious sensibilities, and legal systems, all of which combine to make a meaningful resolution difficult. While #MeToo in the USA undoubtedly impacted how accusations of sexual violence were received by those who believed the accuser and those who believed the accused, there is still a long way for society to go before achieving a level of ethical awareness that make reform possible. Consequently, the court of public opinion becomes that arena where the debates necessary to make such advances are thrashed out. While those debates and contestations do not produce true justice (and can even lead to a witch hunt or mob justice, or even subvert judicial processes by poisoning the public mind with prejudice), yet they are also useful for a society to see itself reflected back.

Much of the criticism of the court of public opinion is that they turn an accused into a victim of the mob. The hysterics of an outrage-driven social media mob, it is rightfully pointed out, can suspend every judgment and people magisterially assume that they know enough of a person's character because they have seen thousands of his/her social media images. With the jury pool infinitely expanded, many commentators want to vie for visibility in the crowded market of public opinion and earn a "top fan" badge on social media when they can summon a following. While some assume the position of a symposiarch or an intellectual, others become unduly provocative and contrarian, all the while insisting they will not yield to the tyranny of empathy. This messiness makes subjecting issues to the court of the public opinion a transitional form of justice with unquantifiable gains. Yet, in several ways, by merely making the accusations, these women altered the etiquette of sexual behavior in Nigeria's conservative culture. The pent-up frustration that would have come from watching the impasse of the Busola Dakolo allegations will find an outlet in the desire to see future cases handled better. For example, while the draft of this chapter was being completed, some journalists led by Kiki Mordi working with BBC Africa carried out a sting operation on lecturers who allegedly abuse their students in Nigerian and Ghanaian universities. Titled, *Sex for Grades*, the documentary featured several lecturers, including one who was also a pastor of his church. The mass outrage from that case at least generated a far more positive outcome: both the university and the church he worked for suspended him from his position immediately.

4 | *"Everything Christianity/the Bible Represents Is Being Attacked on the Internet!": The Internet and Technologies of Religious Engagement*

The Pentecostal churches, noticing the spell that internet technology can cast in modern religious practices, embedded themselves within the lifeworld of social media. Like secular organizations have done, churches too used internet technology to enhance church operations, expand their sphere of operations, promote their pastors' charisma, aestheticize faith practices, democratize access to religious rituals, reinscribe faith into our increasingly automated world, and also bring God and his agents closer to the people. Within the vast expanse of virtual land, they carved their distinctive spaces and filled them up with sacraments, prayers, liturgies, and theologies to serve a worldwide network of audiences. With the seeming boundlessness of the Internet, Pentecostalism astutely expanded its operations across time and space.[1] Churches livestream sermons, post clips of sermons, announce forthcoming programs, show off their corporate social responsibility activities, and share prayers, admonition, photos, and testimonies. From pastors' personal pages, they share pictures of themselves and their families and stories about themselves. With the operating sphere of faith now expanded, and spiritual revelation practices merging with the culture of the Internet, Pentecostalism is further entrenched as a global culture. Worldwide, people have also responded to the emerging techno-cultural reality by turning the Internet into a sacramental space where they show up for prayers, sermons, and connections to a worldwide religious community.[2]

In addition to religious solicitations to which Nigerians actively contribute, they also generally maintain an active online culture,

---

[1] Asamoah-Gyadu, "Anointing through the Screen"; Asamoah-Gyadu, "'Get on the Internet!' Says the LORD."
[2] Campbell, "Spiritualising the Internet."

effusively investing social networks with their invisible yet tangible labor of engaging discussions on social and political life in the country.[3] With few or almost non-existent public venues for either leisure or deliberation in the country, social media became a viable space where people "interact to form opinions in relation to which public policy must be attuned,"[4] thanks to the proliferation of mobile phones imported from China, the relative affordability of data, and the Nigerians in the diaspora who maintain an active engagement with their fellow Nigerians at home. Perhaps unanticipated from the new social developments was how the relative sense of freedom people cultivated from the virtual culture that allowed anonymized identities, contrarian attitudes, free and unregulated speech, and networking of interests, would be extended from frequent critiques of political life to the religious culture. As the new media technology made possible expressions of dissent along with the enunciation of other aspects of sociopolitical life, religious authority suffered some collateral damage carried over from antagonisms of social life expressed in the virtual sphere. Since the dispersed audience of social media performances is more intensely networked than those of earlier forms of media such as the television, it was only a matter of time until the partisanship online culture promotes would also touch their religious leaders and lead to contestation of their authority. This chapter explores such contest of power with Pentecostal leadership, the most visible personification of power identity.

The deliberative nature of social media is one of the major factors that has made social media participants, religious and non-religious, inveigh against faith and pastoral authority in their online engagement. Social media also made it easier to garner a congregation and accelerate ideas among people who gather to participate, partly because of its novelty. Like previous forms of modern technology, the new media upended traditions and traditional authorities by taking away the ability of the entrenched authority to set social agenda and sometimes leaving them barely enough room to moderate agenda. This makes the much-touted "new" in the "New Media" not necessarily a description of its relative nascence but means that the network of users is still

---

[3] Tatarchevskiy, "The 'Popular' Culture of Internet Activism."
[4] Poster, "Cyberdemocracy."

discovering the technology's most creative and radical uses. Social life narrations are now incomplete without acknowledging how embedded technological devices are in our mundane life and easily transfer our political disgruntlement and social tensions into virtual spaces. With its hyper-individualistic nature, the Internet has achieved two things for contemporary Pentecostalism: (1) it took religion from the private convictions of an individual and further privatized it; what people upload as the tenets of their individual convictions through various fora are intensely subjective and yet (2) it compels promotion of the private self as a religious subject. As such, faith is not just a private affair between a person and God; it is now between a person, God, and their social media followers. We share our faith with the public by plugging the performances of our faith into the endless currents of the activities of self-representation that mediate social media either through status updates that narrate our belief or images that demonstrate it. The traditional idea of witnessing one's Christian faith to strangers and hoping to convert them now takes other supplementary forms such as regularly clicking the various "share" buttons to circulate Bible verses, sermons, personal testimonies, prayers, prophetic declarations, reflection on one's faith, selfies taken in church, videos of the self while praying, polemical arguments about religious conduct of others, and status updates of people who validate our faith. Because social media prioritizes the visual, people show themselves performing their faith and such display has preeminence over simply telling others what and how one believes. People who identify by a faith practice now converge in a place and show off their belief modes, and the practices of their faith get further embedded into social life as mediated by virtual spheres.

Despite the notion of sources of power as supernatural, religious leaders have been pragmatic enough to appreciate that for that power to make things happen, it always needs political potency to back up the force of its pronouncements. Religious leaders work to achieve this efficacy by imitating the trappings of political power and by fraternizing with political authorities. Such association entails religious leaders lending the symbols through which they produce spiritual power to consecrate popular politics. This trade-off can be damaging if politicians fail in their promises of developing the conditions that make for social flourishing. The exposure of religion to the contentious arena of high-stakes politics also means that as a faith movement like

Pentecostalism moves from the margins to the mainstream, it also shifts from being a countercultural movement to becoming an integral part of the political power structure. The resistance impulses that dominant ideologies incite in the public space would eventually touch the leaders of faith too.

In Nigeria, since 1999 when the Fourth Republic started and the Pentecostal movement began to gain greater national attention, much of the promises of a more fulfilling existence within the emergent democratic system have not materialized. Governance itself, as Nimi Wariboko describes, has in fact, become a source of collective trauma.[5] People have not only grown disillusioned, they are also increasingly alienated. Optimism about social change has waned as different government administrations got into power and failed to fulfill the promises of a better life. The discontent and the uncertainty mean that the traditional voices of moral authority falter as they struggle to hold society together. People who cannot immediately access the spaces where state power is produced eventually create an alternative sphere where they express their disillusionment, and also build up influence and social prestige, symbolic forms of capital commutable to other forms.

With globalized modern technology, the ubiquity of technological devices, and the multiplication of social networks, social media was the site where people seeking more organic sources of authority turned. As the appurtenances of social media technology have exploded in Africa, so has also social media use and political participation.[6] Some people, in the emerging tradition of social media influencers, do the work of public intellectuals, demonstrating the ability to critically reflect on social conditions. While not always academics or even scholarly in their approach, they nevertheless generate their moral weight by building a competency profile on social networking sites. Their embeddedness in internet structures and their mastery of the vernacular of social media means their contributions take the convivial, contrarian, and abbreviated natures of social media dialogues. With their consistency in providing useful and accessible commentary on social situations, they have acquired influential power

---

[5] Wariboko, *The Pentecostal Incredible*; Wariboko, *Ethics and Society in Nigeria*.
[6] Chatora, "Encouraging Political Participation in Africa."

by establishing themselves as credible experts in a specialized line of thought or industry, generating an appeal to a niche audience, building a community of loyal disciples and followers, and eventually acquiring clout as a form of authority. Not quite rising enough to be designated "celebrity activist" or online celebrity, and not quite qualifying to be described as "online activist" either, these social media users are regular people whose activities appeal to an audience broad enough to make them distinct influencer figures. In their own way, they are thinkers and intellectuals who have found a platform on social media to interest different people with similar aesthetic inclinations, grievances, and taste for notoriety for both civil debates and contentious exchanges.

In this work, I will be referring to this category of people as opinion entrepreneurs, meaning that they are organizers of culture whose mixed measures of intellectual capacity, warmth, social standing, perspicacity to pinpoint and weigh in on current issues, and passion for social causes gives them the impact of an influencer. Part of the appeal of their work is created through presentation of their digital self in everyday life.[7] By sharing snippets of their work/life, personal and family images/videos, random thoughts, ideas, witty remarks, and even some notoriety as a demonstration of their innate subversiveness, they put forward a curated performance stand as "authentic" credible interveners in social causes and also as bricklayers in the construction of meanings that determine society's ethos.[8] From Facebook to Twitter, Instagram, YouTube, TikTok, blogs, and various social media networks, these people do a lot of cultural work discoursing on ongoing world affairs. They are digital intellectuals, entrepreneurs of thoughts and opinions. The degree of labor and the almost endless hours involved in producing commentary and moderation of their page(s) might not be immediately apparent, but the comments of their regular followers indicate they are appreciated for the work they do. Their deft storytelling skills, timely response to ongoing social and political issues, ability to develop and cogently articulate thoughts

---

[7] This is obviously an allusion to Erving Goffman's famous *The Presentation of Self in Everyday Life* that treated daily life as a performance.

[8] As noted, authenticity in this context is also constructed. As Elizabeth Ellcessor noted, "Instead of the distant aura maintained by stars in classic Hollywood, celebrities online are constructed through the presentation of (seemingly) authentic, accessible, backstage selves that are nonetheless exceptional" ("'One Tweet to Make So Much Noise,'" 257).

within the crowded marketplace of opinions and regular outbursts of social media, do not just underscore their authenticity but are also a measure of their credibility and competence to lift cultural weights.

Now even considered a legitimate career trajectory thanks to models of digital capitalism, the ability of these entrepreneurs of opinion to gather a crowd and consecrate ideas also return some commercial gain for those who have successfully discerned audience tastes and desires. This category of intellectuals and their social media followers are a product of new social arrangements that have not only thrown them up as part of the production of power that calibrates balances in society, they are also strategically placed in various corners of social media for niche audiences. In this chapter, I will also be exploring how the dominance of Pentecostal culture and its charismatic proponents – the pastorate, mostly – in public and political spheres opened them up to virulent attacks by a growing subculture of these social media intellectuals, opinion entrepreneurs, and a wider public that have come to consider their prominence in political spheres as a part of the oppressive networks of power in the country. With the ease and ability of religious groups to communicate with a far more expansive audience has also come challenges to the stability of religious authority and the nature of established religious practices.[9] Much of the challenge to the Pentecostal force of authority in contemporary Nigeria takes place on social media networks, a space so open that it could collapse various values, motives, and even religious beliefs into homogenized chunks of resentment and pushback. Here, I explore what significant development in the universe of Nigerian Pentecostalism like technological empowerment – and the subsequent buildup of dissension that reverberates from the religious to the social to the political – among participants in virtual spaces portends for faith and moral citizenship.

Much of the contest that I explore in this chapter took place between 2017 and 2018, when an online radio presenter in Lagos, Ifedayo Olarinde, popularly called Daddy Freeze, started a social media campaign against the practice of tithe payment in churches. That drive would eventually become the *Free the Sheeple* campaign. I consider Daddy Freeze an opinion entrepreneur because his advocacy agenda on tithe, based on a rereading of familiar scriptures, gained ground and

---

[9] Bunt, *iMuslims*; Grant et al., *Religion Online*; Hipps, *The Hidden Power of Electronic Culture*; Howard, *Digital Jesus*.

exploded among the populace. His campaign was influential; his confidence in what he vehemently propounded resounded with the populace and shook the Pentecostal church establishment. His ability to touch on something within the social culture demonstrated his cultural savviness and the perspicacity to apprehend a truth that riles people and which must be addressed. Pentecostal pastors were not new to harsh criticisms of their practices, but when it did not threaten their power identity or the modes by which they performed it, they have almost always acted impervious to them. However, the popularity of Daddy Freeze's campaign pushed them from their seemingly impregnable positions into defensive – and even discrediting – stances. What started with social media posts and commentary on the subject of how paying tithes lacked scriptural backing found an online audience of people for whom the level of power and influence wielded by pastors had already reached an unaccountable height.

Amidst the hoopla that *Free the Sheeple* generated, Mrs. Funke Adejumo, the wife of the president of Agape Christian Ministries in Akure and a well-known preacher in her own right, remarked in alarm during different sermons that "Everything Christianity represents is being attacked on the Internet! Everything the Bible represents is being attacked online!"[10] In one of those sermons that have now been archived online, she warned the congregation,

Everything the Bible represents is being attacked online. Tithing. It is an attack of the devil to diminish Christianity. One man in China said that in 100 years' time, there will be no more Bibles in the world. One hundred years after, his house became the printing press for the Bible. You can't fight against God. It was God that instituted tithing. Don't join them o, just pass .... They use their mouths and pens to attack men of God and say all sorts of things. Don't join them! Their suffering is loading. Just pass.[11]

The moral panic she voiced betrays the fear with which powerful pastors now have to contend: the destabilization of the religious truths and traditions that Pentecostalism has established, thanks to the empowering tool of the Internet that gives the public an avenue to undercut the dominance of pastoral authority. Her specificity in locating the looped distribution network of the Internet as the chaotic arena

[10] "Pastor Funke Adejumo Joins the Tithes Controversy in This Ranting Speech." NijaBox, June 11, 2018. www.facebook.com/nijabox/videos/222444281690137/
[11] www.youtube.com/watch?v=1pTML1YcHXY

where people congregate to challenge their moral authority also acknowledges pastors' powerlessness in the face of social media's ability to "instigate alternative politics of belonging" in competition with the regulatory power of political and religious authorities.[12] In the pre-Internet era, for a campaign like *Free the Sheeple* to go through the media, it would have had to contend with gatekeepers who could have considered criticisms of pastors a disruption of social stability. The gatekeepers' decisions might even have been incommoded by the thought of the massive revenue that media entrepreneurs generate from the churches who buy airtime or media space to broadcast their programs.

The Internet, however, is a borderless space with multiple entry points. With a technological contraption in their hand and rebellion on their minds, people can follow the lead of an intellectual figure in pulling down the pillars of culture or carve their own smaller individual paths. Similar to how Pentecostal leaders established themselves on the social scene through the force of supernatural power that translated into social power and moral influence, the Internet grants dissenters similar pulpits from where they could antagonize their way into the sphere of moral authority that Pentecostal leaders have dominated. These cadres of influencers have become popular and their follower-ship ranks swelled, and that is also because there is no foolproof means of barring participation in these debates. Virtually anyone can set up social media accounts and dedicate them to circulating memes and caricaturing Pentecostal practices and pastoral conduct, or impersonate men of God to critique pastoral authority, write critical social media posts denouncing pastors' sermons, create YouTube channels or even make live videos to comment on doctrines and practices, and acquire a following while doing any or all of these. If the criticisms of pastors had been formalistic theological disputes on church doctrines and practices, that could have been a turn-off for this excitable online crowd. In this case, however, what was required to lead or participate was mostly any form of response to the constant stream of digital stimuli. With such diverse and relatively easy means of taking them on, pastors have more anxiety about being ridiculed in these bursts and cycles of social media performances than from legalistic arguments.

---

[12] Meyer & Moors, *Religion, Media, and the Public Sphere.*

From controversies to scandals, people jump on trending conversations to dissect and critique, and in the process, also psychologically and socially stimulate themselves to a higher level of interactivity. As social media following has become monetizable in contemporary times, some of the thought leaders – like social media influencers – around whom people gather, have had to become more innovative and even employ marketing tactics to attract followership and induce participation.[13] The will to partake in these digital conversations, the Pavlovian urge to give an urgent and immediate response to an ongoing discussion, becomes more intense among social media users, and the stakes of participation are thus raised. In cyber engagements, people do not always jump on conversations arbitrarily. They tend to cluster around influential figures, and, depending on the issue at stake, they gather around a specific thinker whose creation of both mentally engaging and equally enjoyable commentary on social issues.

When Daddy Freeze started taking on well-known pastors with his opinions shared on social media, he was stimulating enough to draw a broad range of participants for whom the *Free the Sheeple* campaign had either resonated or who had shown up in defense of their leaders. The scathing criticisms of pastors on social media that he led, though grounded on the Bible, also included pointed personal attacks. Different groups of commentators responded, leading to crossfires and thrilling exchanges that also satisfied the desire for entertainment. That in itself – the satiation of the unending desire to be tickled – made those campaigns a potent strike against pastoral power and moral authority. They extended the issues among different camps of social media users who also wanted a cut of the benefits of leading those arguments.

As an idea triggered in a remote corner of someone's personalized social media space becomes a social performance that virally infects the attitudes and sensibilities of others, so does the playfulness of the actors draw a large online audience of those poised for some kind of show-down. Given her experience as a Pentecostal pastor, Mrs. Adejumo must have instinctively understood how these various social media users, led by a band of opinion entrepreneurs, influence public culture and could also acquire some level authority through their demonstrated ability to grow and affectively move an audience or give weight

---

[13] Hund & McGuigan, "A Shoppable Life."

to a public opinion. Given time, these opinion entrepreneurs could even shift the norms that generate social meanings, possibly undermine pastors' place in the cultural production of power, and negatively impact how Pentecostal Christians perform their power identity in the social sphere. Hence the charge to the congregations whom she repeatedly warned about how the Bible and Christianity were being diminished through the agency the social media has made possible for a contemporary public: *don't join them*!

Freeing the Sheeple: Daddy Freeze and the Awakening

For many years, pastors in Nigeria had used the Bible to justify their aggressive demand for tithes – that is, 10 percent of one's personal income given to the church – and were hardly ever challenged on the doctrine from the scriptural point of view. They have preached that it was a covenant obligation for material success. Failure to pay tithe would lead people to financial ruin because God would curse them for failure to meet to their responsibility. There have been issues raised about the morality of pastors taking percentages of people's income, but none of the contention gained traction like *Free the Sheeple*. By the time Daddy Freeze started speaking and mobilizing the denizens of the internet space who shared his postulations on tithes, not only had payment of tithe become a standard practice in Pentecostal churches, there were a lot more other specialized forms of church offerings that pastors also regularly demanded for various reasons. In 2017, a video of Pastor Enoch Adeboye, the leader of arguably the largest Pentecostal assembly denomination in Nigeria, asking members who could donate one billion naira each (going by the exchange rate that year, that sum was roughly $2.8 m) to see his secretary after the church service went viral. Even though pastors demanding an outrageous amount of money from the congregation was not new, casually asking for one billion naira during a church service still seemed like an overreach and abuse of pastoral office. Within the context of a society where corruption was endemic, people questioned if the pastors who could ask for such a whopping sum of money from the congregation ever spared a thought to consider if the source of that money was legitimate.

By the time Daddy Freeze started raising questions about the validity of tithe payment in churches, the foundation for the enthusiastic reception of his message had been laid by the degree of resentment that pastors' conduct around money had caused. Daddy Freeze at first did not look the image of a prophet or reformist. Like most pastors who went into church ministry, he was not a trained theologist, neither was he known to have attended a seminary or similar institution. He was an online radio presenter and entertainer with social media handles claiming the authority of divine revelation just like most pastors too had done when they started their ministry. But he was a Pentecostal Christian too, and according to Daddy Freeze himself, he also enjoyed studying church and Bible history. When he emerged on the social scene armed with questions for pastors, he did not come with mere curiosity. He also displayed a confidence in his knowledge of the Scriptures that caught the public's attention. The crux of his argument was nowhere in the Bible was tithing mandated for Christians and, despite pastors' insistence, the tithe was not a route to divine blessings and prosperity as pastors preached.[14] He said if Nigerians studied the Bible by themselves and did not merely rely on the words of their pastors, they would see that the supposed commandment to give a tithe in the book of Malachi 3:8–10 were not meant for present-day Christians but the Levites, a priestly lineage and one of the twelve tribes of Israel.

He denounced the whole practice of tithing, saying it was exploitative and making poor people pay tithe was a subversion of the principles God put in place in ancient times to protect the poor and the vulnerable.[15] He frequently challenged pastors to show him one place where Jesus or any of the Apostles collected tithes or even offerings from the people who congregated around them. In one of his media interviews he looked straight at the camera and with his finger pointed in the direction of the viewer, he said,

If you pay a tithe to any Nigerian pastor, you are a goat. Especially if you neglect what you are supposed to do. I have had people argue with me, *so you think I am giving my money to my pastor? I am giving it to God!* Hello? The transfer of earthly wealth to spiritual wealth was done in the Bible in Matthew 25 and it has nothing to do with pastors. You want to give your money to Jesus? The Bible says the people who are in hospitals. Matthew 25. It is right there. The people who are homeless, the people who are hungry, the people who are naked. Jesus said each time you give to those people, you

---

[14]   www.pulse.ng/communities/religion/daddy-freeze-any-pastor-who-takes-tithe-from-the-poor-is-putting-his-family-under-a/jk1sdnp

[15]   www.pulse.ng/communities/religion/daddy-freeze-religious-activist-insists-that-jesus-is-against-tithing-seed-sowing/wdwr10z

remember me. So if you want to give to Jesus, those are the ones you should help and not the private jet-flying Daddy G.O. who should be giving to you.[16]

His campaign agenda was the climax of years of criticisms of pastors and their management of church finances. However, this time, the discussions snowballed through the intoxicating power of the new media that enabled the instant and wide circulation. People began to respond to Daddy Freeze on social media, newspaper op-eds, daytime TV shows, and vox pops. People agreed with him on pastors' attitude toward money and their lack of accountability to the same public that gives the money to the churches. Those who had expressed similar sentiments in the past dredged them up again, now emboldened by how the advocacy was catching on with the public. This moment instigated by Daddy Freeze was different from past criticism of pastors, because it was fueled by easier access to social media and other forms of accessibility sponsored by digital technology. *Free the Sheeple* was a far more interactive and communally based performance of freedom to speak back at established authority. Technological affordances and the ubiquity of internet-enabled devices had spawned new forms of religious engagement, appropriations, and remediations in Africa,[17] and the intensity with which people responded to *Free the Sheeple* was consequent of the brave new world they now inhabited.

The popularity of *Free the Sheeple* – advocating intense public scrutiny of church finances – registered public disenchantment with pastors who, having acquired immense symbolic capital and social power, also accumulated a matching level of resources over the years. The campaign seemed confusing terrain for the leaders to navigate. Although their production of a sacred economy that nurtured God was based on market-driven operations appropriated straight from secular economies, the means of making money was largely not disclosed. They have not only been beneficiaries of capitalist and neoliberalist enterprises, they have also flaunted their worldly goods as testimonies of God's promises of abundant blessing.[18] Like other social actors in a late capitalist economy whose exhibition and consumption of material goods is disconnected from any tangible production sites, pastors

---

[16] www.youtube.com/watch?v=ZWPjBzau_W8
[17] Hackett & Soares, *New Media and Religious Transformations in Africa.*
[18] Lewison, "Pentecostal Power and the Holy Spirit of Capitalism"; Ukah, "Piety and Profit (Part 1)"; Ukah, "God Unlimited."

actively promote the mystique of the "occult economy,"[19] that is, the belief that money can be magically produced. Without visible connections to the social relations of power and entrepreneurial savviness that actually produce money for churches and pastors, the money they exhibit acquired a self-legitimating autonomy that enabled pastors to raise their public images above the actual exploitation that goes into processes of wealth generation in capitalist economies.

For instance, in one of the churches that I attended some years ago, the pastor narrated how he was once stranded in a hotel room and prayed hard and passionately for money. By the time he woke up in the morning, his bedroom had been filled with dollar notes that had rained throughout the night. This kind of story of a God that could command a global currency and iconic marker of capitalism for the use of his servant is strategic in its telling. The pastor was promoting a myth of how money can be magically (or miraculously) acquired over the carnal human systems that are actually involved in making money materialize as a reality. Such accounts are intended to avert the congregation's eyes from looking directly at the amorality that typifies the capitalist system of exchanges and instead look up to the heavens and perceive money as a miracle. By redacting the social processes, entrepreneurial struggles, market systems, and political relationships of power that organize the rewards that translate into wealth, this pastor could also effect a disconnection between his spiritual gifts and a potential accusation of simony. As several scholars have noted, Nigerian Pentecostals pastors have not only preached the prosperity gospel and encouraged people to sow their financial seeds into God's business, they have also taken up entrepreneurship in many forms that have diverged from their primary vocation as pastors.[20] Despite their ventures into mercantilism using funds mostly generated from the church, they still do not consider themselves the kinds of businessmen who should be subject to the secular standards of accountability.

The *Free the Sheeple* campaign challenged the assumption that the noble duty of producing a sacred place put pastors beyond the crass pursuit of money. The campaign also gave vent to latent unease with

[19] Comaroff & Comaroff, "Occult Economies and the Violence of Abstraction."
[20] Hackett, "The Gospel of Prosperity in West Africa"; Ukah, "God Unlimited"; Ukah, "Prophets for Profit." See also: Ukah, "Building God's City"; Ukah, "God, Wealth & The Spirit of Investment"; Ukah, "Piety and Profit (Part 2)"; Ukah, "Those Who Trade with God Never Lose."

pastors' wealth and how they have flaunted it as proof of divine favor. Perhaps the biggest achievement of the anti-tithe campaign was the forceful centering of money into the social relational practices that have also imbued pastors with their consecrating authority. Calling out Pentecostal pastors to account for the wealth that defined their public images can furthermore be construed as a conscientization agenda, an awakening to the human factors in the mix of resources that generated their grandiose wealth. The campaign was, to that extent, an attack on insensitive capitalism that underlay the foundation of cathedrals; the ungodly indifference that sidesteps the actual social processes of funds generation; and the unethical conditions that produced money for pastor's use and which compels them to treat it as a natural outcome of religious ritual and faith. In the ideological arena where pastors had operated, they had nurtured an economy of relations that made it acceptable for them to own so much without a concomitant level of accountability for their resources or concerns for social justice.

The pastors at the receiving end of Daddy Freeze's barrage of attacks were unprepared for the turn of events where the Internet that had broadened their sphere of influence would also be the site of its contestation. Until social media made it possible a crowd of people to converge in a place to challenge them, pastors had largely enjoyed a world where much of their authority was vertical. Most of the communication channels were controlled, quite unlike now when people can easily assemble in the vast grounds of the Internet to speak back. When pastors were pressed enough to respond to Daddy Freeze on the controversy, their answers mostly came in the form of *ad hominin* attacks. According to Daddy Freeze, when he began talking about tithe, "every pastor, every G.O., every senior pastor, every reverend priest, had something to say about the tithe debate." Because they came at him "guns blazing," he realized that "it is not God we are worshipping, it is mammon."[21] Some of the pastors' attacks at Daddy Freeze were so indecorous that they further played into the hands of supporters of the campaign, and the (wo)men of God incurred on themselves a level of ridicule and antagonism that would have been previously unthinkable for their social status. The pastors probably imagined that Daddy Freeze's attack on their practices would

[21] Personal interview.

fizzle out, but *Free the Sheeple* garnered supporters who agreed that there was no indeed biblical support for the payment of tithe and that pastors should not have an infinite allocation of resources placed at their behest.

I met Daddy Freeze at his Lekki residence in Lagos, Nigeria, in summer 2019, for a conversation on how the campaign had played out. He delved into the problems of Nigerian religion and why the shortcomings of the Pentecostal church necessitated the freeing of the "sheeple" from the clutches of predatory preachers. He had many criticisms for how churches had wired people to connect salvation with money such that every idiom of spirituality is currently about boosting personal prosperity and acquiring more worldly goods. For instance, he cited a popular phrase like "unmerited favor," which Nigerian Pentecostals have used to describe miraculous happenings that have improved their lives, usually by improving their financial lot. For Daddy Freeze, the idea of "unmerited favor" ought to describe the undeserved salvation that sinners received from Jesus Christ. Rather, churches have taught people to orient the ideas encoded into such phrases toward getting richer. Even worse, they encourage the procurement of such undeserved wealth in ways that did not accommodate moral compunction. The wealth people pass off as divine blessings can be directly linked to the mechanisms of corruption in the society. The idea of "unmerited favor" would allow them to side-step the immorality, capitulate to the corrupting forces in the society, and institutionalize an ethic that would promote ill-gotten wealth as divine favor, an "unmerited" one.

Daddy Freeze ramped up the scale of his criticisms to the point that pastors could not ignore him. When he narrated his experience with the pastors, he recalled he had his greatest moments of clarity when he went public with the revelations that he had been receiving from Christ. At some point, he had hoped to be wrong with his claims and expected the pastors to set him straight.

I could not believe that the G.O. (General Overseer) that was in his '70s, who has gathered 10 million people all over the world, could ever be wrong and I would be right. I waited for them to come up with some strong arguments of their position on tithe, but they came with nothing. They shared experiences of how tithe has worked for them, but nothing from the Bible.[22]

---

[22] Ibid.

To his consternation, the rebuttal he received was more personal attacks than theological positions drawn from the Bible. Pastors attacked his personal life, they preached against him on the altar and even cursed him, but they still did not advance a biblical stand to support their position. He said,

A pastor whose church I attended for more than 11 years; a man that was entrusted to teach the word cursed me. He said he gave me 24 months to see my end … why? Because I dared him to show us in the Bible where the apostles who were our first pastors and Daddy G.O.s collected tithe. This was a man to whom I entrusted my tithes and offering for 11 years. I contributed to the building of his current temple, and he curses me?[23]

The pastors' best argument, he eventually found, was that the gospel they preached to people was working, and that should constitute enough proof of its efficacy. While the pastors that contended with him had an idea of supernatural operations whose ends justified the means, Daddy Freeze contended that the means and processes matter far more and experience should not override scriptural authority. He said, "*'It is working'* is not a doctrine. It cannot stand the test of time unless it founded on the Scriptures. They (the pastors) don't know much, the only thing they know is the worship of the God they created. They became experts on that, and they were leading people into sin."

Some pastors, he said, labeled him a demon and called him a "God-hater," "Jesus-hater," and "pastor-hater." The overwhelming scale of attacks did not just come from the pastors but also the Pentecostal congregation who pushed back against his irreverence. According to him, even his job as an entertainer was attacked. When they could not get him fired at Cool FM, the radio station where he worked in Lagos, they got some advertisers to pull back from his show. Those moments, anyway, he said bolstered his firm resolve to "free the sheeple" from the clutches of Pentecostal dogma and pastors that propagate it. With the spate of attacks that followed *Free the Sheeple,* Daddy Freeze said he became emboldened to further demystify Christianity as presently constituted and introduce a more rational form of faith that would empower people to clarify between doctrines of God and human traditions that are contingent on social realities. He told me about a certain pastor who, ten years prior, had requested that his church members

---

[23] www.youtube.com/watch?v=1pTML1YcHXY

give their tithes in N1,000 notes (the highest denomination of the Nigerian currency) rather than smaller naira denominations. This pastor, Daddy Freeze said, told his people that if they gave in bigger notes, they would receive their blessings in bigger packages.

Now, people go to church and make electronic bank transfers and so that pastor no longer preaches that people should bring their offerings in N1,000 notes anymore. The Holy Spirit opened my eyes to that the reason the pastor ever demanded the bigger notes in the first place was so they could count the money they collect as offering more easily. It saves time and labor of church workers if they are not dealing with smaller notes. But the pastor made it into a doctrine and taught the people it was God's will. It is unfair to manipulate people with your personal agenda.[24]

Therefore, his goal was to teach people the word of God in an empowering manner so they could learn to study the Bible on their own and learn to separate between doctrines of God and contingent church traditions. He said, "The church is not a building, or the physical structure. That one was brought down by Jesus who also fulfilled his promise to replace it in three days." Pastors, he said, would not preach a gospel of spiritual temple because it would entail a de-emphasizing of the need for the huge cathedrals they raise money to build, and even the flashy wealth they get to exhibit as proof of the effectiveness of their gospel.

Daddy Freeze also consistently referred to himself as "teacher of the Word" and it did not matter to him that he was not formally ordained by anyone because, according to him, neither Jesus Christ nor Charles Fox Parham (an ascribed founder of what became the Pentecostal movement) were formally ordained either. None of the pastors taking him on, he contended, were formally trained in the Scriptures either: they operated based on divine revelation. Daddy Freeze said his goal was for God's Word to be taught to God's people, and the delivery of the gospel to the people need not impoverish the congregation in its packaging and transmission. Rather than incur heavy expenses in the logistics of assembling people under one roof, he could make videos of his teachings, share them, and respond to his "congregation" in the comments section of social media. The goal of his model of "churching" was to teach people God's Word based on an undiluted ideology

---

[24] Ibid.

as Christ intended it to be, not as powerful preachers have fashioned for their own uses. His end mission is to breed an independent Christian-hood where people can read the Scriptures for themselves and come to their own understanding. Interestingly, Daddy Freeze does this church-ing business, particularly on Instagram, along with his other vocation as an entertainer/public commentator. This seamless combination of roles often blurs the line between the "pastor" side of him and the OAP.

Daddy Freeze's argument's about non-ordination also underscores an important idea in the liberalism of Pentecostalism. If, as Edward Cleary noted of Pentecostalism in Latin America, one of the greatest theological achievements of Pentecostalism as differentiated from orthodox churches is the right to free expression – that is, "almost anyone accepted by the Pentecostal community is allowed to interpret scripture during worship, to moralize about the conditions of life, to preach about changes needed in personal conduct, to pray spontan-eously, to offer suggestions for the community's response to an evil world," it follows that members would also extend that freedom to contest power with their pastors.[25] That kind of development, expect-edly, makes pastors more conservative as they scramble to protect their moral authority from spontaneous outbursts of dissonance among congregations.

Quite antagonistic of the present church system and how much time it robs from daily productivity, Daddy Freeze had the opinion that churches should even have fewer meetings. He said while Jesus attended the synagogue on Sabbath day, there was no record that he did so *every* Sabbath day. While one can argue that there is also no proof that Jesus did *not* go to the synagogue every Sabbath day, his point is that people should not have to go to church perform religious rites all the time before being deemed Christians. Given the level of social development in Nigeria, he believes there is a need for a critical reevaluation of the ethics and values of a faith movement that has failed to give the people the succor that they seek from God. People should not spend all their time in churches; they should have enough time left in their daily lives to do other things than congregate to pray. A church, he insisted, should not have to set up expensive and massive buildings at the expense of people who are massively poor and make them contribute to church wealth.

[25] Cleary, *Power, Politics, and Pentecostals in Latin America*, 7.

He argues that pastors' obsession with putting up church monu-
ments has made them more invested in the relentless competition to
build the largest church complex, a factor that is driving them to
manipulate already impoverished people who should be fed with the
truth of God's Word. Nigerian churches have lost their way, he says,
and become too invested in projects of self-aggrandization. They are
personalizing and paganizing the gospel, he complained. "You see, the
early churches used to fight principalities and powers in terms of the
financial and political systems that tried to suppress the will of God.
Today, they – the Nigerian pastors – have all but reduced 'powers and
principalities' to personalities, the aunties in the village (un)doing
you."[26] In our conversation, Daddy Freeze slides easily from
a mishmash of references from Freud to Max Weber, European church
history, and social history to criticize the present Nigerian Pentecostal
church. "In Lutheran times," he said, "the church leaders could hide
things from people because the Bible was in Latin. These days, they just
dumb down the Scriptures." To stop people from venerating pastors'
word over God's, Daddy Freeze says he is committed to
a demystification of the pastors and the spiritual hold they wield over
the people. "I want people to know that pastors are mere humans. They
are not more anointed than they are, and they cannot harm you." The
threat of harm that could come upon anyone who spoke against
a pastor, and which they had held over the populace for a long time,
was empty. Daddy Freeze said after he challenged all the pastors in
Nigeria to curse him with all their spiritual powers – and some did, they
publicly pronounced he would die – and nothing happened to him, it
became obvious to him that all the supernatural power with which they
had always instigated reverence for themselves was mere
superstition.[27] By announcing that he did not die despite all the curses
and death pronouncements they made against him on the altar, he
believes he demystified the faith leaders. Or, at least, he lessened their
"pastoral (bio-)power," that is, their authority as God's representatives
on earth to determine to proclaim social, supernatural and eventually

---

[26] Personal interview.
[27] In one of his interviews, he mentioned how when he first stopped paying tithes,
he feared he would die because of the years of teaching that had made him
believe that the sanction for not paying tithes was death. After about four
months of not paying he still lived, and he got bolder. www.youtube.com/wat
ch?v=eIaOy4AZqR8

physical death on an erring person, one of the techniques of fear and submission that charismatic religion has exercised.[28] That experience of freedom from the threat of imminent death also taught him that if more people could study the Bible independently, they would not merely accept pastoral authority but would be more questioning of their teachings.

The *Free the Sheeple* moment Daddy Freeze prompted also influenced other people who needed to speak their minds on church financing and lack of accountability; others who saw an opportunity to generate social media content by taking on powerful and famous pastors also joined the debate. Since pastors are considered powerful public figures, they were the prime targets of a society that had not only had enough of their overwhelming influence, but who have also found in digital technology a viable means of confronting them on their doctrines and public conducts. People found in the Internet a significant means of defying oppressive doctrines through the weaponization of their social media content. With opinion entrepreneurs, the church now has to contend with social media reformers whose social media handles and witty content ceaselessly nail theses to the church doors. Pastors, whose power identity has been based on their ability to spontaneously act under the influence of the immanent Holy Spirit while on the pulpit, now contend with the burden of hyper-surveillance and the nagging worry their sermons could become a meme online. In the next section, I will be looking at the aftermath of Daddy Freeze's campaign and the various performances it spurred among a general class of people who demonstrate their civic citizenship and dissension with ruling authority by taking on pastors in the same way they now take down their politicians and public leaders on social media to the extent that the latter advocate some degree of regulation.

The Radical Congregation of Social Media

One of the pastors who responded to the fracas about *Free the Sheeple* made an interesting observation about contemporary religion and the expressions of discontent with its practices as are done on the Internet. While he was responding on the issue of tithes, Bishop Emmah Isong, currently the national publicity secretary of the Pentecostal Fellowship

---

[28] Katsaura, "Theo-urbanism."

of Nigeria, decried the "anti-church elements" that "live inside the internet." He said these people are the ones who ensure that "if a pastor steals yam, it goes viral."[29] Bishop's Isong's frustration also underscores the reality of the futuristic world that we already inhabit: we no longer "go online" as a form of transcendence of spaces that we log into and out of, now and then. We are now permanent – and connected – residents of the digital cosmos whose engagement on social media spaces is homologous to our inhabitation of physical and social spaces. The advantage of social media networks over earlier media forms is their ability to collapse many conversational arenas into a solitary sphere, enabling mobility between discursive spaces. The fact that church business is one of the many topics of discussions on the broad forum of social media adds another dimension to previous scholarship on religion and new media, much of which has been overly optimistic in assessing the prospects that lay ahead of faith practices in the digital era.[30]

People are literally living "inside" the Internet, and from their habitation of virtual reality, they are firing scud missiles at errant pastors. New technologies have always facilitated the expression of disenchantment with religion and religious leaders, although scholars sometimes treat such radical expression as a novel meeting of religion and technology. They, still attached to the idea that religion is subjective and therefore, antithetical to the universal, empirical, objective, and rational science that founded technology, look for convergence points.[31] According to Jeremy Stolow, in this manner of thinking, there is an underlying supposition in these ideas that religion and technology,

exist as two ontologically distinct arena of experience, knowledge, and actions. In common parlance, the word *religion* typically refers to the intangible realms of ritual expression, ethical reasoning, affect, and belief whereas the word *technology* points to the material appurtenances, mechanical operations, and expert knowledge that enable humans to act upon, and in concert

29 Uchechukwu, "Tithing Is a Scriptural Injunction, Mandatory, but Not Compulsory – Bishop Isong."
30 Brasher, *Give Me that Online Religion*; Campbell, "Challenges Created by Online Religious Networks"; Campbell, "Religious Authority and the Blogosphere"; Campbell, *When Religion Meets New Media*; Hammerman, *thelordismyshepherd.com: Seeking God in Cyberspace*.
31 Radde-Antweiler & Zeiler, *Mediatized Religion in Asia*.

with the very tangible domains of nature and society. The locution *religion and technology* thus operate along a series of analogous binaries including *faith and reason, fantasy and reality, enchantment and disenchantment, magic and science, fabrication and fact.*[32]

Rather than religion and technology supposedly struggling against each other's innate attributes, *Free the Sheeple* and its aftermath exemplifies how the devices with which people access the Internet are far too fused with their bodies and minds to distinguish between religion and other activities that take place on the cyberspace. There is no "religious" use of the Internet (social media, that is) that is not at the same time social and political. With the imbrication of humans to their internet-enabled devices, the performances of citizen dissent in cyber-spaces are enmeshed with the urgency of their sociopolitical and socio-economic conditions, which makes the expressions fiercer and intensely radical. This, of course, does not mean there is a standard behavior of all "netizens," as individual dispositions are called "subjective" for a reason. However, like-minded people find each other online and take behavioral cues from one another. These connections have been made easier by the configuration of algorithms that track our psychographic behavior online and "serendipitously" sends matching sentiments and affects our way. The overlap between religious and political dissent cannot but happen when the spheres of religion, politics, and economics are open to each other, and their values transmute. Thus, religious leaders find that they have to be answerable to spiritual forces and temporal concerns expressed on social media as well.

With the multiplicity of cyber-fora linked to social media pages and run by different individuals, *Free the Sheeple*'s anti-tithe movement generated many comments codified into memes, videos, images, blogs, vlogs, street vox pops, YouTube videos, TV and radio interviews, social media discussions, and online commentaries. Many of the discussions were aimed directly at the pastors and their conduct. As some of the commentaries were rather cutting, people worried that undermining pastoral authority would deplete the force of Christianity and attributed the development to a demonic attack on the church. They pushed back furiously, but even their participation only ramped up the scale of the controversy. As the issue raged, multiple bloggers further expanded the scope of the discussion by taking snippets of pastors'

---

[32]　Stolow, *Deus in Machina.*

responses to Daddy Freeze on the tithe debate and compiling them into a whole to run commentary on them. By framing disparate responses into a coherent set of material, they made their blogs, social media accounts, or YouTube channels the proverbial village square where those looking to gather and talk about the issue could converge. On YouTube particularly, by attaching Daddy Freeze's name to the title of their videos, theirs would be the video that would come up in the search. Also, by annotating the videos they had posted, they fore-grounded the engagement and triggered more uproar.

For instance, in a vlog posted by Summer Aku on her YouTube channel and titled, *Nigerian Pastors Unite against Daddy Freeze: The Full Compilation of Pastors' Responses (Tithe Drama)*, the video starts with texts rolling up the screen that introduce Daddy Freeze as the subject matter and then cuts to an interview where Daddy Freeze challenged Christians to challenge their pastors to teach Deuteronomy 14:22–25 and Matthew 25, verses of the Scripture that said people would eat their tithes but which pastors would never mention because it would affect their ability to generate income.[33] At some point in the interview Daddy Freeze said, "Let me see them stop collecting tithes. Let them stop for one year. Let's see who will still be a pastor ... Stop collecting tithes."[34] Then he faced the camera directly and stated, "Preach the world that Jesus preached. At least Jesus did not collect tithes, Jesus fed the 5,000. In Nigeria, the 5,000 feeds these thieves." As Daddy Freeze spoke, the blogger used an onscreen text to highlight that Daddy Freeze was sharing "more verses" and "and more verses" and "even more verses" of the Scripture, a preface to how she wanted his arguments to be read in comparison with the pastors she would also feature.

After the Daddy Freeze segment of the video, she introduced the pastors' collated responses with onscreen text that says, "AND ALL THE REACTIONS BEGAN." The pastors were not reacting to that interview by Daddy Freeze, but she selectively edited the clips to make them appear as a linear drama between him and the pastors. The blogger briefly analyzed the pastors' rhetorical strategies and anno-tated the points in the video that she wanted people to note: where the

---

[33] www.youtube.com/watch?v=KzB2l3J-q38
[34] My choice of this clip was deliberate because it contains a compendium of responses by the pastors to Daddy Freeze.

pastors lacked Biblically based defenses, name-calling, bragging, mis-
quoting the Bible, threatening, vibrating with anger, throwing allegations, and being overly defensive.

The video began to show pastors, some of the biggest names in
Nigerian Pentecostalism responding to the tithe debate. The first
was Pastor Adeboye who was speaking in a church service where he
said:

I saw a clip on the internet by a fellow who said he was talking about tithes,
that we shouldn't pay tithes. At first, I didn't want to listen but God said,
"wait na." (At this point, the onscreen text showed "God said, wait na") and
I continued to watch to see what he had to say. Then he said *tithe is supposed
to be used to buy alcohol so we can drink in church*. I said, well, now we
know who is talking. Even mad people don't go to church to drink alcohol.
No matter how crazy somebody is, the moment you said this is a church, ask
him to come and drink, he will say *ehn ehn ehn, I am not that crazy*. Because
even in his madness, he knows when you say this is a house of God, he knows
the house belongs to God. [italics are points where Pastor Adeboye takes on
the voice of another character]

By highlighting the portion where Pastor Adeboye said God spoke to
him in Nigerian pidgin, a creole variant of the Standard English, she
undercut his strategic attempt to delegitimize Daddy Freeze's credibility. What Pastor Adeboye put forward as proof of his close relationship
to God – nudging him to watch a video – became the joke when
Adeboye insinuated that God spoke to him in a colloquial language
(one that is also considered the lingua fraca of a non-formally educated
underclass). The screen went dark, and the blogger prefaced the next
clip with texts that read, "And Signs of Anger & Frustriation [*sic*]."
The video showed Mrs. Adejumo speaking while the onscreen text
read, "Cursing and Name Calling." In the video, she was saying:

Don't listen to any idiot telling you what to do about your money [some
scattered applause could be heard in the church] on the internet. Hear me!
I meant that statement, "idiot." Because anybody that is against the
Scriptures is a fool! That is what the Bible says [the onscreen text asks,
"Where is This in the Bible?"] Who told you not to pay tithe and who told
you to pay it? Put the two of them on a scale and weigh them and choose
who to follow [onscreen text reads: But no Bible verses]. Somebody telling
you not to pay tithe. What right has he to determine how you spend your
money? [scattered applause]. I know what happened to me. If an angel

comes now and tells me not to pay tithe, I am too convinced to be confused about it. [onscreen text: still no Bible verses]. Not all pastors are stealing money o! [onscreen text: Then Bragging]. When I was coming this year, I said *God, I gave N54,000 every Sunday last year by your grace. What should I do this year?* I heard in my spirit, 'Double it!" So every Sunday, N110,000.

Then came Apostle Johnson Suleman. As he started speaking, the screen text came on and indicated he would be "Bragging and Bragging." Apostle Suleman began talking,

... about somebody talking about tithing. I have a PhD in theology and a PhD in Human Resource Administration not to argue. The Bible says in first Corinthians chapter two verse 14 [onscreen text: Quoting the Bible and Avoiding the Topic], the natural man cannot receive the things of God. They are foolishness to him. He cannot know them because they are spiritually discerned. It is stupidity for me to sit down and speak over spiritual matters with [onscreen text: Still Avoiding the Topic] logical reasoning. The Bible says in John chapter two from verse 20 down, it says you need not any man to teach you, but the anointing which you have received teaches you all things [the video cuts to a congregant nodding her head vigorously]. Your pastor or social media should not teach you about tithing. Go and ask God. We must be careful [onscreen text: Then Threat] so we differentiate religious rascality from spiritual maturity. There is so much religious rascality. To talk is cheap. To post things on the internet is very cheap [onscreen text: More Bragging]. I have read the Bible from Genesis to Revelation 36 times. Omega [that is the name of Apostle Suleman's church] began in 2004 and I was already a millionaire before we started [onscreen text: And Then Big Lie]. The tithe I pray every Sunday is more than the tithe all of you pay for two Sundays. I am a dangerous tither, and I don't hope to change.

Mrs. Adejumo came up again on the video (as excerpted previously), and then followed by Pastor Matthew Ashimolowo who said he would be responding to the tithe debate said,

Some bunch of yoyo somewhere should not determine what we believe. Some guy who beats his wife, throws her out, throws his children out of the house should not determine what we believe. Not only that, he broke his own son's knees while trying to defend his wife. Not only that, he drinks alcohol, sleeps with women and he is trying to preach to preachers?

The onscreen text indicated that he was "name-calling" and "showing anger." When it came to Pastor Paul Adefarasin, the onscreen text cheekily said, "Now it is time to go to Galaxy" as the pastor started a message that truly took the issue to another planet entirely. He said,

God created the universe, he took a tithe: the Milky Way. God created the Milky Way, he took a tithe: the Galaxy. God created the Galaxy, he took a tithe: our Solar System. God created the Solar System, he took a tithe: Planet Earth. God created the Planet Earth, he took a tithe: Israel. God created Israel, he took a tithe: Jerusalem.

Other pastors featured including Pastor Ayo Oritsejeafor who said anyone who asked the congregation not to pay tithe simply wanted to kill them and they would die quickly if they did not pay. Just like Mrs. Adejumo, Pastor Oritsejeafor asked the congregation to compare the lives of their pastors who asked for tithe with that of the person who asked them not to, and they would see that the clear difference. Then he added in pidgin English, "The Bible says, the difference, is clear." Again, the onscreen text noted that phrase, "the difference is clear" was a 7Up slogan and not from the Bible. Another pastor featured was Bishop David Oyedepo whose message compared tithes to excrement that must come out of the body, otherwise one would be discomfited. The final one was Pastor Adeboye again saying in what turned out to be a brief clip, "Make it clear to them. Anyone who is not paying his tithes is not going to heaven. Full stop." At the end of the video, the text comment came up: *But why haven't they raised their voices like this about corruption in Nigeria?*"[35] By attaching all the pastors' angst on tithe to one of the problems that faced Nigeria, the issue of corruption, she could connect the performances of pastors with the angst of every-day life in Nigeria and thereby indict the pastors' priorities.

The controversy of The Great Tithe Debate eventually cooled, espe-cially after some other senior pastors such as Bishop Mike Okonkwo, Pastors Sam Adeyemi and Tunde Bakare intervened and clarified in their sermons that it was not (and should not be) doctrinally necessary for Christians to pay tithe. By taking that stand, they directly contra-dicted the other pastors who said those who fail to pay tithes were cursed and would not make it to heaven. They also noted to their fellow pastors that it was not necessary to frighten people to make them pay tithes. People should only do so if they desired to give to God.[36] Those

---

[35] Aku, "Nigerian Pastors Unite against Daddy Freeze."
[36] "Pay Your Tithes Willingly and Not out of Fear – Bishop Mike Okonkwo"; Okoduwa, "Do Not Pay Tithe by Pastor Abel Damina"; "Pastor Sam Adeyemi

pastors, who also run megachurches and are also visible public figures, more or less officially removed one of the many threats of death and punishment hanging over the lives of people and which further complicate their already precarious existence. For a certain social class, tithe payment might not matter to their overall financial capability, but for millions of already impoverished people, not being under a spiritual obligation to pay could free up some money from their income so they could do more for themselves and their families. After people understood that tithe payment did not carry the punishment of death or the curse of poverty, and that they would not miss heaven at the end of a challenging life, they could still give 10 percent of their income to their church. Only now they would be doing it willingly.

However, the controversy also made it easier for pastors and the church to become regular fodder for social media talking about the flaws and foibles of powerful pastors. While Daddy Freeze's goal of reforming what he thought was lacking in the church was clear, others seemed to be looking to build an influencer base by initiating debates on polarizing topics of religion. For instance, a blog like NijaBox, linked to several social media handles, regularly posts articles and videos on social media with titles such as, *How Nigeria's Pastors Are Rich, Yet Their Church-Goers Will Never Board Their Private Jets*; *Popular Pastor Beaten in Church by Members*; *Nigerians Perceive Pastor Adeboye's Latest Prayer Leading to Corruption and Nepotism*, and so on. On its Facebook page where the blog has a far more active presence, NijaBox shares videos of church activities that include deliverance sessions, sermon clips, miracle performances, pastors performing frivolous acts (such as the videos of Pastor Chukwuemeka Odumeje dancing with his friends in church while the altar space is littered with currency notes they had sprayed on themselves), and other similar materials.

Some of the videos and reports NijaBox feature are already annotated with magisterial comments even before asking people their opinion. For instance, they will share a video and ask, "Pastor Matthew Ashimolowo warns his congregation to stop listening to controversy on social media around tithing because it is a command after the order of Melchizedek. He also went on to argue that seed sowing in monetary form is in the Bible. Your thoughts?" Another one states: "CONFESSION. This

Says the Practice of Tithing Has Expired, No Christian Should Feel Guilty for Not Tithing."

prophet is the son of Alph Lukau. He was seen last year making money appear from the Bible in South Africa. Today it looks like he is saying something else. The question remains has he repented from his magic tricks?" NijaBox sometimes also posts videos announcing church activity or videos where the pastor is speaking what it calls "the truth" (that is, denouncing activities of roguish pastors). The videos, meanwhile, are not limited to Nigerian preachers. For instance, they also shared a video of a preacher in Tennessee in the USA, Perry Stone, who – in the heat of praying and speaking in tongues – stops to check his phone. Other social media activities frequently fact-check pastors' messages, and provide critical commentary that can sometimes verge on rudeness.

Another example of how the acts of hyper-surveillance on church activities by social media users bothers the pastors is when Pastor Adeboye advised the youths in his church not to marry women who are lazy, cannot cook or do household chores, or cannot pray non-stop for an hour. He spoke in his church on fulfilling marital relationships but the message got on social media where what he preached attracted a lot of rude remarks.[37] He had spoken to both men and women, but the content about woman got far more attention. He said,

Don't marry a girl simply because she can sing! In the choir there are some people that can sing but they are fallen angels! Marry a prayer warrior! If a girl cannot pray for one hour, don't marry her. Don't marry a girl who is lazy! Don't marry a girl who cannot cook, she needs to know how to do chores and cook because you cannot afford to be eating out all the time. Don't marry a girl who is worldly! If you do, you have carried what you'll worship for the rest of your life! Don't forget what I am telling you. It's very important. There are those who I have advised before but ignored my advice. They later came back to me and said: "You warned us." I am warning you now.[38]

While this kind of injunction has always been passed in churches without complaints, this remark got on social media and was attended by an outrage that subjected Adeboye to a lot of opprobrium by people who thought his ideas of balanced family life were outmoded. His critics called him "ignorant" and denounced him in strong language for feeding into patriarchal notions that the preponderance of the spiritual and physical labor that makes for a good family rests on the

---

[37] www.bbc.com/news/world-africa-53488921
[38] "If a Girl Cannot Pray for One Hour, Don't Marry Her, Says Adeboye."

woman. By pushing back against his words with trending social media activity, they denied his moral vision for family life and his attempts at universalizing it using his gravitas as a representative figure of a faith movement that identifies by power. The pushback on that issue were so intense that he had to put up another comment on Twitter where he stated, "My messages are not for everybody. So I plead with you, ask God to speak to you specifically."[39] The frequency of the attacks has embarrassed his church to the point that Adeboye himself pleaded with his church members to stop putting his words on YouTube.[40] The irony is that even that appeal ended up on social media. From the exchanges that followed the criticism of Adeboye's ideas of what roles women should play in marriage (and in other instances where he had spoken on rape, social relationships, and wifehood), one could also see undertones of feminist ideology. When he wrote a birthday message for his wife on his Twitter message, and noted that his wife of about fifty years remained submissive to him and even still cooks his meals and trims his nails, he got fierce backlash against his male chauvinism.[41] The media that reported the pushback noted that those who took him up were "feminists," an indication that the ideology was percolating into society, but not through structured channels of academic debates, rather through deliberation and opinion entrepreneurship mostly on social media spaces where ideas are weaponized against influential pastors still wedded to patriarchal ideals and power.

Testing and Attesting Power Identity

That said, none of the encounters with social media opinion entrepreneurs make the Internet the Pentecostal graveyard, and the next chapter will dwell on the modes by which leaders' authority is maintained even within an economy of public ridicule. Like earlier church reformation movements, the one that stems from the digital universe is more about believers trying to reclaim the essence, the potency, and the standards of spiritual practices of the early church for the

---

[39] www.pulse.ng/communities/religion/enoch-adeboye-my-messages-are-not-for-everybody-pastor/g472ew7

[40] Udodiong, "Pastor Urges Church Members to Stop Putting up His Videos or Quotes Online."

[41] https://punchng.com/feminists-at-war-with-adeboye-over-birthday-message-to-wife/

present day.[42] Since churches are powerful organizations, and government agencies can hardly regulate their activities without inviting claims of persecution, it is more helpful to think of social media as a site of self-reinvention and a gradual generation of progressive cultural habits. For instance, earlier in 2017, when *Free the Sheeple* began to take on pastors, a government agency, the Financial Regulatory Council of Nigeria (FRCN), tried to implement a clause in the Corporate Governance Code that fixed tenure for leaders of corporate organizations including non-profit enterprises such as churches. The code, meant to improve organizations' financial accountability, indicated that a leader who had spent twenty years or more as CEO should leave their position. The code also barred those retiring leaders from handing their position over to a family member. Pastor Adeboye was one of those affected by the implementation of the code. He announced in church that he would retire as the General Overseer. He also named a successor, Joshua Obayemi, who would oversee the local church in Nigeria while remaining the worldwide leader and overseeing RCCG in the 192 countries they were now domiciled. In that same church service, he also registered his displeasure with government's interference in church affairs. He was quoted as saying, "The government has been showing increasing interest in church affairs. Unfortunately, for us in RCCG, it might not be very helpful."[43] As the news of his retirement hit the airwaves, it was instantly read as one of the many attempts of a Muslim president to muzzle Christianity and Islamize Nigeria. Pastors claimed that the government had no right to push them toward retirement since they were appointed by God and not by the state. Within forty-eight hours after his announcement and the furor that followed, the Executive secretary of the FRCN, Jim Obazee (also once a RCCG pastor), had been sacked and the code suspended. When the code was revised, it left out the churches. That affair with the FRCN was perhaps another reason the *Free the Sheeple* movement resonated with people when it began later that year.

The church leaders who would be affected used the weight of their public influence to make the government capitulate. With such a level

---

[42] Drescher, *Tweet if You [Heart] Jesus.*
[43] www.premiumtimesng.com/news/headlines/220007-breaking-buhari-sacks-official-whose-actions-led-adeboyes-exit-rccg-leader.html

of power available to Pentecostal pastors to influence public policy, it is obvious that churches cannot be made accountable in their financial dealings through formal and structured means. Nigeria's ruling elite needs pastors as much as pastors need them. Pastors would not have been able to identify by power if they had not co-opted power to their side, and politicians cannot attain a needed level of moral authority without pastors. This balance of patronage means it is almost impossible for one side to try to check the other's excesses. As raucous as the rhythms and rituals of social media participation could get, it also generates affects that are propped by social disaffection and all-round political disempowerment that seeks to engender reforms in the social and moral order. Opinion entrepreneurs mostly lead the argument; others pick up the beat, and for various reasons. The hope of Nigerians standing up to the power and influence that pastors have accrued, to challenging them to some level of accountability in their dealings is, for now, largely tied to the irreverent activities of opinion entrepreneurs. Not only do opinion entrepreneurs frequently challenge pastors, but politicians too have also faced a similar level of scrutiny. One cannot divorce the criticisms of pastors' deficiencies in moral and financial accountability from similar demands made of elected political leaders. Like many regular activities, "political activities on the internet are embedded in larger social processes, and the Internet itself is only one element of an ecology of media. The Internet does not create an entirely new political order; to the contrary, to understand its role requires that we understand much else about the social processes that surround it."[44]

The sensibility that propelled *Free the Sheeple* partly owes to a political awakening by people let down by their moral and political leaders and who have found a conducive space to take on these issues. It is hard to say one propelled the other – whether criticisms of politicians and their corrupt handling of the nation's financial resources launched a sentiment that transferred to pastors or the other way round – but the ways Nigerians use social media to mobilize against their religious leaders is not in isolation of their resistance practices against their political leaders. This does not mean that changes to policy have been automatic because of the power of social media. In reality, democratic practices also still require analog modes of communication to drive

[44] Agre, "Real-Time Politics." Also see Papacharissi, "The Virtual Sphere."

policies.[45] However, Nigerian leaders now know to watch the social media conversation to check the pulse of the public on their policies. The Internet medium is becoming an arena where the cogitations that congeal into public opinions are spawned, the space where the "engine of deliberation … generates and exports deliberative habits to other settings of political decision making."[46]

As the political uses of social media gain traction, elected and appointed leaders get just as jittery as pastors that their legitimizing traditions are being threatened by the irreverence the Internet enables. Nigeria has tried – and is still trying – to propound harsh laws and regulations that will curtail social media activities such as sharing false information, and attacks that can cause disaffection for the state.[47] Those laws are ostensibly to reduce the rate at which people dispense fake news and use social media for the mischief that folds over into social relationality, but they also fear the radical potentials the lack of regulation of the Internet promotes. To curtail revolutionary ideas, the government breeds its own troll farms[48] and even some churches use their media department to forcefully push back against the contempt that social media fosters against authority figures. Such responses are understandable if one considers that what is at stake for religion and political authorities – power and material and symbolic rewards – is too much for anyone to passively cede spaces to online activists. This cynical manipulation of democratic ethos that allows everyone the freedom of – and space for – self-expression is a strategic countermeasure that helps sustain power through the introduction of chaos into the internet sphere. Piling on commentary using trolls can contain the spirit of the revolution because people get eventually overwhelmed with opinion overload and either withdraw entirely or retreat to corners of the Internet where people deal with issues that do not require much emotional processing.

There is some irony to the challenge of the pastors, though. While much of the criticism began with pastors' acquiring excessive power

---

[45] Rasmussen, "Internet and the Political Public Sphere."

[46] Evans, "Who Wants a Deliberative Public Sphere?"

[47] www.bbc.com/news/world-africa-35005137. Kazeem, "Nigeria's Lawmakers Are About to Pass a Bill Which Could Gag Citizens on Social Media"; Adegoke, "Nigeria's 'Frivolous' Anti-Social Media Bill Just Won't Go Away"; Iroanusi, "Nigerian Senate Reintroduces Bill to Regulate Social Media Use."

[48] Journalist and professor Farooq Kperogi, also classifiable as an opinion entrepreneur, uncovered the presidency's troll farm in the early days of the Buhari administration: www.farooqkperogi.com/2020_01_02_archive.html

without a matching level of accountability, the best-known social media creators who attack these attitudes eventually professionalize their own campaigns too. To maintain a certain level of aesthetic appeal for their opinion production, particularly for those who run blogs and channels, and considering that pushing out opinions is a job (so to speak), they get to the point where they need financial resources to keep going. Some generate this through ad revenue. But to get to the stage where their content makes money, they have to build up their clout and generate traffic even if that effort entails being controversial and disrespectful for its own sake. Apart from ad revenue, one blogger who consistently criticizes pastors lists pullover hoodies on her channel for sale. The prices range from $25 to $40. When one clicks on the link she shared, it redirects from the YouTube channel to an online store where the hoodies have texts such as "Blind no more," "Na so we go dey dey?" (which is pidgin for "is this how things will continue?") and "God dey weep for us" ("God is crying for us"). To each of the store pages have also been appended notes such as, "More and more people are no Longer blind to the deceptions and lies of false prophets and fake pastors who steal in the name of the Lord," "Sometimes when we look at the situation of Nigeria we can't help but wonder whether no say we go dey dey? will there ever be a change?" and "With the present state of things right now . . . God must be looking down and weeping for us."[49] These displays of merch and commoditization of radical content tempers the excitement that the Internet is "the site and subject of liberal democratic practice" especially because such enhancement of capitalism over the purported ideals of democratic freedoms can lead the public to become cynical of all motives.[50]

In the interviews I have had with several partakers in these social commentaries, some were quite dismissive of Daddy Freeze and other social media critics. They saw them as clout chasers and even demonic agents who should be resisted with weapons of spiritual warfare. "It is an attack of the devil on the church," some reasoned. "This is a satanic attack on the body of Christ, and we must be vigilant." To this set of people, the whole crisis was a demonic conspiracy, and that was all there was to it for them. They would not throw their pastors to the

---

[49] https://teespring.com/blind-no-more?cross_sell=true&cross_sell_format=no
     ne&count_cross_sell_products_shown=3&pid=212&cid=5839
[50] Dean, "Why the Net Is Not a Public Sphere."

wolves of public culture to gnaw on, because it would make the church vulnerable. Whatever flaws pastors might have, they still represent a religious constituency in a political culture where such a high-profile representation can ward off one's social erasure and the constant threat of violence. They would rather God deal with His pastors rather than an online crowd. In such a culture where people remain resolute in their support for their religious leaders, for *Free the Sheeple* to have gained ground at all is interesting. According to Daddy Freeze, his campaign's success could only be because the Holy Spirit inspired and fueled the moment. While this answer represents a spiritual perspective, a more material one is that the disaffection against corruption and public leaders' liberalism with finances peaked and resulted in those outbursts. However, if the whole of Nigerian Christianity is not up in arms against the pastors, it is also because the churches remain about the only spot in the country where there is a discernable link between the money people give as tithes and offerings, and the edifices and infrastructure that spring up.

In many of the discussions that I had with Pentecostals over Daddy Freeze, the pastors' supporters would point to the efficacy of churches – the many people they had supported and mentored, the various enterprises they had built and which were functioning effectively, their acts of charity, the church buildings they were putting up, and even the public roads leading to their churches – and use that to challenge the idea that pastors deserved the antagonism of *Free the Sheeple*.[51] For instance, Nigerians live in a country where they are subject to multiple taxes that are indiscriminately introduced by various levels of government but, for the most part, they do not see the results in public infrastructure or any other aspect of public life. When they pay tithes and give different offerings, they see results in the modern structures that churches put up. As someone remarked in one of my conversations with her, "Pastors are not the ones who ruined Nigeria!" Many Pentecostals see their pastors as prudent managers of resources in a way that their elected leaders are not, and it is therefore no surprise that their impulse for radicalism is tempered. That is part of the

---

[51] The successes by the church range from their intervention services in areas such as education, finances, security, social services, and even infrastructure such as motorable roads. For some of the examples of their social activities, see: Ade-rufus, "'Why Should We Praise Him?'"

dynamics of how the power identities of their leaders are sustained with the acquiescence of their followers.

When Daddy Freeze said "it is working" is no doctrine, he overlooked a crucial detail in how the Nigerian public, forever imperiled by dysfunctional administrations and processes, have come to appreciate the activities of pastors in the Nigerian social terrain. The Pentecostal doctrine in Nigeria is calibrated on demonstrable proof of "it is working" or at least, "it works for me" rather than hardcore theology. The fact that pastors, as the shepherds of the movement, have been successful in the areas where the government has failed means that churches are seen as development agencies.[52] They have become a constituency around which the power identity of ordinary congregants is anchored and, therefore, must be protected from collapse. If it goes down, an ethical vision of Nigeria's modernity – along with the notions of empowerment many congregants derive from their belonging to a faith movement like Pentecostalism – will crumble too. Technology might have empowered people to take on their leaders and challenge religious authority to reform their theological ideas in the face of new realities, but the infrastructure itself is not enough to dislodge the construct of religion outright. That is why, as I observed, people's demands for change from pastors are radically expressed in their social media activities and internet use, but they are ultimately oriented toward change and internal reforms rather than total destruction of Pentecostal pillars.

Some others were far less conservative in their reasoning of why *Free the Sheeple* gained traction though. They said even though their personal pastors were attacked in those debates, they still supported Daddy Freeze's arguments. Their sentiments were based on what they perceive as an overdue need for reformation in the church and in the polity. They thought the church must set the standards for the society, and the necessary agitation that will make such changes happen should not be outsourced to non-Christians. They compared *Free the Sheeple* with other reforms in church history, and said without someone standing up to powerful leaders, there would be no progress in religion. While they remain convinced that God called their pastors, they also believe that pastors are humans who could lose their way due to the corrupting influences of the world. When that happens, even pastors need God to restore them to righteousness. In that case, they reasoned,

---

[52] Wariboko, "Pentecostal Paradigms of National Economic Prosperity in Africa."

Daddy Freeze's *Free the Sheeple* could, in fact, be God intervening to correct whatever was wrong with his church. To these Pentecostals, all the furor was not mere happenstance, it was God sanitizing his church as he did many times in the Bible. They even referred to Martin Luther and the church reformation movement in Western history to buttress their point that such debates are important for such progress. The allusion to the Lutheran reformation is quite apposite, considering the role that a new form of media technology, the printing press, played in upturning religious authority of the day.

While they were equally critical of pastors, they were not going to give up on Christianity because some aspects of their faith practices were flawed. They held on to their conviction in the inherent efficacy of the Pentecostal truth, and they were quite clear that they were not interested in seeing the church they have invested their lives and labor in collapse. Instead, they want to set the terms and conditions by which they can continue to be Christians in the modern world. They also want to raise their children without being encumbered by suffocating ortho-doxy and promises empty(ied) of meaning. So, they would remain in the faith and reform it according to progressive ideologies rather than yield to the seduction of secularism. As someone said to me while talking about the imperative of pastoral accountability, "Pastors are human, and they too can fall off just like anyone of us. It is important to remind them that God called them for us his children, and not the other way around." It is about disciplining and curtailing the expression of power identity lest it becomes errant and monstrous in its exercises of the self.

5 | "God Too Laughs and We Can Laugh Too": The Ambivalent Power of Comedy Performances in the Church

At a church vigil where members had gathered for a night of prayer and worship, where music ministers and prayers warriors would wage a battle against the kingdom of hell, a stand-up comedian too waited in the wings to be called on the church altar. This comedian, Aboki4Christ, had performed in many churches over the years and had honed his skills in making God's people laugh. Still, each performance was a different experience and the character of every congregation had to be properly gauged to determine the kind of jokes that would tickle them. People had to laugh, but equally important to him was that people go back to their homes with a moral lesson from the jokes along with a feeling of refreshment from having been in the house of God. In his later retelling of that night at Winners Chapel, Calabar, Aboki4Christ said,

The church vigil was titled "Operation fire for fire." That was supposed to be a night of prayer where you fire the devil and his demons out of your life. So I did a joke about the devil to prepare the mind of the people to understand the nothingness of the devil, how minute the devil can be. We tend to exaggerate the devil so much. We tend to give him the accolade he doesn't really deserve. Everything that happens, oh, it is the devil! We ascribe so much to the devil even the devil gets surprised that he wonders, can I do this thing they said I did? . . . I typically make jokes to belittle the devil and let him see he is insignificant in the life of the child of God.[1]

Unlike the '90s when drama groups like Mount Zion Faith Ministries International performed inside the churches, entertainment has shifted to mostly comedy performed during special programs such as vigils, anniversary celebrations, conventions, and crusades. Stand-up comedy, unlike stage drama, is easier to stage because it requires fewer

---

[1] Personal interview.

176

resources to put up in the church. A solo performer, or a pair, with a mere microphone, would fit into an interlude between regular church activities and perform before the congregation much more readily than drama artists. As one of the comedians noted to me, they also make people laugh, unlike church drama artists who are so bent on teaching morality lessons they "always get too serious."[2] Some of these artists are also well-known comedians who already perform in the entertainment industry while others grew up in Pentecostal churches and turned into comedians. Their primary audience is thus church congregations although they also perform at secular gatherings.[3] Both categories of comedians are thus "crossover artists." However, given how fused both secular and religious spheres in Nigeria have become, both sets are easier to categorize as artists who go almost wherever they are invited to perform for an audience.

For ease of referencing in this work, I will refer to performance genre as "gospel comedy" and everyone who performs in a church as a "gospel comedian" throughout this chapter.[4] My preoccupation here to look beyond the function of humor to ruffle and rupture, and instead at its performance as part of the dynamic construct of power identity through a balance of public affirmation and private contestation. As stated in the previous chapter, the proliferation of internet technology has exposed Pentecostalism and its powerful leaders to a lot of ridicule and satire that cannot be mitigated due to the endlessly open nature of social media. Understanding the power of mockery, churches co-opted the business of jest-making by inviting popular comedians to perform. That way, they get to retain some level of control over the production of the jokes circulating in the public sphere. When a comedian has appeared in a church, stood on the altar to perform, and devoted comic material toward validating the man of God, such an artist would be hesitant to make jokes ridiculing the pastor or the church. I should also note that the trend of gospel comedy is not limited to the Pentecostal churches in Nigeria – it extends to some of their branches in North America, par-ticularly in the United States, and the United Kingdom.[5] Nigerian

---

[2] Personal interview.   [3] Taiwo, "From Jagua to Ali Baba."
[4] Egbo E. Imo attributes the rise of gospel comedy to the proliferation of churches. Due to the high number of churches in the national sphere, the church easily becomes the space where emerging artists gravitate for their career launch.
[5] The diaspora churches either use comedians in their local communities or invite popular ones from Nigeria to perform in their churches, particularly during special services and celebrations.

churches abroad either use a local Nigerian comedian affiliated to their church or fly in a comedian from Nigeria.

When they perform in church, comedians also do the cultural work of mockery that, though it might satirize faith practices, also mitigates the jokes in such a way as to ultimately reinforce the power and authority of the church leadership. From my interviews and assessment, most church members who go to church believing in the power of the man of God's anointing and its potential for their transformation do not leave church believing that either their pastor's or their own power identity has suffered because the comedian caricatured what they believed. They mostly consider it harmless fun. Not everyone is on board with this practice of comedy in church though. One of the most notable criticisms of the practice came from filmmaker Mike Bamiloye (see Chapter 1), who tried to call people's attention to what he saw as a problem,

For a long while I have questioned . . . the fact that the comedians brought in are allowed to make jokes of scriptures, the Blood of Jesus, speaking in tongues, the throne of grace etc. AND WE SIT THERE LAUGHING! What are we laughing at? What is funny? Mocking God and Christ and the Holy Spirit and the Word is funny???? We hear of other religions where they are obsessed with protecting the image of their Leader and we gleefully allow people to MOCK our Leader JESUS CHRIST and the Holy Spirit and thereby indirectly MOCKING GOD!!! They look at us with disdain because we are BAD AMBASSADORS of our faith![6]

Those who disagreed with Bamiloye reminded him that when he started taking drama performances to the church in the early '90s, some people also kicked against staging plays in church. They saw it as a mockery of God's sacred space. If the church could advance despite drama performances that Bamiloye once staged in church, some professional comedians told him, it would not collapse because a comedian stepped on the altar to make jokes.[7]

As these comedians perform in churches, they do important cultural work that complicates the notions of the disruptive power that cultural studies have attributed to comedy and laughter. For instance,

[6] www.pulse.ng/entertainment/celebrities/mike-bamiloye-actor-thinks-comedy-has-no-place-in-church/7vrglqk
[7] https://dailypost.ng/2016/12/13/lied-not-sin-invite-comedians-church-enenche-enenche-replies-mike-bamiloye/

a secularizing logic is evident in how Aboki4Christ understands and plays his role as a comedian whose performance stage includes the churches. He considers most of the misfortunes that Pentecostal churches, with their fixation on the demonic and the occult, attribute to the devil as a dubious fantasy of Christians who either want to or even have already relinquished personal responsibility for their failures. His jokes about the devil are to reflect such thinking to those people. They are free to hold their views of demonic figures, but by turning the misfortunes they attribute to spectral forces into comedy material, he downplays the force of its power. The devil as a foreboding specter already haunts the Christian imagination, but armed with jokes, he tries to lessen its effect. By subjecting the congregation's impression of demonic powers to the collective censure of contempt and laughter, he undermines the paralyzing belief in the devil and points them toward more rational modes of thinking about their social condition. Through jokes, he challenges their received knowledge of supernatural causality and subtly urges them to confront their social issues without necessarily attributing them to metaphysical factors.

If comedy were an effective weapon of social transformation as often stated, this effort would elevate the gospel comedian into a vanguard for moral and social progress. On the other hand, such an abrupt conclusion about the role of a comedian could be an overstatement of the transformative mission of the comedian given that the conditions under which their comedy gets produced makes them orient its content toward social conservatism. This is not to say that every aspect of gospel comedy has a conservative agenda or that this is all there is to it. It could also politicize issues in a way that opens the door for more progressive thought. For instance, by "joking with the devil" in church, the comedian also alleviates the fear of those who see the leisure and pleasure in bringing comedians to the church space as a worldly distraction leading the people of God to spiritual famine. Instead, he suggests that through his anti-devil jokes, Christians get to relax. They should also not have to fear making themselves vulnerable to demonic attacks because laughing at jokes in the church is not a surrender of their spiritual vigilance, but a reiteration of it in other ways. Aboki4Christ's perspective on the supernatural is to help people transcend their taught ideas of the role of the devil in their lives, attenuate the terror it stimulates in their imagination, and challenge them to look beyond supernatural myths to solve existential problems.

By redefining the power of the devil and pushing people to look at other ideological alternatives, he is opening their minds to make room for critical doubt in their beliefs.

While scholarly studies have examined other aspects of worship that are considered entertaining like music and dances, comedy in churches is rarely considered because it is still relatively recent and uncommon outside the Pentecostal church circles.[8] Jokes, we know, are funny because of their subversive nature – they can distort the view of reality and make us question accepted perspectives. They are weapons in the hands of those who use them, whether the performer on the stage or the audience whose laughter completes the act. Laughter has political uses that can either be considered therapeutic for those seeking to escape the violence of their postcolonial condition and at the same time, it can make the pain more tolerable.[9] The reflexive insight the dispensed jokes grant – at least when delivered by a virtuosic performer – clarifies contradictions and identifies the gaps in reality. Gospel comedy brings some nuances to comedy's putative power to expose the artificiality of social constructions of reality because it throws up the question of how the things of God become a "laughing matter," and how the church affords the distancing necessary for them to laugh at sacred concepts and practices.

At first glance, comic performances seem incongruous to the sacred construct of the church, and many critics of the practice state as much. As spontaneous combustion of human emotions, laughter can both be eruptive and disruptive, and a violation of the hallowedness of worship. Laughing at jokes shared on the church altar feels somewhat contradictory to the discipline and self-restraint that religion typically prescribes. From the perspective of the diversity of church practices through time (apart from drama, other entertainment forms have included choreographed dances), stand-up comedy in church might be transgressive but laughing in church is neither novel nor radical. Religion provides the material for comedy, either to ridicule the faith or to find some comical aspects in its practices. Ritual performances and certain religious experiences both produce a jouissance that makes

---

[8]   Carl, "Music, Ritual and Media in Charismatic Religious Experience in Ghana"; Kalu, "Holy Praiseco"; Patsiaoura, "Transcending Distinctions between Religious and Secular Musicianship"; Ryan, "Negotiations of Faith and Space in Memphis Music."

[9]   Afolayan, "Hilarity and the Nigerian Condition."

people laugh (such as the time they talk about "laughing in the spirit").[10] Comedy and laughter are as consistent with faith practices as they contradict it.

People who have tried to explain comedy in church look into their religious texts for instances of people laughing and find a theological justification for mirth in a church. The gospel comedians and the pastors (at least the ones who accept the trend) that I worked with for this chapter do not think of laughter and faith as merely conterminous. Their rationalization of laughter in the church is that it is intrinsic to worship and quite consistent with Pentecostal theology. "God too laughs," several of the comedians say, "and since we are made in His image, we laugh too. We *can* laugh too." To clarify this further, they pointed me toward the Bible where God's laughter was recorded in the book of Psalm 2:4, 37:13, 59:8. In the first verse, God was laughing derisively at those plotting against his anointed. In the second verse, God was laughing at the wicked who were scheming against the righteous but did not know that their own end was imminent. In the third verse, the Psalmist attributes laughter to God and sets the stage for an impending victory. The three verses where God laughed had one thing in common: presumption of their human abilities and power over the weak was the joke, and God's laughter was the response. God's laughter was a precursor to unleashing divine judgment on those who victimized His children. The Psalmist narrator uses God's laughter as a prayer and pre-emption of an imminent victory against the presumptive oppressor who underestimates the weaker party's ability to marshal God's power in their favor. What does this scriptural model that posits laughter as triumph and conquest portend for Pentecostals who make jokes in church? If laughter is a form of divine judgment, what – and whose – is the victory?

The question of who or what is defeated when comedians describe their performance using Scriptures that gesture toward victory calls for an exploration of how they imagine their roles as performer in the church, and how that perception could structure their attitude to their work. Critical studies of comedy have argued about the expansive functions of social and political criticism, therapy/catharsis, strategic

---

[10] See, for instance, Capps, *A Time to Laugh*; Capps, "Religion and Humor"; Claassens, "Laughter and Tears"; Ellis, *Humorists vs. Religion*; Geybels & Van Herck, *Humour and Religion*; Laude, *Divine Play, Sacred Laughter, and Spiritual Understanding*.

ridicule/entertainment, and building community.[11] A number of the studies that have explored the performance of comedy, humor, and jokes as social critique construes them as a form of "resistance politics."[12] That is, the weapon of the weak and the dispossessed against powerful hegemonies (usually defined as the state authority and a conniving elite class).[13] The thrust of these studies prop up the unsettling nature of laughter and how its impulsive expulsion from the body can undo the official attempt by hegemonic political forces at constructing faux reality as a veneer over the surface of actual social life.[14] For instance, Donna Goldstein's study of women in the shanty-towns of Rio De Janeiro points out jest-making as a coping mechanism, an "absurdist discourse that produces laughter," particularly in a political context with a "moral and legal system incapable of addressing grievances."[15] The dissension with hegemonic political power that satire, ridicule, and other forms of laughter-inducing performances represent is one of the few ways the silenced masses and the self-muted subject give a visual and aural sound to their experiences.[16]

A clear departure from the school of thought that treats comedy as a weapon includes postcolonial theorist Achille Mbembe, who complicates the relationship between the powerful and the dominated in the post colony. Mbembe argues that the conviviality in the relation between the powerful and the dominated zombifies both sides, and

[11] Banjo, "What Are You Laughing At?"; Cheruiyot & Uppal, "Pan-Africanism as a Laughing Matter"; Devlieger, "Rome and the Romains"; Halliwell, "The Uses of Laughter in Greek Culture."; Hillenbrand, *Underground Humour in Nazi Germany, 1933–1945*; Obadare, "The Uses of Ridicule"; Provine, "Laughter as an Approach to Vocal Evolution"; Weitz, *Theatre and Laughter.*

[12] This is a reference to James Scott's *Weapons of the Weak*, where he shows that the weak are not entirely powerless and manifestations of their agency do not always come through singular and spectacular acts of heroism, or similarly organized revolutions but through everyday actions.

[13] See, for instance: Helmy & Frerichs, "Stripping the Boss"; Pearce & Hajizada, "No Laughing Matter"; Sorensen, "Humor as a Serious Strategy of Nonviolent Resistance to Oppression."

[14] Examples include: Beard *Laughter in Ancient Rome*; Dubberley, "Humor as Resistance"; MacKenzie, Francis & Giappone. *Comedy and Critical Thought*; Niebylski, *Humoring Resistance*; Sorensen, "Humor as a Serious Strategy of Nonviolent Resistance to Oppression."

[15] Goldstein, *Laughter Out of Place*, 271–272.

[16] Hammett, "Resistance, Power and Geopolitics in Zimbabwe"; Kuhlmann, "Zimbabwean Diaspora Politics and the Power of Laughter."

does not necessarily lead to social ruptures.[17] Similar arguments resonate through critiques of humor and ridicule in works by Nwira and
Lipenga, Bozzini, and Pype, where they too use various examples to
illustrate that humor can be reifying of the power structures it purport-
edly seeks to dislodge.[18] In critically teasing out the "resistance" narrative from various comedy performances, analyses have focused on
how comedy performances affectively connect with marginal subjects
in staging acts of daily refusals to cooperate with hegemonic power,
thereby generating a momentum that can lead to larger social transformation. This approach to finding social correctives in comedy
weaves "unspoken linkages between ethics, power, and agency," limits
its assessment of successful comedy to its revolutionary ethos, and
ultimately overlooks the fact that even resistance politics can be
conservative.[19]

A middle position is to treat the art of making and performing
comedy as, according to Obadare, ambivalent.[20] By *ambivalence*, he
considers humor as a "neutral weapon which can be used by and
against both the 'strong' and the 'weak.'"[21] In the same vein, I also
consider humor as a neutralized weapon open for uses toward causes
that enhance the power identity of both the already strengthened and
the ones looking to transcend their status. Rather than humor as
upsetting political power, my analysis explores the both the possibilities it generates and the limits of its performance. Humor is so versatile
that in one context it might generate laughter that heals and bonds, but
also creates more pain especially for those who are at its receiving
end.[22] What in one context might be taken as a pushback against
power may, in fact, be a self-ridicule where the disenfranchised stage
their lack of agency against the unrelenting power of the state.[23] As
a performance practice that functions as both a social and a political
tool, it has multiple edges that cut through the social fabric, but only

[17] Mbembe, *On the Postcolony*, 111.
[18] Bozzini, "The Catch-22 of Resistance"; Ngwira & Lipenga, "A Country
Laughing at Itself"; Pype, "Funerary Comedies in Contemporary Kinshasa."
[19] Brassett, "British Comedy, Global Resistance."
[20] Obadare, "The Uses of Ridicule."   [21] Ibid., 260.
[22] Halliwell, "The Uses of Laughter in Greek Culture"; Peacock, *Slapstick and
Comic Performance*.
[23] Willems, "Comic Strips and 'the Crisis.'" See also Davies, "Exploring the Thesis
of the Self-Deprecating Jewish Sense of Humor"; Herzog, *Dead Funny*;
Thurston, "Social Dimensions of Stalinist Rule."

with the level of force that its wielder can muster. The power of making jest is also tentative because, "things first expressed in jest may later be articulated in serious terms."[24]

In the next section, I will elaborate on the nature of gospel comedy and the laughter it causes to explore the notions of anti-authority power in comedy performances. If "jokes are a metaphor for understanding the distribution of power and the nature and dynamics of social relationships within given configurations,"[25] how is this expressed in gospel comedy that is performed in Pentecostal church settings where both slave and master moralities, the dominant and the dominated, converge under the same roof to worship?[26] What are the inherent attributes of gospel comedy that may or not give it social transformation possibilities? To rephrase that last question in tandem with Aboki4Christ's idea of what comedy can achieve, does joking about demons really transform our psychological relationship with them? How does joking with the things of God change the structures of relationship with the anointed men of God who produce the signs and symbols that structure faith? In most studies that characterize humor and laughter as resistance against power or as reinforcement of it, analysts at least have clear ideas of what constitutes the apparatus of hegemonic power and its dichotomy, the subaltern. There are no such clear-cut hierarchies in the church structure.

Gospel Comedy: The Motley and the Cassock

According to Olatunde Taiwo, the stand-up comedy industry in Nigeria is largely a culmination of years of labor by different humor merchants from the earliest days of the introduction of television to Nigeria in the late '50s. Their labor was not often well rewarded until around 1995 when second-generation comedians like Atunyota Alleluya Akpobome (popularly known as Ali Baba) emerged on the scene, professionalized the industry, and turned comedy into an act performed before upper class or elite audiences who could afford to pay decent amounts for their shows. The third-generation comedians, a sizeable number of them Pentecostal Christians and who had grown

---

[24] Bernal, "Please Forget Democracy and Justice," 308.
[25] Obadare, "The Uses of Ridicule."
[26] Wariboko, "African Pentecostal Political Philosophy."

up in a country deeply suffused with Pentecostal ethos, evolved the evangelical angle of those comedy performances.[27] This third generation, most of whom began to perform in their churches from around the early 2000s, were young people who had been raised in a church. They saw how many singers and drama artists began their careers in church, and they grew to see the altar as a stage to both use their gifts for God and launch their careers.

One of the comedians told me his comedy career began when he saw himself in the same place as the biblical Moses whom God asked what he had in his hand. When Moses responded that it was a staff, God helped him weaponize it to free the Israelites from slavery. For him, every talent or any similar intangible possession of the Christian is usable for the church as long as its result will glorify God. Again, considering this set of young comedians were socialized within the Pentecostal culture, they had also imbibed enough of its social practices to generate resource materials for their professions. Akpororo said,

I broke in[to the industry] with one joke which talks about a mad man who went to a church to give a special number. I shared this joke at the 'Laugh and Jam' organised by Basketmouth [real name: Bright Okpocha, a fellow comedian]. It was a joke that just came about. In my church we have a programme we call, 'E-mad men'. We take care of mentally ill people. We don't discriminate. But when you hear me talk about madmen, it is because I have studied them. When you hear me talk about pastors, it is because I am a church boy.[28]

Another comedian who also attributed his career trajectory to the opportunities the church afforded him was Oladipupo Daniel of the performing duo, StillRinging. He said his path to gospel comedy started when he realized that church services were becoming too routine and required variety.[29] He felt it was his calling to introduce new forms into the church, and comedy was the tool he had to do so.

By now, everyone knows the order of service. If they say service starts at 10:00 a.m., you can be certain that by 10:10 a.m., they are on praise worship. People get bored when there is nothing new to engage them. It was during one of our fellowship programs that I started thinking of what I could do to bring

27 Taiwo, "From Jagua to Ali Baba."
28 www.tori.ng/news/4103/hunger-pushed-me-to-start-comedy-akpororo.html
29 The names of the StillRinging duo are Oladipupo Daniel and Ogunsina Ayodeji Samuel.

some more life to the service. When I first started this, one of the pastors at [a well-known church] told me, "Your comedy is good but too churchy. Take it to the world. Take it to the poor. Take it everywhere. What you will be doing is planting seed. If you perform in a pub, somebody will remember that there is church tomorrow and come. When they hear StillRinging is coming to our church, they will want to come because they want to see you." He laid hands on me and blessed me.[30]

Oladipupo Daniel was not the only one encouraged by his pastor to take his church gift to the world. For several comedians who began in church, their pastors played the role of producers and talent hunters. For instance, according to Akpororo (real name: Jephta Bowoto), even his iconic stage name came in a moment of inspiration that had to do with his pastor who already knew he had the talent for making jokes. Akpororo said, "One day I was raining abuses on a guy in church and I said to him: *You wey your head look like Akpororo* ... My bishop then looked at me and said, 'why don't you change your name from Holy Son to Akpororo?' That's how the name became mine from that day onward."[31] For Holy Mallam too, his pastor had a role to play in helping him discover his talent. He said,

I was an undergraduate at Lagos State University. The Foursquare Campus Fellowship, then led by Pastor Seyi Jaiyeola organized an event at the LASU car park. One of my Church members knew the pastor, so she introduced me to him. He auditioned me for about five minutes before he gave me the opportunity. I spent about seventeen minutes on stage. It was explosive. From then on, I began to get a lot of invitations to different churches, fellowships and events. There was a particular night vigil where I worked as the Master of Ceremonies and got paid N500.[32]

Another gospel comedian, Olusesi Adebesin, also referenced the role the church and the pastor played in the making of his career. He is a member of the Winners' Chapel, one of the largest churches in Nigeria, and acting with the church drama unit helped him to hone his skills. He said,

Stand-up comedy began like a joke for me. I used to be in a drama unit in my church ... and each time I acted no matter the role given, it was always funny

---

[30] Personal interview.
[31] www.tori.ng/news/4103/hunger-pushed-me-to-start-comedy-akpororo.html
[32] www.vanguardngr.com/2013/08/i-hawked-bread-pure-water-to-pay-my-school-fees-holy-mallam/

because I used the Hausa accent. One day, I attended a programme at our church headquarters in Ota, there I saw a comedian named 'Holy Mallam' performing and he was doing clean family-friendly jokes with a Hausa accent. So I said to myself I can do what this guy is doing. And when I got back to my local assembly anytime we had youth programmes or other special programmes in the church I asked the pastor to spare me five minutes to do jokes and he obliged me once after which he kept giving me more opportunities. That was around 2002 and 2003.[33]

Rather than discouraging the comedians from following a career trajectory that could lead them down the slopy path of worldliness, their pastors actively encouraged them to engage church members with their comedy and broaden their spheres before a non-church audience too. By mentoring these artists, helping them see their potential as performers and giving them space within the church to perform, these pastors midwifed a generation whose talents could have been lost or misused because of lack of opportunities. When they became well-known performers, many remained beholden to their faith, pastors, and church background.

Comedians and their performances of humor in the church bring a combination of pop culture star power and secular entertainment. The roles of the stand-up comedian and the Pentecostal preacher are already similar in the use of technique, affects, stagecraft, and their overall goals. As Iain Ellis said, "both concentrate power, control, and purpose on a stage within a singular being whose task is to convince and win over audiences ... both are teachers whose 'sermons' must be carefully constructed and paced in order to move spirits."[34] The gospel comedian, like the preacher, strives to give the audience a pleasurable experience through laughter. While a pastor's use of humor is complementary to the sermon, the gospel comedian's goal is primarily to make the church laugh. Their brand of comedy ridicules virtually every and anything. Just like they do in their non-church performances, these comedians make fun of poverty, witches, police, ethnic stereotypes, mental health, disabled, sex-based relationships (without being explicit), and political elites. They prance about on stage in church while they freely make jokes about violent and anti-social behavior. The only people typically spared from ridicule are the pastor and his wife.

---

[33] www.thisdaylive.com/index.php/2016/10/01/i-started-stand-up-comedy-in-the -church/
[34] Ellis, *Humorists vs. Religion*, 61.

StillRinging's brand of comedy mimics regular church services, and it is this detail – the similitude of church worship, prayer, and parodied reenactment of actual church situations creatively interjected with comedy – that makes the group distinct. Their act mimics the lively relationship that sometimes exists between preachers and their "interpreters" (that is, those who stand beside the preacher on the altar and translate his words into indigenous languages for those in the audience who either do not understand English or prefer to hear the sermon in local languages). Here is how it works: one performer mimics the church leader's stagecraft while the other interprets. They use simple sentences already familiar to the audience because they are randomly lifted from actual church sermons. While one of the comedians "preaches," the other performer translates it into Yoruba language but deliberately misinterprets the meaning of the "sermon." Rather than a direct translation, the "interpreter" inserts witty comments derived from gossip from popular and social culture into his translation, thus changing the meaning entirely. The main preacher – played by Daniel – would feign shock and annoyance at the interpreter, who sometimes pretending to be unaware and sometimes acting unfazed, will continue to mangle the sermon to the delight of the audience who would roar with laughter. For instance, in one skit by StillRinging that took place during a church vigil tagged "Audacity of Praise," this exchange occurred:

PREACHER: (Points to someone in the audience) You cannot be selfish and be transformed!
INTERPRETER: (In Yoruba) You don't want to take a selfie near (an electric) transformer.
PREACHER: Because when light comes upon you ... You will be shocked by the glory
INTERPRETER: (In Yoruba) When electric light shocks you, you will dance "shoki" into glory.

(Audience roars with laughter)
PREACHER: I will pray for you quickly ... I know you are all children that will obey
INTERPRETER: I know you are not "wobe" children.[35]

---

[35] www.youtube.com/watch?v=tCaVCC0hWnw

Sometimes, as the punchline is delivered and the audience burst into another round of laughter, the comedians let the laughter subside by filling the gap with the "preacher" acting frustrated with his mischievous interpreter. Here is another instance of their exchange,

PREACHER: You know you are a father of many nations ...
INTERPRETER: (feigning shock and responding in Yoruba) Ah-ha!
    When one is not Tuface![36]

(Both preacher and interpreter break character and burst into laughter along with the congregation).[37]
The Tuface that the "preacher" referred to here, meanwhile, is one of the most popular artists in Nigeria and Africa, and he has been fodder for many comedy routines because of his rather cavalier personal life that saw him having multiple children with women to whom he was not married. This public aspect of his private life provoked laughter from the knowing audience, clearly showing that contemporary Pentecostals are not sequestered from pop culture. Their familiarity with lingo from popular music like "wobe" and urban dance like "shoki" shows they are active participants in this secular sphere, along with its undercurrents of gossip and ridicule.

The joke itself in this kind of performance lies in the transposition of the message of the gospel – presented by mimicking the voice or the mannerisms of a pastor when making his spiritual declaration in church – with banal comments from popular culture and its attendant gossip. The efficacy of the joke lies in the way familiar signs from the Bible connect with signs from popular culture and street vernaculars, along with the delivery tactic of linking an open end of one system of signs with another. This near-seamless conjoining of prayers and various biblical references with popular culture references is striking because the transmutation of one to another, effectively, was an unexpected sleight of hand. By decontextualizing the Bible and its prophetic blessings of making the listener the father of many nations (the promise God made to Abraham in the book of Genesis), they also created an interpretive framework to understand the Scripture in both sacred and profane forms. "To obey" became "wobe," a slang for "street urchins"

[36] www.youtube.com/watch?v=RAioInibFxw
[37] Older generation Nigerian comedians have used this technique of language mistranslation to satirize the colonial era where the words of the "master" are mistranslated into the language of the "native."

and to be delightfully shocked by God's transformative power such that it feels like an electric current was commuted to shoki, a freestyling popular dance. The joke works, first because of the flexibility of the language and the creativity of the users. It also resonated with the audience because of their double consciousness as both Pentecostal and social subjects; their twinned subjectivities that place them in the social spots where they can understand two languages: Yoruba and English; religious and secular; spiritual and frivolous. The congregation is able to migrate along the spectrum of church and the world to see the shift in meanings from the things of God – delivered with dense seriousness by the supposed man of God – to secular registers.

Those use of quips by the "interpreter" to the prayers by the "preacher" is also a subterfuge. It cheerfully points out to the church member the irony of the prayer that they intone an "amen" to, without necessarily disarming the larger spiritual import of that prayer in their minds. Suddenly, the prayer about being "the father of nations" was no longer about the expansiveness of promised divine blessings, but the irresponsibility of an unbridled libido. These jokes, meanwhile, are sometimes performed in the church space and on the church altar too. There are times when the comedy performances occur within a church during special programs, at another venue outside the church, or at special church programs too. Either way, there is an altar or a stage where the preacher stands and which becomes a consecrated space. That same sacred place is where the comedian – and in this case, the StillRinging group – also stand to mimic the meaning-making utterances the man of God puts before the audience. The congregation that watches, from the same altar, an emanation of both their pastors' prophesies and comedians' parody of the process, finds themselves also playing the role of an interpreter. As they laugh, they also sieve through the existing range of ideas and meanings to fuse a coherent narrative from the performance they are watching. Sometimes, the comedy act precedes the sermon and is slotted into the same interregnum where gospel music (by artists mostly invited to the church for that occasion) is also performed. Sometimes, the gospel comedy is inserted in the intermission between one session of the sermon and another, when people must have been yearning for decompression after listening to the pastor for an hour or more. As the congregation participates in this exchange through their laughter, they are simultaneously seekers of spiritual experience and seekers of pleasurable experience, both occurring within a single church program. Sometimes, as the previous example shows, the "interpreter" perhaps challenges the "man of God" to consider the irony in some of his prayers and prophecies.

Although these comedians mostly insisted their brand of humor is divinely inspired, they are not shy to admit how much they keep up with current events of popular culture for material for their performances. This means that the audience that comedy performances cultivate is open to various cultural influences that make the material familiar and relatable. Meanwhile, as comedians extend the same jokes and brand of delivery to secular engagements, they are mindful that their act does not "churchify" those spaces and make people uncomfortable while listening. Daniel said, "Some people (the program organizers, that is) don't even want you to mention Jesus, Jehovah, or the devil in your performance. Those words can make people uncomfortable and so they replace a word like 'Satan' with 'the enemy.' We leave that for strictly church settings."[38]

With gospel comedians' professionalization of their act arose the need to define themselves even when they cross over into the non-church arena as performers. Some artists make only what they call "clean jokes," or contents deemed fit for church. As Holy Mallam says of his art, "I noticed that there was nothing like Christian comedy, and I decided to start that …. I started ethical comedy in Nigeria and I chose to be clean."[39] As a form of self-definition, "clean" meant that he marketed himself as a Christian who performed a non-vulgar kind of comedy that he labeled "ethical comedy." Holy Mallam, whose comedy routines in churches consist of exhortations and prayers, is a member of one of Nigeria's biggest churches, Living Faith Church, (aka the Winners' Chapel). His performances are usually prefaced with expressions such as "Praise the Lord" and "thank you Jesus." He does not stop at just making jokes, he also preaches, prays, prophesies, and peppers his act with an occasional "Amen?" His jokes mostly consist of tales about his Christian social life and lots of self-denigrating ridicule about living his formative years in acute poverty. In one of his acts at the *He Lives Bible Church* at Bletchley in England, he told his church audience, "When people see me, they expect that it's the usual comedy

---

[38] Personal interview.
[39] www.vanguardngr.com/2013/08/i-hawked-bread-pure-water-to-pay-my-school-fees-holy-mallam/

that they hear everywhere that I do, but I was not called to do that. I was called into an assignment. There is gospel comedy, amen? Say to your neighbor, 'gospel comedy.'"[40] On his social media pages, he markets himself as an "ethical gospel comedian . . . with family friendly jokes." He says of his kind of art,

Ethical comedy is the only way out as far as I am concerned. It's about the only kind of comedy that makes sense . . .. One of the things I learnt which helped build my career is ethics. The ethics of a profession are the principles that guide it. It sets a borderline that we must not cross. It stipulates what is acceptable in a profession. I understood this before I started comedy. And it has helped me. Ethical comedy is an acceptable and non-vulgar comedy. Ethical comedy does not only cut across all spectra; it's also relevant everywhere, unlike the others . . .. Insulting people, 'yabbing' them and doing vulgar jokes are, to me, totally unacceptable. Nevertheless, you may find some people who appreciate them. I have a right to do what works for me. This is what works for me.[41]

He is not alone in this self-positioning. Several others who grew up in the church, such as Aboki4Christ and StillRinging, likewise take themselves seriously as mediators of the sacred experience. They moderate their jokes even in non-church settings, and they say they take good care to not overstep bounds so as not to corrupt their brand. They are fiercely insistent that what they do is the work of God, and, as ministers, they do not want to be seen as flippant. Others who make the usual stand-up comedy and perform in church get called out when they cross the line of acceptable public conduct for people who perform in church. An example is Akpororo who removed his shirt and displayed his bare torso while performing at a church event.[42] That was not the only time he was criticized for his excesses. At the 2018 *TheExperience* show – an annual gospel music festival (and perhaps Nigeria's biggest music show), featuring local and international Christian artists and typically attended by thousands of people all over the country – Akpororo's comic routine generated some controversy.[43] After he had spent some time saying he wished he had "annoying anointing" to punish the people who irritated him, ranted

---

[40]   www.youtube.com/watch?v=nCoux0Oz3dQ
[41]   www.gistmania.com/talk/topic,206840.0.html
[42]   https://punchng.com/why-i-slammed-akpororo-for-performing-shirtless-
        sammie-okposo/
[43]   http://theexperiencelagos.com/2018/

talked about tithes payment, and excoriated Daddy Freeze (see Chapter 4) over his campaign against tithes, Akpororo moved to valorizing the spiritual power and the righteousness of the senior pastor of House on the Rock and the convener of the *TheExperience*, Pastor Paul Adefarasin. He joked about the pastor's wife, Ifeanyi, who was sitting beside her husband at the program. Akpororo said the pastor had an overdose of anointing because of his wife's captivating beauty. He said her beauty was so spiritually intoxicating that the couple communicates in their house by speaking in tongues only. Her husband's spiritual power as a pastor, he says, is boosted by his wife's looks. Akpororo proceeded to speak in tongues himself to demonstrate this point.[44] His speaking in tongues as a joke, beamed on live TV and streamed on multiple social media networks, was not well-received by some Christians who thought he went too far and subsequently criticized the church for permitting such excesses. Some even criticized him for saying he correlated a sacred gift like anointing with dealing with annoyance. However, at that festival, he was on a roll. In the second joke he made which also triggered mixed responses – roars of laughter followed by howls and boos of surprise at the sheer audacity – Akpororo said that in Warri, Delta State, the city in the southern region of Nigeria where he comes from, "people" would walk out of the church if the pastor's wife was not as beautiful as Pastor Ifeanyi Adefarasin. Mimicking the voice of those "people" he posed a question (in pidging but which I have trans-lated to English), "If the pastor does not have the eyes to see and marry a beautiful woman, how can he have eyes to see our future?"[45]

I should note that that was not the only time Akpororo would make a joke about the looks of a pastor's wife or even the pastor himself. This eroticization and sexual fantasy directed at the pastor's wife from the church stage is recurrent in his act. For instance, in 2015, during the sixteenth-anniversary celebration of COZA, he also made a similar joke. Akpororo's niche is his "Warri boy" image which gives his performance its traction, and which helps him escape accountability for certain transgressions. Warri is an oil-rich city and its notoriety has been iconized in popular culture with the trope of "Warri boy" or "Warri pikin," a stereotypical image of someone who is irreverent of all authority, uncouth, noisy, rough, and somewhat quick to instigate violence. When Akpororo gets on stage, he enacts that characteristic

[44] www.youtube.com/watch?v=SFpXSt7hiHo   [45] Ibid.

unruliness with his whole body. His gestures are animated, and his voice booming out of the microphone turned up to the highest decibel as he prances around on the stage. On this occasion at COZA where he was performing on the altar, he said to the congregation (in pidgin English but which I have once again translated to English), "I tell people, when a man of God is so handsome and also has anointing, how can a demon go near him? It is even from a distance that such pastor casts out demons."

At this point, Akpororo whistles at an imaginary demon from a distance and shoos it off with his hand. The video cuts to the pastor and his wife laughing heartily and some members of the congregation jumping on their feet while laughing and clapping excitedly. Akpororo then descends one step down from the steps on the altar while looking in the direction of the pastor's wife sitting on the front row opposite him. "Mama, you are fresh! You are like today's bread." He shouts "heyyyyyyyyyyyyyy!" and the video cuts to that of the pastor's wife laughing at the joke along with her husband. Those sitting around them join in laughing and screaming and clapping while also casting glances at the couple to watch their reaction to the jokes. Now thoroughly stimulated, Akpororo walks up and down the altar. Behind him on the altar wall was a life-size virtual projection of his image with exaggerated facial expressions. He puts the microphone back to his mouth and mimics a preacher's technique of ensuring participation by asking the congregation to turn to their neighbor and shout "hey!" Then he continued,

But seriously, if church can look like this on earth, how would heaven be? Look at your neighbor and say, "I want to see you there!" Don't miss the road! Let us meet there! Ah-ha! Look at the groove! *Chai*! Look, if you don't know Jesus, you are missing! No joke. Unbelievers go to club, but as Christians, this (the church) is our club.[46]

In drawing attention to the physical appearance of the pastor and his wife – and even fantasizing about the wife's body by comparing her to the allure of freshly produced food – one sees a Christian eroticism which O'Neill says "re-politicizes believers to take to their soul rather than the streets" (to protest, that is).[47] Though the joke makes both the

---

[46] www.youtube.com/watch?v=L_AXLJZCjXI
[47] O'Neill, "I Want More of You: The Politics of Christian Eroticism in Postwar Guatemala."

pastor and his wife objects of sexual fantasy, their non-availability for consumption by the laughing congregation (who are looking in the couple's direction even as they laugh) strengthens their power in the imagination. They are desirable, but their not being available to the audience who watches them from a distance reifies the idea of the power they embody. The audience laugh at Akpororo's antics on the altar. Several times, the video cut to scenes of the congregation laughing with gusto.

The focus on the audience reaction to the performance brings me back to the theorization of comedy as "resistant politics." The laughter instigated by gospel comedy does not appear as subversive, but is in fact, a re-inscription of class power and domination. For the churches that preach prosperity gospel especially, the whole enterprise of comedy on the altar is to facilitate an excitable environment that galvanizes belief. The reifying of pastors' spiritual authority and the intense laughter by the congregation, are more a conservative politics of power than a challenge of it. In a context where Akpororo's comedy conflates pastors' physical beauty with social class and spirituality, and those that laugh included not just the congregation but the pastor, his wife (and on some occasions, the crew of politicians that sits by the pastor in the front rows watching the comedian on the altar), which laughter can be said represents subalternity and which is that of power?

Interestingly, in one of his jokes at *TheExperience*, Akpororo commented on someone's testimony of overcoming poverty. He said when the person narrated their experience before the crowd, "the rich people sitting in front said '*awwwww*' while the poor people sitting at the back wondered thought, '*So? Is that one even a story of poverty?*'" He then proceeded to challenge that person's account with a worse narration of what the poor go through by ventriloquizing their voices and the resolute acceptance of their lot. At that moment, the comedian first acknowledged the unevenness of the power dynamic of class differences in the gathering but spoke to the stratification by ridiculing poverty rather than critique the conditions that nurture it. By painting graphic cases of poverty to show the many ways things could be worse, he helped the testifier enhance the miracle of what had been overcome through the power of God and a consequence of the anointing of their pastor whose spiritual calling had helped the person break the strangleholds of poverty. To remind the congregation how poor people were outside the bounds of that church event was not a conscientization of the rich people and the political leaders sitting there, it was playing the stories for laughs and making it seem the poor enjoy their poverty. Gospel comedians recognize that the space they are granted on the church altar is a privilege, and they consciously orient their performance toward the church's corporate priorities. Their much-touted artistic freedom as jokers, and which is often valorized in theoretical analysis, is willfully constricted at that moment. Joke-telling, the so-called weapon of the weak, in the hands of a comedian committed to the service of reifying the power identity of the pastor, is ambivalent.

Gospel Comedy and the Unlikely Space of Resistance Politics

If there is any subversive politics to the practice of bringing comedians to church to perform, it is not so much in the contents of the jokes to produce "social inversion, 'the-world-turned-upside-down' scenario where slave governs master or man bites dog; the ridiculing of foolishness, narrow-mindedness, and the rigid insistence on the inflexible systems of living; and comic transfigurations that permit the investigation of alternative identities or suspensions of law governing the bodies."[48] Rather, it is in the sheer incongruity of having comedians perform in the church at all. Allowing comedians space to make jokes about the things of God, demonic forces, deliverance, speaking in tongues, heaven, beauty, social differences, and supernatural power is a level of transgression that celebrates the dominance and the self-assuredness of the Pentecostal movement. As mentioned in previous chapters, the gospel of prosperity facilitated some of these changes in church activities. Having shifted the congregational focus from the afterlife to an idea of "heaven on earth," the church services likewise had to reflect the enjoyment of what the world had to offer. And the congregation members too have become amenable to gospel comedy, happily laughing over gossip from popular culture as they would do in a secular assembly. By listening to various stories, including ones that praised their pastor's spiritual power, wealth, family, and also watch his wife's physical looks glorified, they are reassured of their choice to identify with an assembly of people who embody collective fantasies of a good life.

[48] Stott, *Comedy*, 2.

The performances of gospel comedies, orbiting around Christian life and social expectations, spiritual warfare, and social attitudes toward Christians do not fulfill the conditions of hegemonic subversion through jest. Comedians themselves do not publicly criticize spiritual authority in their performances. They may occasionally criticize the Christian social life and its doctrines, but they skirt around the man of God and his foibles. They are mindful of the cultural power that pastors wield and do not want to risk offending them or their devoted church members. If the "oldest, most basic role of the comedian is ... role of *negative exemplar*,"[49] that is, a social or moral deviant who can take on the part of a spokesperson for cultural sensibilities (because they are first a spittoon for collective scorn), then gospel comedians find themselves in a spot where they have to balance that supposed social marginality and the creative license that it grants them with other spiritual sensibilities. They must foreground their performances by saluting the pastor and reifying his spiritual authority before performing. On some occasions, some comedians start their performance on the altar by prostrating before the pastor fully – and of course, God – thus underscoring the power dynamics that condition the production of the jokes and how their delivery would proceed before the audience. This statement of deference to his authority is practical and also reflective of the reality of control of the market by powerful pastors in a society already saturated by religion. The comedian's success capitulates to the gravitational pull of business constraints and can hardly dare the inordinate radicalism of comedy. So, no matter how radical their performances may be outside church circuits, they do not risk touching the anointed of God because of the possible fallout. Their job is to enhance his power identity before the congregation who also need a continuous guarantee of their pastor's social and spiritual power.

It is also understandable why the content of gospel comedy hardly defies the authority of the church and political establishment that solicits church leaders within the church space. The church is the place where both the working class and the elites meet, and that is also the place where their tenuous differences – and the circumstances that shaped them – are momentarily dissolved in the spirit of worship. For the dominated who come to church – particularly a church that preaches the prosperity gospel – seeking to escape their difficult social condition, a radical agenda that disrupts the power of the clergy is not the first thing

---

[49] Mintz, "Stand-up Comedy as Social and Cultural Mediation."

in their minds but an aspirational desire for the power wielded by the dominant class. Therefore, the suspension of dominant norms, the affront to moral orthodoxies, and the inversion of attitudes by comedic acts is not found in the content of the jokes or the mode of delivery of gospel comedy, the aspects with which most analyses of comedy obsess.

Church members too wield social and economic power that could determine the comedian's career trajectory, so comedians subjugate the radical potential of comedy under the governing power of spiritual hierarchies. Church members who attend services with gospel comedy surveyed for this chapter remain clear about their spiritual expectations of God from their church services and insist they are not carried away by laughter but remember where they were. No matter the social atmospherics, their national and political situations remain real, and personal and spiritual problems have to be solved. That they are amused enough to laugh aloud does not mean they lose themselves to the point where they will tolerate insults to their pastor or his anointing and what it promises to them.

Interestingly, where some dissension occurs is not in the comedy on the stage but the sober space backstage where both comedians and pastors have to negotiate rewards for the artist. Almost all of the gospel comedians interviewed for this work stated that their church performances pay relatively poorly – few pastors treat what they do as a profession and pay these gospel comedians what they see as fair wages. Even when some pastors pay at all, they only offer a pittance and they call it "money for fueling the car." According to some of these comedians, they sometimes do not get paid because the church's presiding pastor is too conservative to consider joke-telling as a job and therefore did not give an order to his administrators to pay for the comedian's services. One comedian said, "When you finish your ministration, some pastors will just pray for you. One pastor told me once, *I see you go places with this your comedy*! I thanked him for his vision, but I told him, 'Daddy, if you want me to go places, you must give me the fare. I will not trek to that place.'" This retort indicates an attitude developed to ensure the comedic vocation is taken seriously. While the comedians reinforce pastoral power through the enterprise of comedy, they also privately challenge them by insisting they will not work for free. The same comedian said,

If every church blesses me as payment, if that is the only thing they do for me, how will I pay my house rent? That is why a lot of those that started their music and comedy career in the church have gone secular. That is where the money is. We cannot shy away from the fact that money is important to grow the ministry. Even the church needs money. If you want the talent and potentials of God's children to manifest, you have to talk about money.

Not all comedians are bold enough to say this to their pastors' faces, however. Some said they cannot publicly protest if they are not paid by the pastors. To do so would be to activate "the spirit of rebellion" and rebellion is not only considered a sin against God, it can promote a disaffection for them among church members whose patronage is integral to their success.

They said they have therefore developed tactics for getting paid, and those schemes are usually carried out in the smaller churches. A comedian narrated that after an endless stream of performances in churches across the country, some of which either did not pay or paid poorly, he had to learn to issue an invoice prior to his showing up on the altar. Sometimes, he said, pastors would promise they would pay and then disappear after church service. So, he started demanding to be settled upfront. One said, "Some pastors are scandalized by my demand for money. They love what I do, but they want me to do it in the name of God, for the love of Jesus Christ. When I talk about money, they say, *how dare you charge God?*' Then I tell them, *I am not charging God. I am charging you!*" By de-anchoring the man of God from God himself, they maintain the clarity necessary to maintain a business stance within a religious ethos predicated on communalism and free gifts of one's talents to God. Another comedian told me that sometimes he would agree to come to the church after the pastor had badgered him or blackmailed him to offer his service to God for free, but he would not show up. After he had done that a few times, he said word got around and they learned to respect that his talents, just like that of the pastors, deserves to be respected. And "respect" is predicated on being paid.

The role money plays in the relationship is significant in understanding the tension between the idea of a church as space where private convictions are legitimized and the church as a corporatized entity. According to Keith Hart, the wage labor system is a mediator of two spheres: the vast endlessness of the market, and the domestic and closed space of the home. The market is the zone of infinite rationality where one's talents are objectively calculated and rewarded with money. The other sphere, the home, the protected and subjective sphere where intimate personal relations makes the bounds of what is called "work" unknown and infinite. This sense of heightened division and duality between the outside world where our humanity is assailed and the home space where it is reaffirmed forms the moral and capitalist foundation of a society.[50] But in a church setting where a performer believes they are working for God and even consider themselves indebted to the church that nurtured them, they also want to be treated as professionals and the binaries of market and home fall short as a descriptor of how one could navigate these spheres. For them, the church represents a market because it is where they get their business, but it is also a home because of the relationships they have built over the years and which has helped them to come this far.

The artists interviewed for this chapter thus created a logic that allows them to mediate between contesting realities and make meaningful connections between themselves as spiritual subjects and as businesspersons dealing with thorny situations of negotiating payment for religious services. This rationality is founded on the practicality and clarity that money brings, and it has helped them to untangle their identity as Christians and as comedians. Yet, at the same time, this reasoning allows them to reconcile the two identities coherently. With money, they can bring a sense of rationality to the subjective relationships of the religious sphere. Also, with money, they maintain a focus on the uses of their gifts and at the same time, the conditions of its exchange. They can synthesize their personal relationship with God and the church with the impersonality of market logic. With money introduced, there is a mutual determination of self-ownership and divine submission. The comedians could own their gift and themselves as the conveyor of comedic talents and structure how they offer it to God. By insisting on being paid – by receiving tangible money (which people have gathered in the church space to pray for anyway) – they can stabilize their identities as Christians, performers, and social subjects with visceral needs.

One of the artists told me that he began to insist on money when he found that he was not given enough honorarium to meet his needs, and he was constantly praying for money. He asked,

---

[50] Hart, "The Hit Man's Dilemma."

Why go to church and beg God to meet your needs all the time when you can just ask your pastor to pay you for your services? They kept saying that we should perform for free so that God will bless us, and then promise us that we can build a platform for bigger things. After I had done that many times, God opened my eyes to see that I already had a platform. I just needed the wisdom to monetize it.

Yet, another comedian reasoned,

They don't regard what we do as a career and that is a problem. Most pastors do not treat us like professionals. They want us to overlook money and focus on God. It is good to serve God but you also have to eat. You see the same pastor that tells you not to ask for money living off his church. They and their children use nice cars, fly private jets, and live lavishly. What gives them the right to profit from the things of God but denies us the same right? We are all called of God, we should all be paid according to our calling.[51]

Yet another one said, "Because we make people laugh does not mean that we ourselves laugh all the time. I am actually a very serious person. I am serious enough to know when my interests are being threatened."[52]

Through such reasoning, comedians use the logic of capitalism to their own ends. They use money as a tangible and objective measure of what they actually give up when they offer their services to God. In some ways, money represents the power to bridge the gap between oneself and one's desire, and the supernatural empowerment to procure that desire has been the core of the prosperity gospel and its theology of give-and-take that pastors themselves preach. With time, church laborers like comedians have watched the church grow from small personable spaces to impersonal corporate organizations and those who demand money from their pastors for their secular services are thus reacting to changes in church structure. They are no longer willing to continuously sacrifice their talents to an institution without tangible rewards even though they have an affinity and investment in its survival.

It is noteworthy that as much as pastors have preached and prayed about money for people, not paying them for their services was often them merely being callous or shameless exploiters of labor. One could also consider that the pastors were redirecting these artists' attention

---

[51] Personal interview.   [52] Personal interview.

away from church as an enterprise and urging them to find their means of support elsewhere. As recently early 2020, there was an open debate about whether churches should be paying artists such as instrumentalists. Some argued that it was only fair since it has become a profession, takes a considerable amount of productive time, and is sometimes the artist's only income. Some others countered saying it was only a matter of time before everybody else in the church begin to demand some payment for their services. These arguments demonstrate a change in the attitude toward church as an organization. For many years, churches have over-valorized service rendered in the church as a seed sown to God for a better life. Apart from volunteer services within the church such as singing in the choir, ushering, altar decoration, protocol officials, hospitality, traffic control, intercessory team, technical team, and working in the media department, people have also worked at construction sites, performed janitorial services, and even offered high-end professional labor at no cost. All of these acts of giving to God have facilitated an attitude of commitment to the church, and it is therefore understandable that pastors will not want people's commitment to church activities reducible to paid employment. If they make it all about money, the attitude of faith with which they approached those actions will be lost as people unabashedly perform for money. Marking what is supposed to be a spiritual contribution with money also means that people can afford to be detached and treat the church as a business center rather than one based on spiritual and social relationships.

However, gospel comedians see this mode of thinking as opening them up to exploitation. When they introduced money and insisted on payment instead of spiritual blessings that pastors typically offer them, they were trying to stabilize the relationship between themselves, God, and his human mediators. Money helps them to draw universal and personal connections between the sacred and secular spheres. By saying that they would rather be paid in cash than with prayers, they bring a secular clarity to a sacred relationship while at the same time sacralizing money. It is not enough, these comedians seem to be saying, for pastors to preach about divine provisions and ways of making money and not live up to the standards of their own message. Their desire for a national platform and media power continues to drive this third-generation of comedians to use the church as a launchpad for their sustained career in non-religious contexts. Besides, they are passionate about their faith. They want to be part of the growth of the church.

They want to be a part of the global movement of the spirit. And they want to be able to do all of these as Christians and as businesspeople.

Finally, for these comedians, insisting on being paid was not all about money but about enforcing principles even as they demonstrated their love for God and the church. They might have forced some pastors to pay, but it was still not about the money. The payment could be quite meagre relative to what they receive for performances for secular organizations anyway, and by insisting on being paid, some churches have started to treat them more professionally. They say they had to insist on payment to redefine the terms and conditions of religious identity in present times. It is no longer one's creative contributions that affirm one's belonging in the church community or the "kingdom business," but money too. Money is also the affirmation of participation. Pastors have long touted church as "God's business" or "kingdom business," and have raised a generation of young people that constructed their work ethics and the associated rewards on principles of faith, divine inspiration, and individual talents as viable routes toward wealth generation and financial stability. By reintroducing those same principles into their relationships with pastors who want their services, they let a secularizing ethos underwrite social relations in the church. Comedy, with its ability to cloak serious matters under the mask of the clown, is perhaps the savviest method of enforcing those principles.

Gospel Comedy and Power Identity: A Postscript

This chapter has looked at gospel comedy as part of the artful construction of power identity that publicly affirms the performances of power by leaders but also privately contests its coercive force. By bringing comedians to churches, comedy's ability to produce happiness is appropriated but its radical edge tempered by its pander toward leadership authority. Now far more exposed to ridicule due to the opening of the public sphere through modern technology, Pentecostal leaders strive to control joke production. By coopting comedians, especially famous ones, these leaders preempt the jokes produced about them. This tactic of consecrating popular cultural forms has helped the Pentecostal culture groom and expand its cultural space. Katrien Pype once described this space thus: "Pentecostal/charismatic popular culture (PCPC) then is a particular cultural space of creativity, persuasion, experience and world making that is distinguishable from other kinds of popular culture through its own artistic, creative and genre features."[53] Indeed, for a time the PCPC was a distinct zone of cultural production while it occupied a countercultural space. Presently, it is so interwoven with the social culture and marketplace systems that some conservatives fear their unique identity as Christians is no longer distinguishable. When Jesse Weaver Shipley wrote about the intersections of popular culture and Pentecostalism in Ghana, his observations about the overlap between the pastors' and the comedians' stagecraft was narrated against a backdrop where both operated in the same cultural sphere and mostly interpenetrated through a measure of mutual appropriation of content and techniques.[54] In recent times, both spheres have become far more intensely linked through performance on the same stage and altar.

One pastor justified using comedians in church to entertain people as being merely realistic. "We now live in a world of 'God accepts me as I am.' To try to give the people, especially younger ones, the old-time religion is to lose them. You have to give them what helps them to stay."[55] Indeed, leaders have to deal with the challenge of maintaining an edge in a hyper-modern and globalized world where competing desires jockey for attention. Contemporary Pentecostalism also competes with other attractions of modernity that offer a very similar vision of social flourishing and community. Particularly from the '90s upwards, Pentecostalism's successes greatly depended on the resourcefulness of its subjects to see the openings in cultural spaces, and they took advantage of it all. Its success now consists opening more cultural spaces to expand its spheres.

This is not to say that everyone accepts this brave new world where people gather in church and laugh. On one side, some Pentecostals are adamant that the admixture of church with secularist entertainment overly dilutes spirituality with the world. They worry that accommodating such forms will lead to the debauchery that will end the idea of the church as it should be known. They argue from the Scriptures that God said, "My house shall be a house of prayer for all nations"[56] – and there is no room for play and amusement in Jesus's prescription of church. They insist that if there is a decline in spiritual fervency that

[53] Pype, "The Liveliness of Pentecostal/Charismatic Popular Culture in Africa."
[54] Shipley, "Comedians, Pastors, and the Miraculous Agency of Charisma in Ghana."
[55] Personal interview.   [56] Matthew 21:13, KJV & NIV.

needed shoring up with gospel comedy, it is due to too much play; of church borders extending to include the secular world. Inviting comedians and other performers into the church is doubling down on the very factors leading to its demise. One pastor claimed, "It is the lack of the presence of God that people now make up with comedians."[57] One of my interviewees who was also against the trend surmised, "Why should lost souls come to church when what they will get here is what they are already getting in the world?" Some others say they are worried that laughing at the things of God will cheapen them, and they think Pentecostals ought to take articles of their faith as seriously as Muslims in Nigeria do – frequently threatening to start a religious riot if they consider their faith blasphemed. On the other side are also Pentecostals who accept the trend as a reality of the times and think a church has to do whatever it can to retain the people who might stray into the world for its amusements. Ironically, these two factions can be present within a single church and vehemently contest these grounds with each other.

When comedians themselves are criticized for invading the church space with their humor and lessening spiritual truths, they counter by making a dynamic interpretation of scripture to justify their perform-ance on the altar. StillRinging said, "I tell my critics that we have made the big men of God who hear from God regularly laugh in church and heavens did not fall. God still answers their prayers. If they can laugh, why not everyone else? Why can't you laugh? Are you holier than them? God too laughs, why not you?" Indeed, it is remarkable how the images of pastors laughing at the jokes made by these gospel comedians circulate as YouTube videos with titles that sensationalize gospel comedy *see how StillRinging comedian made Bishop Oyedepo almost fall off his chair laughing!* Pastors' laughter to comedy perform-ances is used for self-legitimation by the comedians and weaponized to confront the critics of their profession. Aboki4Christ too retorted on the subject of whether comedy should be performed in churches:

When they say we should not make comedy in church, I asked them what is church? Is the church the building? I ask where we can make comedy, they say maybe at weddings, birthdays, and secular events. I now ask them, who told you that is not in that place? Do we limit God to the four walls of the

---

[57] https://punchng.com/ill-query-any-pastor-who-hosts-comedian-in-church-okoroafor-assemblies-of-god-head/

building we call church? As far as I am concerned, the building is not the church. You and I make up the church. If I can make you laugh at your wedding where God is also present, why can't I make you laugh in the place where you go to worship? I carry the presence of God everywhere I go, I not only have the presence of God in the building called the church. If I can make people laugh outside the building we call church with God indwelling within me, why can't I make them laugh inside the building that you and I molded and called the church? Why assume the building is the only habitation of the Almighty? God is too big to be enclosed in that place. There is nothing wrong in making people laugh in church. The building is not the church, the people are.[58]

What is interesting here is not just the appeal to the Scriptures to justify his careers as a co-spiritual laborer with pastors, but how he also articulates the understanding that the borders between the spaces called church and the world are collapsed. This is particularly true when viewed against the constant absorption of secular performances in the church and the secular sphere's overfamiliarity with church performances until there is no demarcation between both spaces. Rather than Christians being tempted to dig into the underground economy of secular and sinful pleasures, their restlessness can now be satisfied by bridging church with every space. These comedians are a testimony to what a church has to do to manage its successes. These comedic performances expose an alternative reality, a counter-world where spirituality and frivolity can exist side by side – where people are comfortable playing with the devil.

If, as scholars have argued, laughter facilitates a sense of community and the shared values that project a common sensibility, then gospel comedy acts as a tool to expand the borders of church and intensify the ideas of ritual practice.[59] Comedy can corrode our concept of church as a space for solemn spiritual praxis, and pluralize ideas of what faith practices can accommodate and the ways we see and relate to the concept of church. Since the Bible says every place and every space that two or more Christian find themselves is filled with the presence of Jesus,[60] the idea of people making the church space by the mere fact of their presence ontologizes any gathering and any activity of Christians, and institutes them into "church." This perception of what is

---

[58] Personal interview.   [59] Merrill, "Feminist Humor."
[60] Matthew 18:20, KJV & NIV.

designated church might as well be extended to every space and the fourth wall – or the four walls that make up the church structures – broken and kept open to maintain a post-structural flow that irrigates spiritual energy and social behaviors with radical openness. After this level of expansiveness, what remains of the church is its roof, which, in the spiritual and theological sense, is the omnipresence of God that dominates everywhere.

6 | "The Spirit Names the Child": Pentecostal Futurity in the Name of Jesus

My research took me to a church in Ibadan, where I was to interview a pastor on prayer. To start such sessions, I typically engage in small talk with interviewees before turning on the tape recorder so both of us can be at ease with each other. On this day, the pastor told me that he had just returned from a child naming ceremony. To keep the conversation going rather than out of serious curiosity, I asked him the child's name. "Jesutunde. We named the child Jesutunde," he responded. Jesutunde? At that time, I was taken aback by what seemed like a strange configuration of names. A name like Tunde catalogs the Yoruba and general African belief in reincarnation, and it should be incompatible with Christianity. The "Tunde" name (meaning: has returned/has reincarnated) name is typically prefixed by Baba (father) or 'Ye (short for Yeye, or mother), and it means that one's dead father or mother has returned (to this world from the dead or the ancestors). So, how does a name like Jesutunde (Jesus has returned/reincarnated) square with the Christian understanding of the afterlife that has no accommodation human souls continuously circling between the worlds of the living and the dead? Inserting the name and persona of Jesus into Yoruba indigenous myths to generate a name like "Jesutunde," seemed like an awkward consequence of replacing or trying to transcend the ethical structures that uphold cultural belief in the supernatural.

Belief in reincarnation is a potent myth in the African cultural repertoire and this is reflected in ritual enactments of ancestral deification and masquerade performances. Unlike Christian mythology, African traditional religions believe "the posthumous survival of individuality is not for the purposes of a future resurrection of the righteous, a reanimation in the materialistic hereafter, but re-incarnation in a new body."[1] The "new body" here is that of a child and, following

---

[1] Olomola, "Contradictions in Yoruba Folk Beliefs Concerning Post-Life Existence."

208

Wole Soyinka's delineation of the African cosmological imagination into the worlds of the living, the dead and the unborn, it shows the mutual correspondence between these three cosmological spaces.[2] This belief in reincarnation is also articulated through naming practices, and that is why the names that echo some of those beliefs are considered "demonic" by Christian converts. They see it as opening up one's life to affliction by satanic forces. In the past, when a child was born, the parents typically consulted the diviner to know which ancestor might have "tun de," that is, which one might be making a return trip back into this world. It is partly due to this belief in the permeability of worlds where the dead can access the space of the living that traditional religious practices are easily demonized by Christians. Also, the ways names are used to mark these epistemological practices carries over into Christianity, where converts from indigenous African religions instinctively understand the roles naming practices play in negotiating the natural and supernatural worlds.

However, this is also the point where the thought behind "Jesutunde" gets clunky: to construe Jesus as an ancestor in a similar manner to those who depart the world of the dead to reenter a child's body is somewhat heretical. The foundation of Christianity is laid on the myth of the resurrection of Jesus and the eternal life he was imbued with as a result of his triumph over death. Taking Jesus as one of the multiple ancestors making the rounds from one cosmos to another reduces his elevated status as an iconized member of the Trinity/Godhead. So, I asked the pastor, "By giving a child that name, is it not a theological contradiction to suggest that an already resurrected Jesus could enter into a woman to be reborn again like our Yoruba ancestors believed?" The pastor shook his head and replied, "Not at all. That name was what the Holy Spirit chose for the child. We do not name our children by ourselves; we do it by the inspiration of God. *Emi ni o maa n so omo loruko.*" That is, it is the spirit that names the child. That last sentence, rendered in the Yoruba language, made me wonder the spirit's underlying political agenda in inspiring a superficially ideologically incoherent name like "Jesutunde." The pastor's justification for the name prompted me to investigate the notion of the *spirit* beyond the obvious allusion he makes to the Holy Spirit as the inspirational source of child naming.

---

[2] Soyinka, *Death and the King's Horseman.*

For a people who perform power and embody it in their everyday expressions of faith, seemingly mundane acts such as naming a child are part of how power is performed. Those that convert to Pentecostalism as adults face identity crisis of their new status and which they sometimes resolve through names.[3] Names that include Jesus are therefore handcrafted to display of status of power found in the name of Jesus. Names are expressions of thoughts, feelings, and wishes, and over time, as they are repeatedly called, are means of cementing status. For the spirit to prompt them toward taking ancestors, deities, and supernatural beings from the mythic spaces of African belief and superimposing Jesus in their stead, shows more than forging of an identity by people leaving an old life behind and embracing a new one as Pentecostals. They are also establishing their power identity as Pentecostal Christians; people who have transcended and triumphed over demonic forces and the historical circumstances that produced them.[4]

As the example of Paul Esupofo in *Agbara Nla* in Chapter 1 showed, personal naming typically accompanies conversion to signify new identity. The names are deeply thought-out to reflect this journey of conversion and the space the convert now occupies in the new faith they have chosen. For instance, the Isawuru character did not merely select names, he chose "Paul" – the name of a character in the New Testament who, as Saul, persecuted Christians – to link his conversion narrative to a Bible character with a similar history. Saul had a personal encounter with Jesus Christ and ended up as a Christian after a dramatic conversion. Paul would eventually become one of the biggest propagators of the faith and he wrote several of the New Testament epistles. Also, Isawuru's choice of Esupofo – Esu (the Yoruba Christian label for the Biblical devil) has come to nothing – is also quite significant. Such artful selections of names shows how the Isawuru character is portrayed as the quintessential Christian convert, especially a Yoruba one.[5] They combine names that align histories written in the Bible with the ones of their indigenous cultures, which

---

[3] https://forums.ssrc.org/ndsp/2013/08/29/the-new-name-its-a-prayer/
[4] Scholars like J. K. Ayantayo and S. Olanisebe have expressed dismay with the way Pentecostals are giving up aspects of their culture and the colorful histories that underwrite them to take up names borne by biblical characters that are not necessarily superior to indigenous names.
[5] I have limited this analysis to Yoruba largely because trying to pull off a study like this across many ethnic groups in Nigeria would have been too unwieldy.

they have termed "demonic," and forge a new living history that will unfold through their performances of their everyday life as people of power. This performance of power identity crafts a personal sense of oneself as an individual who embodies the traits of Jesus as a victor. Having overridden beliefs (such as the idea of heaven and the afterlife) and substituted the gods (pantheon, ancestors, and their histories) with the symbolism of Jesus' name, these converts define the spirit that influences the culture of the collective.

In scholarly studies, "spirit" has been variously defined. In Hegelian terms, spirit means the principle or the underlying ethic that animates social consciousness and the actions that ensue. In religious studies, spirit could mean both the Holy Spirit – the pneumatic force that inspires people and prompts them to take creative action – and the immaterial beings who participate in activities on this material plane.[6] Spirit relates to spiritism, the study of the phenomena that link the spiritual world to the immediate physical one humans inhabit.[7] "Spirit" has a universal resonance as an incorporeal being, one not necessarily anchored to Judeo-Christian religious mythology, but as a transcendental energy or superhuman agent that can impinge upon or activate human agency. The pastor in my example, of course, construed the spirit as the stimulating force of the outpouring of the divine into the ethical life of African Pentecostals. Throughout this chapter, I have settled for an approach that takes *spirit* as an approximation of social ethics, order of living, obscure instincts, sounded drives, and the culmination of a certain sensibility from which a dominant collective derive their power and influence, and through which people are ultimately impelled to express beliefs and act upon certain expectations. Humans can create the spirit of a society through their gathering together in a place and carrying out concerted action.[8] Doing things with language is one of the ways they create and express the defining spirit of the times. When the spirit names the child, especially with "Jesu" names, the spirit uses each individual to build a network of influential power to ultimately transform the world into its image. In a world the spirit is already reshaping, those children's lives further create a multiplier effect. For the spirit to name the child, the spirit not

[6] Anderson, *Spirit-Filled World*; Yong, "On Binding, and Loosing, the Spirits."
[7] Vasconcelos, "Homeless Spirits," 14.
[8] Wariboko, Nigerian Pentecostalism, 116.

only relates to the significance of child naming, especially in African cultures; the spirit is also hyper-aware of the need to implant its power and influence into the still-blank slates of the lives that are just beginning.

By choosing to name the child, the spirit chose a significant cultural site to demonstrate its politics.[9] Africans consider names an important determiner in how one lives one's life "authentically."[10] They are also important to a community because they are an "open diary" where people both store the information about the social order as it was at the time of a child's birth, and by which they also reinforce such data.[11] The political economy of names is so crucial that they say that only a "mad person" does not care what (s)he is called.[12] This spirit is invisible and immaterial, yet omniscient and omnipotent enough to galvanize even personal decisions such as child naming. The spirit is also dynamic enough to mesh into social configurations, demonstrating that Africans' conception of the "spirit" as a revelation of the Christ personality is distinct from the Jesus in Bible history.[13] The spirit connected to African cosmological imagination, the earth from where the deities, gods, and ancestors spring, and turned these sites into a palimpsest where it could write a new African genealogy with the name of Jesus Christ.

Names are given to be called and for the bearer to respond, and that format of call and response recalls theologian Clifton Clarke's methodological proposal for the study of African Pentecostalism.[14] According to Clarke, the dialogical and dynamic nature of "call and response" aptly describes African Pentecostalism. The "call," he notes, is the authoritative prompting of African Pentecostalism through the Bible as the received Word of God for theological practices; the history of the church delineated into epochs, the practices and legacies that have framed contemporary Christianity, and the religio-cultural context that gives African Pentecostalism its distinct flavor. The

---

9   "The act of naming is an act of power. Parents naming children, conquerors naming new lands, and organizations naming themselves all involve the assertion of authority and control. Names allow us to communicate through the development of shared meanings." Guenther, "The Politics of Names," 412.
10 Sarajlic, "The Ethics and Politics of Child Naming."
11 Akinnaso, "The Sociolinguistic Basis of Yoruba Personal Names."
12 Osundare, *African Literature and the Crisis of Post-Structuralist Theorising*.
13 Ngong, "African Pentecostal Pneumatology."
14 Clarke, "Call and Response."

"response" is Africans' reaction to these stimuli through their various performative and corporeal activities that form the lived theology of their Pentecostalism. Call-and-response, as a form of interaction, thus expresses the many facets of African histories and culture: the past and present; the contact of human and supernatural worlds; indigenous belief systems and their manifestations in contemporary Pentecostalism.

One area where "call and response" remain unexplored, however, is where its antiphonal nature is virtually literal: names. In the relatively dynamic and straightforward exchange of giving someone a name and calling out the name while expecting some kind of response (and giving a response as a call in itself), there are dense historical cadences, cultural impulses, and the ethical agenda of the name giver. The name bearer (who might also be the name-giver, as seen in instances of self-renaming after conversion) considers the outstretching of his or her social existence as a series of unfolding performances that respond to the name called at one's natural birth (or spiritual rebirth). Thus, "call and response" is an apt analysis of naming practices and the ways they are performed through the meanings they evoke when sounded.

Like many Africans, Pentecostals do not treat names as an objectified label that floats above a person but as a codification of history and belief imposed on a person at birth to be recycled in demotic enactments. They take names seriously both as Africans with a distinct worldview and as Christians steeped in Judeo-Christian traditions, and who understand the mythic significance of names from both perspectives. As Africans, they understand that names are powerful because they reflect the socio-ecological structures that hold up the terms of social relations, familial tensions, and even human–divine relationships. Yoruba people express the interactive nature of names with a proverb that translates thus: Because of people's propensity to run into trouble, everyone is given a name to individuate them. There is also another proverb that says that a person's name haunts their life and its events. The different ways onomastics are discursively treated in proverbs and folk tales index names as a predictive force or symbolic charm that has power beyond the physical to activate singular life experiences.[15] To them, names also measure historical changes, register ethical progressions, and reflect apprehensions of situations and the

---

[15] Fakuade & Adeosun, "Yoruba Personal Naming System."

subsequent systematization of knowledge accrued from those experiences.

The name given at either natural or spiritual birth represents a social condition activated to further speak to those condition, demands a response, and creates a sequential interaction between bearer, society, and those circumstances.[16] The power of a name lies in its ability to touch the "psychic substrates associated with superstition, ritual, irrational belief, and primitive behavior."[17] Names, by their nature too, are forms of praise, rewards, highlights, or allusions to certain symbolic references that are either mutually shared or which the name-giver hopes to impress on the social system. The Jesu naming traditions can also be described as "mythic onomastics," a process that stimulates in the imagination, "the primordial functions of names as descriptors of human reality."[18] Thus, names are a creative site for people to express ethics. For Yoruba people, the malleability of their language means new categories of meaning are easily introduced from existing ones through the use of "prefix to roots, stems, or a given syntactic categories."[19] The rites of naming itself form part of the social processes that reflect the realities and the values of the society. By "reflect," these names are not merely a mirror that reflects parallel social events but a constitutive element of the fabric that shapes the society.[20] This reality is also expressed in the Yoruba proverb that urges one to consider the condition of one's household before one names a child.

As Christians too, they understand that names are a force of power. One of the parts of the Bible they refer to on the importance of naming is the creation story. In the Bible, one of the clearest demonstrations that God had given the first man He created, Adam, total dominion over His creation was the authority he gave him to name everything, including Eve, the first woman. According to the Bible, the name Adam gave all living creatures is what they are called, an added detail that shows that the significance of a name goes beyond its invocative or the illocutionary force embedded to the registration of the circumstances

---

[16] Agyekum, "The Sociolinguistic of Akan Personal Names."
[17] Kaplan, Bernays & Kaplan Educational Centers, *Language of Names*, 16.
[18] Compagnone & Danesi, "Mythic and Occultist Naming Strategies in Harry Potter."
[19] Orie, "Yoruba Names and Gender Marking."
[20] Latour, "When Things Strike Back."

that determined its choice.[21] Putting the name of Jesus in names such as "Jesutunde" is thus an objectification of faith and a desire to expressively live out Jesus's mythic power, glory, and history. The name is the "call" and the unfolding outcome of the person's life is the "response." To ensure they get the right call they would be responding to all through their lives, the Christian imagination condemned the invocation of deities and ancestors compressed into some of those names. They described these names "demonic" and banished them. Like the example of "Jesutunde" shows, some started to inscribe Jesus into those spaces.

After my conversation with the pastor at the child naming ceremony, I began to gather Pentecostal Christian names among Yoruba people that were prefixed with "Jesu" or other similarly iconic Christian symbols. Just like "Jesutunde," an appreciable number of them, on the surface, appeared like contradictory worldviews of Africa and Pentecostalism. Names like Jesurinde (where the *-rinde* means "to walk back home after a journey into the afterlife") reads as a rather tenuous reconciliation of differing worldviews. Such contradictions are, however, instructive because their semantic and linguistic outcome also marks an ongoing formation of the interconnections of previously disparate pieces of theological thought into an essentialized African Pentecostal identity. As the example of Jesutunde (or a female variant, Jesuwande, as a substitute for Yewande) shows, the *Jesu* part that prefaces those names that symbolize African beliefs about life after death itself becomes a new creation, the meeting of different religious and cultural myths to shape a new frame of references. Pentecostalism, like other similar waves of Christian religious movements, is absorbing existing forms to create new meanings that respond to questions evolved by time.

African Christian naming practices have been through several epochs. At first, the earliest converts chose Western and "Christian" names such as "John," and "Matthew" to separate themselves from their "heathen" and "pagan" family that still practiced indigenous religion. In another phase, cultural nationalism and anti-colonial sentiments drove a number of Africans who were being socialized into Western/Christian culture to change their attitude toward names. They chose names in their local language to sound more "native" and

---

[21] For a study of names and speech acts, see Yost, "The Speech Act of Naming in Context."

names like "David Brown Vincent, J. H. Samuel, and Joseph Pythagoras Haastrup ... became Mojola Agbebi, Adegboyega Edun, and Ademuyiwa Haastrup, respectively."[22] In the current phase, Pentecostals fashion names that reflect their Christian identity, their power over the demonic forces that haunt them through familial and historical affiliation, and at the same time, they retain their Africanness.[23] The Jesu- names that they are opting for are not merely about Africanizing Jesus. These names resonate within local cultural contexts in a way that "Christian" names like John and James might never do, and that is why they are an important tool of registering their cultural power and triumphs into the public consciousness. That is, apart from the current Pentecostal practice of giving their children allegorical names such as Vision, Wealth, Testimony, Hallelujah, Miracle, Faith, Glory, Dominion, Power, Blossom, Flourish, Bible, Anointing, and Winner, the "Jesu" names rendered in local language to meet the exigent demands of a new identity that bespeaks power; power in the name of Jesus. The same Africanness that earlier converts once tried to delink themselves from, now provides means for contemporary Pentecostals to ground their identity as the people of power.

Names and the Spirit

In this section, I will first establish the notion of the *spirit* as it pertains to Pentecostal practices to assert that contemporary naming practices of Jesu- among Pentecostals are a performative act of response to the call being made by history, the times they live in, and the shaping of their desired society through what Lee Edelman describes as "reproductive futurism" (that is, the belief that all our political actions are motivated by the conviction that we are fighting on behalf of our children's future).[24] This section will therefore engage the notion of a society's ethical order as a spirit and reflect on how the dynamics might play out in the context of an African social life. Here, I also establish how the orthodoxies of a social order that has been reshaped by the dominance of a cultural movement like Pentecostalism can express its new spirit through naming practices. For the Pentecostal power identity to resonate, the society has to be made conducive

---

[22] https://forums.ssrc.org/ndsp/2013/08/29/the-new-name-its-a-prayer/
[23] Olanisebe, "Elimination by Substitution."   [24] Edelman, *No Future.*

through changes to language and social thought. This makes
Pentecostal naming practices a rich site to explore how names signal
the call-and-response of history and culture: the ideological imperatives
that undergird the shift in reformulating language, the circumstances
that enable Pentecostal self-making and remaking, the Pentecostal
absorption of foreign encounters and subsequent creative inclinations,
shifting class values, and the conditions of altering or producing new
orthographies for local languages.[25]

Through names, they call upon the spirit to wage wars to expel the
occult and demonic forces they deem as underlying subsisting names,
transcend the founding ethics of their African society, and inaugurate
a Pentecostal world order. In Wariboko's conceptualization of the
spirit as "the culmination to which all social practices are heading …
a kind of *principle* that inheres in organized human activities,"[26] he
also argues that while the spirit is contingent on social performances
and structures, its emergence within a place also relies on corporeality
since bodies are what connect the physical and spiritual realms. The
unique placement of the body as the anchor point between the spiritual
or the social can become "spirit" when a web of human agents assemble within a site of a clearing to initiate actions that not only dictate
a new collective ethic but, by the substance and consistency of their
practices, also normalize the ethos. As he conceives it, there is always an
antecedent to the generation of the spirit where "bodies and minds, and
the interconnections between them … are responsible for the site
emerging."[27] Consequently, the "spirit that arises in relation and in
response to the dynamics of focused concentration and attunement of
humans in the common."[28]

For my purposes in this section, I will illustrate the antecedent to the
"spirit" now manifesting through a mesh of Jesu- names and the
cultural sites where they have emerged through the African classic by
Chinua Achebe, *Things Fall Apart*. Then I will demonstrate how
Pentecostalism as a contemporary culture also offers people the
means of standing apart and above the values circulated within the
social clearing through their own Pentecostal naming practices too.
According to Achebe, one can measure how good life has been to an

[25] Komori, "Trends in Japanese First Names in the Twentieth Century"; Makoni,
    Makoni & Mashiri, "Naming Practices and Language Planning in Zimbabwe."
[26] Wariboko, *Nigerian Pentecostalism*, 128 and 140.   [27] Ibid., 125.   [28] Ibid.

Igbo man through the names he gives to his children.[29] That was apparent in *Things Fall Apart*, where, prior to Christianity coming into the society to impose a new call of history that ruptured the ethical foundations of her community, the existing social spirit gave resonance to the call-and-response in the names a character, Ekwefi, gave her children. In that homogenous society of Umuofia, there were congruences between individual moral characters and the communal values that gave the community its identity.[30] For Ekwefi, who suffered the losses of her children as they died in infancy, the names for each successive child she had afterward became a rhetorical strategy to pass a commentary to the community in both obvious and sublime ways.[31] A child's name also condenses the parent's history, and is therefore a repository of memory, prayers, beliefs, anxieties, desires and autobiographies; an expression of individual and collective values, prayers and kinship ties; and a description of the world as it is or as it should be.[32] As a rendering of speech that conveys more than only personal emotions, names also describe how the name-giver contributes to the society's ethos and the structures of their symbolic universe through the performative quality of names. They call out to society, the society responds, and the response becomes another call, thus forming a cycle of dialogical engagement. Names are about the only thing we are given or which we acquire that are meant to be used by others. The economy of that use is expressed in the ways they are chosen for the politics they announce, the values they propagate, and the ethics – social and collective – that they collate. Names are a fiction, a product of imagination expressed in language, and like all fictions, they forth-tell, perform, and control.

A subplot in *Things Fall Apart*, Ekwefi's story is of a woman who cannot fulfill her expected role of motherhood within the social structures of her village. She is plagued with what is known as Ogbanje

---

[29] Achebe, *Morning Yet on Creation Day.*
[30] Wariboko, *Ethics and Society*, 74.
[31] Ogbaa, "Names and Naming in Chinua Achebe's Novels"; Wamitila, "What's in a Name."
[32] Agyekum, "The Sociolinguistic of Akan Personal Names"; Ogie, "Edo Personal Names and Worldview; Omoloso, "A Speech Act Analysis of Selected Yoruba Anthroponyms"; Oseni, "A Guide to Muslim Name, with Special Reference to Nigeria"; Oyěwùmí, *What Gender Is Motherhood?*; Smith, "Child-Naming Practices, Kinship Ties, and Change in Family Attitudes in Hingham, Massachusetts, 1641 to 1880."

children – a malevolent set of supernatural beings who are "born to die." Called Abiku in Yoruba mythology too, these children's transversal journey from the chthonian realm to the world of the living is made through near-endless rotations of life and death through the same woman.[33] In the case of Ekwefi, she had borne ten children and nine of them had died in infancy.

As she buried one child after another her sorrow gave way to despair and grim resignation. The birth of her children, *which should be a woman's crowning glory*, became for Ekwefi mere physical agony devoid of promise. The naming ceremony after seven market weeks became an empty ritual. Her deepening despair found expression in the names she gave her children. One of them was a pathetic cry, Onwumbiko – "Death, I implore you." But death took no notice; Onwumbiko died in his fifteenth month. The next child was a girl, Ozoemena – "May it not happen again." She died in her eleventh month, and two others after her. Ekwefi them became defiant and called her next child Onwuma – "Death may please himself." And he did.[34] (italics mine)

There are two points to note from the world of Umuofia that Achebe describes. The first is that the societal ethos is adjusted on a clear definition of roles. The men occupy and dominate the public sphere, and this is illustrated by their use of the village square for associations and public gatherings on political and social issues. When women are present, it is mostly during festive periods or spectacular parades where their participation is relegated to the margins as audience and side commentators. Men are at the top of the social hierarchy, especially if they are rich, physically brave, older, or all three.[35] The women's

---

[33] The Abiku–Ogbanje phenomenon in southern Nigeria has been a subject in critical exploration of the interface of folk beliefs and modern science and has also been applied as a metaphor for disjunctures in the rites of weaving cultural memories. Achebe, "Literary Insights into the 'Ogbanje' Phenomenon"; Falola, *A Mouth Sweeter than Salt*; Ilechukwu, "Ogbanje/abiku and Cultural Conceptualizations of Psychopathology in Nigeria"; Ilechukwu, "Ogbanje/Abiku"; Maduka, "African Religious Beliefs in Literary Imagination"; McCabe, "Histories of Errancy"; Ogunyemi, "An Abiku-Ogbanje Atlas."

[34] Achebe, *Things Fall Apart*.

[35] Achebe, reflecting on *Things Fall Apart* at its fiftieth anniversary in 2008, mentioned that Igbo culture premises masculinity and makes a show of all of its trappings – power, strength, and success – without giving its feminine side as much of a chance. This feminine side, however, is there but sublimated into the culture. It speaks with a gentle voice, with vocal cords so soft and so gentle that one has to "make a special effort to listen to hear it." From Achebe's

participation in Umuofia is mostly dependent on the varying dynamics of their domestic and nurturing roles.[36] A woman's crowning glory is the birth of children, and Ekwefi's failure to successfully sustain the lives of the children she produces has significant consequences for her and her relationship with society.

This first assertion leads to the second one: In this context, the barren woman is relegated to the margins since her worth in the overall social construct is based on fulfilling her biological destiny. The space where she exercises her power is mostly the domestic sphere. Consequently, her agency against the ruling power of the community over her and which she can deploy is through naming her Ogbanje children. The names she chooses are a self-reflexive call to the metaphysical being responsible for her misery – death, that is – and to the ethical ears of the community. In African cultures, it is not unusual to use a child's name to speak to the members of the community to challenge them to live up to collective interests, a trait that J. A. Sofola describes as a form of "moralistic activism."[37] A similar trend was observed by Susan Suzman in her study of changes to Zulu personal naming practices, although she also noted that the trend is being altered by changes to the family unit such as urban culture and evolving family patterns.[38] Equally, it is noteworthy that Ekwefi's story is similar to that of another character in the Bible (Genesis 29), Leah, who also named her children to make a commentary on her existential condition.[39]

Since the community's values rest on the seeds of family relationships and the larger interconnections of the individual to the society, a childless woman like Ekwefi is disadvantaged for failing to spawn

---

reflection, one concludes that one of the fears that haunted the Umuofia community, and which was viscerally expressed through the actions of the protagonist, Okonkwo, was feminization. Achebe, cited in *Listening to the Gentle Voice*, 311–312.

[36] Whereas Umuofia would manage the cataclysmic changes that challenged its idea of masculinity with relative prudence and strategic redefinition of its traditional ideals through a reevaluation of the concept of bravery, Okonkwo's strong-headed wedding to the old ideals proved his tragic flaw – a point Joseph Slaughter makes in his allegorized rereading of the "simple" tales women weave in their retracted spaces. Slaughter, "A Mouth with Which to Tell the Story."

[37] Sofola, *African Culture and the African Personality.*

[38] Suzman, "Names as Pointers." See also Chitando, "Signs and Portents?" 145; Kadenge et al., "Anthroponyms of Albinos among the Shona People of Zimbabwe."

[39] Genesis 29.

offspring that would carry forward either the dynamics of the domestic sphere or the political power of the public sphere. Her means of appealing to the community and the unseen forces that mediate affairs between various worlds was through a vocalization of her desperation, trauma, pain, and supplications through her children's names. It was an individual calling on the spirit, the values on which the community was founded, and beseeching it to understand her situation. Her children's names become an oral performance, an entreaty to the conscience of the community who sees her suffering and also understands that her displacement in the order of things is beyond her control. Those names were also a response to the standards – the call – which the community had imposed on everyone. As Achebe said in his reflections, in the society that Umuofia represents, material achievements are lauded (or "loud-ed") to the detriment of subterranean voices from the margins that women occupy. Ekwefi's means of speaking up and cutting through the din of the celebration of material achievement is child naming, a rhetorical strategy implicitly understood by all. As Chima Anyadike said of the politics of the rhetoric deployed through this gentle voice, "The sense of the rhetorical in use here is not so much that of the elaborate and fanciful as that of the effect and persuasive use of language."[40]

For Ekwefi, this instrumentalization of names is a means of sublimating her failures into the social order. She is not a threat to the survival of that order because the marriage and family structure is polygamous. However, the order is a threat to her well-being as an individual because where she fails in her duty, her husband's co-wife succeeds. With the co-wife's celebration of multiple sons, Ekwefi's case drives her further down to the level of an unfortunate outlier. By using the oral function of the names to speak to the metaphysical forces that had taken her children and the physical human ears in the community, she was also inviting them as engaged spectators to the drama and vicissitudes of her life. Through these names, she expresses her cycles of emotions to them – a mode of communal communication that uses the intangible and subconsciously understood semiotics to narrate the dynamics and cruelty of fate. Such embodied oral gesture is a moral plea, a call, for them to understand her plight and respond by bearing with her, giving her fate a chance, and letting her live without the jeers

---

[40] Anyadike, *Listening to the Gentle Voice*, 313.

and shame that attend women who cannot fulfill their biological roles. The names represent Ekwefi's astute awareness of what is required of her, her failure to live up to it, and her self-conscious appeal to the custodians of the social order not to condemn her as the cause of her own predicament or disregard her basic human dignity. While Ekwefi's dialogical use of names reflected the society in which she lived, her place within the community, and her trauma, there was no rupture to the ethical structure of the society. She sequenced her experience through her children's names, but it was also a cyclical conversation with the society as she tried to negotiate wider social issues. The call-and-response within such homogenous and traditional societies was a dialogue between an individual and the community, until missionary Christianity interrupted them. The new faith ruptured the social context in which this communication was meaningful. By the time they re-fused, the myths and symbols of Christianity had become a part of its ethos.

When colonial missionaries began to propagate Christianity, existing African names was one of their targets because they understood the power to irrupt the social configurations of a place. For example, colonial modernity used the inscriptive processes of identifying, labeling, and differentiation to rename people, either by giving them new "pronounceable" names to facilitate interaction with European missionaries or because they thought those African names stemmed from their pagan heritage that had to be scrubbed off to make the conversion project complete.[41] Their mode of urging those converts to a name change was not always subtle. It was administered through the demonization of their ways and/or by recreating the African social site so that admittance to social services such as education, health, and class benefits were tied to religious conversion and conformity.[42] Those who were renamed or chose to rename themselves after their Christian conversion could access "new possibilities, new attributes, new values, reshaping ideologies and creating new concepts of the self as well as redefining the groups from which the self operates" through the " . . . complex nature of onomastic erasure and de-erasure and the resuscitation of dormant identities."[43]

---

[41] Oduyoye, *Hearing and Knowing*, 33.
[42] Ajayi, *Christian Missions in Nigeria, 1841–1891*; Ayandele, *The Missionary Impact on Modern Nigeria, 1842–1914*; Taiwo, *How Colonialism Preempted Modernity in Africa.*
[43] Pfukwa & Barnes. "Negotiating Identities in Guerrilla War Names in the Zimbabwean War of Liberation."

As personal names serve a psychic function to the African conception of the self, the self in relation to others, self-esteem, and self-autonomy,[44] the name-changing process amounted to more than a switch in label. The sonant practices of calling the converts by their "Christian" names and their bearers' responses had far-reaching effects of varying the ethos of their social cultures. The names became part of the politics of class inclusion and exclusion, structuring the systems of relations in the social marketplace, and helped construct the category of the "enlightened Christian" against the "African heathen." The cultural process triggered by the missionary preceded the changes to the society's ethical structures and made continually possible, the generation of a new religious spirit within the polity. The site that would emerge from the interconnected bodies and minds of those earlier Christians would become the norm, the spirit against which several social and religious relations interchanges and conflicts would serially occur through history, and which contemporary Pentecostals are once again redefining through Jesu- names.

With incursions of new religions came a gradual rupture of the spirit of the society that changed even their naming practices. Gradually, "the pathway between moral principles of a people and their ensuing concrete mode of existence or way of being" was gradually forgotten as it yielded to a new order.[45] "Christian" names became customary for Yoruba Christians (and Muslims who converted while accessing social services such as education) from the nineteenth century to the early twentieth century to signify their severance of ties with their paganistic origins and embrace of modern culture.[46] In *The History of the Yorubas*, first published in 1921, Samuel Johnson spoke extensively from a nativist's perspective about this trend in local culture. He complained that modern naming practices were erasing the creativity and the epistemic content embedded into the culture. He worried that modernity's preoccupation with arranging things into alien categories was violently disruptive of how Yoruba people understood naming and lineage tracing. As people adopted the arrangement of having first names, middle names, and surnames,[47] they were forcing their own

---

[44] Gilmore, "Some Notes on Community Nicknaming in Spain."
[45] Wariboko, *Ethics and Society*, 74.
[46] Oyěwùmí, *What Gender Is Motherhood?*, 198.
[47] Surnames, according to Yonge, are also a relatively modern invention even in western cultures.

culture into the constricting box of Western modernity's structure of names to ridiculous results. For example, a married woman becomes Mrs. Taiwo (a name given to the twin child who comes out of the womb first) although she has no twin in her family and her husband is not a twin either. Or, a name like Babarimisa, typically given to a child that was born after the death of his patriarch, becomes a surname and is transmitted across his generations even while the patriarch was yet alive! Johnson ended his disgust of the corruption of Yoruba naming practices with the hope that, with education and further enlightenment, people would see that names like "Phillip Jones or Geoffrey Williams" were not more Christian than names such as "Adewale or Ibiyemi."[48]

If Samuel Johnson could see into contemporary times, he would likely be amused about the different levels of change that Yoruba names have undergone since then and how education has not purged the inclination to change names to reflect social and religious identity. The epochs of African Christianity, like the nationalism waves referenced earlier, produced different attitudes to names. For example, African nationalism once triggered pride in African names,[49] whereas Pentecostalism resulted in both symbolic and inventive indigenous names. In the late '80s to the '90s, born-again Pentecostals changed their surnames that connected them to their ancestral roots to ones that reflected their new heritage in Christ. Through the years, a generation of people whose surnames mark this point in history have not only grown up, they have raised their children with first names that are now more directly connected to their Pentecostal identity; children who will, they hope, raise their own children to do the same. These developments have shown the integration of different social and ethical strands, how much they have plumbed the depths of civic organizational structures, the internal divergences of the faith movement, social impulses, and the "underside" of their oral and embodied theology.[50]

Social and modern infrastructural politics have adapted to accommodate these various changes such that anyone who takes Samuel Johnson's concerns seriously enough to revert to the "old" ways as far as nomenclature is concerned would be an outlier who runs against the grain of societal spirit. The precedence of colonialism that triggered

---

[48] Johnson, *The History of the Yorubas*, 86–89.
[49] Ayandele, *The Missionary Impact on Modern Nigeria, 1842–1914.*
[50] Chitando, "Theology from the Underside," 23.

both the antecedent and consequent of spirit-making gave us a new "call." The "response," through name changing practices, continues to reproduce the social encounters and the ethical changes as seen in Pentecostal naming practices. In the next section, I will provide a list of names, first and last, given in contemporary times and which are specific to Pentecostal practices to consider how they are part of the project of the formation of a power identity that shows how these Pentecostals monumentalize their recreation of the cultural site and its values.

The Spirit of the Spirit

For this work, my assistant and I collected over 200 Jesu- names borne by people who identify as Pentecostals. We sieved through them for trends and new directions in naming practices. Our efforts resulted in the collation of other names such as Gospel, Kingdom, Victor, Victory, Hallelujah, Success, Power, Miracle, Testimony, Dominion, Anointing, Anointed, Divine Heritage, Divine, Winner, Overcomer, Abundance, Prosperity, Billionaire, Faith, and Light, but these do not feature into this analysis for two reasons. One, while those names are mostly borne by Pentecostals, they are not exclusive to them. I found an agnostic who had named his children Vision and Power, and he insisted that his choice of names had nothing to do with the Pentecostal movement. The second reason was that a section of Nigeria, specifically the Niger Delta area, uses names such as Government, Goodluck, Godspower, Chief, Godswill, and Godschild that are quite similar to those of Pentecostals, but their choice of names does not always have a direct correlation to the contemporary Pentecostal movement in Nigeria.

Consequently, we focused on Christological names: the names that have *Jesu* attached to as either prefix, suffix, or part of the stem. Although many of the names collected for our study were first names, a substantial number of them are also surnames that have been altered by the bearers. Among those who had first names were many people who were named at their physical birth by their parents, while some others renamed themselves after conversion. Also, those with "Jesu" surnames are mostly those who altered their family names after their conversion. There were also those that grew up with Jesu- names given to them by their parents, but who had also altered their surnames to reflect their Pentecostal identity. Thus, such name bearers carry names that demonstrate the power of Jesus such as Mosimilejesu Jesusanjo (the first name: I rest on Jesus; second name: Jesus has redeemed the lost time).[51] Such names not only demonstrate where the parents' of the name bearer stand in their conception of their Pentecostal selves, they do so in an ostentatious manner such that when the names are read out either in public or even in a classroom as the child grows up and relates in social settings with their peers, the names ring out to the listeners and tag back to the politics of identity the parents were playing when they made those selections.

We broke our name list down into four categories, although the four groups are not hermetic. Their meanings, origins, and what they attempt to subvert overlap. (Please see Appendix for translation of Jesu- names.) In the first category are names traditionally associated with deities and lineage gods such as the "Ifa" oracle (and prefixed with *Fa-*), Ogun, Osun, Sango, Oya, Esu, Ore, Orisaoko (prefixed as *So-* as in Soyinka), Obaluaye (prefixed as *Oba-* as in Obasanjo), Obatala, Orisha (prefixed as *Osha/Orisha-*) but whose monikers have all been substituted with Jesu. These are names like Jesurinde, Jesujimi, Jesugbemi, Jesumoroti, Jesugbohun(mi), Jesudele, Jesuranti, Jesugbamila Jesutoyinbo, Abajesude, Jesubunmi, Jesuwale, Jesugbero, Jesutola, Jesuwole, Jesukeyede, Jesusina, Jesudele, Jesukoya, Jesukorede, Jesudiran, Jesudipe, Jesugboye, Jesufunke, Jesulabi, Abajesude, Jesuloni(mi), Jesudunmomi, Jesugbamila, Jesuniyi, Jesulana, Jesulola, Jesulere, Jesulokun, Jesulade, Jesudairo, and so on. The names in this category are both first names and surnames, but mostly the latter. Some of their bearers confirm their names have undergone the process of renaming after their born-again conversion or some other life-altering experiences. They claim various reasons for the change, such as divine instructions received directly from God or their spiritual leaders encouraging them to disengage from their "satanic" lineage deities, extricate themselves from negative connections to histories of ancestral and "demon" worship in their families, and make a performative disconnection from ancestors whose incarnation they are supposed to be.

Some of the respondents, born to born-again parents, were named with Jesu right from their births. Some say they consider the name

---

[51]   This name has been altered to protect the identity of the bearer.

prophetic and it forefronts their identity as Christians, while others merely shrugged and said, "it is just a name." Ironically, while some of the bearers of these names have Jesu appended to their first names, their surnames still bear evidence of their familial links to Orishas. This Jesu–first name and Orisha–surname configuration happens mostly in cases of parents or grown-up converts who have had to keep their surnames intact for various reasons: not wanting to sever nomenclatural links with family members who will read other meanings into such a move; being unable to go through the hassle of name-changing and issuance of new documents; wanting to maintain the social capital the family name has accrued in the society; and simply ambivalence toward the actual impact of one's surnames in one's destiny. However, such people, both parents and the converts to Pentecostalism, still chose Jesu–first names because the power that is summoned through the call-and-response of names is believed to be far more reflected in first names than surnames. If they would be identified by power, it is not in the surname shared with other family members but their first names. Besides, as one person mentioned, maintaining both a first name that shows Jesu and a surname that links to an ancestor shows how far they have come in their personal histories. An example of such a combo is a name like Jesugbemi Fajemirokun (Jesus has blessed me, Ifa has allowed me to see the oceans).

In the second category are names that have been traditionally attached to concepts such as Ola (wealth), Olu (the chief, or the Lord), Ayo (Joy), Akin (the valiant one), Omo (child), Ibi (birth), and so on. The examples of the names are Jesutunmise, (or Jesutunwase), Olajesu, Oorejesu, Similejesu, Mosadijesu, Jesujimi, Jesufela, Jesujuwon, Jesutosin, Jesuwumi, Jesujomiloju, Jesusegun, Jesulowo, Jesubukunmi, Jesubukola, Akinjesu, Wurajesu, Jesuwole, Jesukemi, Jesusina, Jesudiran, Jokotijesu, Mojokotijesu, Mojokotolajesu, Jesusogo Jesuwale Jesugbolahan, Olajesu, Ifejesu, Jesufunke, Jesulabi, Jesuniyi, Diekololajesu, Jesulana, Jesuseun. This category is rather expansive because some of the names modified or implanted with Jesu here are similar in construction to the names in the first category. For instance, as there is Falola, there is also Omolola. For those in this category who renamed themselves or gave their children Jesu- names, much of their reasoning stemmed from the jadedness of the traditional prefixes listed here. Traditionally, Yoruba Christians have always been inventive with the language to create "Christian" names, unlike

Muslims who consider their (indigenized) Arabic names Muslim names. Names such as Oluwasegun (God – the Christian one, that is – triumphs) and Oluwatobiloba (God is a great king) are traditionally Yoruba Christian names; they are peculiar to Christian converts who carved such names as indigenous expressions of their faith ethic.

However, the Jesu angle is a more recent development and a culture that will be self-reproducing for many years. That is because even Oluwatobiloba has gradually evolved into Jesutobiloba, and a name like Iyanujesu (the miracle of Jesus) is preferred over Iyanuoluwa (God's miracle). These choices index how people who want to demonstrate their identity as Pentecostals relate it closely to Jesus, the one whose name is the power of self-expression is drawn to define the spirit of the culture. Also, some of the bearers are the Christian Pentecostals of the '80s generations who have grown up and now give their children names with Jesu because, according to some of our respondents, prefixes like Olu/wa, Ola-, Omo-, are jaded and "ambiguous," and no longer distinguish them from Muslims or even nominal or fellow Christians who belong to orthodox denominations. A Jesu- name, they say, has far more edginess to proclamation of their faith.

In the third category are names that are newly created by Pentecostals and do not seem to have any traditional precedent. These Jesu- names seem showier and overtly partisan in appearance, and are also proclamatory of Jesus and the gospel. Such names include Jesuloba, Jesulayoayemi or Jesulayomi, AgbaraJesu, Ayanfejesu, Okiki Jesu, Jesutisomiji, Jesuloluwa, Abajesurin, Obajesu, Obanijesu, Jesugboromiro, Jesudolapofunmi, Jesudolamu, Tijesu or Tijesunimi, Teminijesu, Ogojesu, Ooreofejesu, Ifejesu, Jesupamilerin, Jesunipinmi, Jesunitemi, Jesunifemi, Jesuniye, Jesunbo, Jesunbowale, Jesudunsin, Jesulolami, Jesudowolemi, Jesunimofe, and Jesufemi. As one of our respondents said, his father gave him the name Jesutobi purely by a divine instruction, which came at a time they were celebrating the birth of what his father thought would be his second and last child. These names, like biblical names, are thought to be both definitive and distinguishing.[52]

Finally, there are names such as Jesutunde, Jesuwande, Jesujide, Jesujimade, Jesudurotimi, Jesujide, Jesugbeye, Jesudola, Jesuwole,

---

[52] Botterweck, Ringgren & Heinz-Josef Fabry, *Theological Dictionary of the Old Testament*.

Jesulaja, Jesugboye, and Jesujaguntolu. In this category are names that were previously abiku names or which depicted a situation around when a child was born but whose meaning has now been usurped by "Jesu," thus giving a different meaning to the names. For instance, a name like "Durotimi" (Stay with me) is a mother's plea to an abiku/ogbanje child not to die. Another example is Dairo (Make this one stay), which is sometimes rendered as Fadairo or Ogundairo. A name like Jesutunde, in a sense, also belongs to this category. When Jesu is transposed into these names, the names take on an entirely new meaning that overshadows their etymological origins as a plea to supernatural power to intercede in repeated cycles of child deaths. A name like Jesudurotimi now becomes "Jesus stays with me" while Jesudairo becomes "Jesus made this one stay." Also, in this category are names like Otegbeye (Conspiracy/strife becomes a thing of honour) and Omolaja (This child has come to reconcile warring factions) that become Jesugbeye and Jesulaja respectively. Some of the respondents in this category claimed that the names had no link to how they were traditionally expressed, and they just coined it because it suited them or their circumstances.

Overall, there are several conclusions to be drawn from the pattern of Jesu- names. One is their tendency toward monotheism, a development that erases the diversity of Orishas and lineage deities in Yoruba land. From the examples of names in our first category, where there were a number of references to Orishas such as Ogun, Oya, Osun, Oba, Sango, and Esu, we see a replacement of these deities or a transvaluation of their ethical systems recalibrated. Their diversity has been stylistically subsumed under the name of Jesus, a singular deity. The contemporary Christians who choose these Jesu- names are going into the imagined place of African origin to rearrange their history. By removing the "devil" and his pagan essences from their names, they can comfortably respond to the call of history made by Pentecostalism by inserting Jesus into their life to retroactively rewrite their origins Their name construction invokes the idea or the belief that a supernatural force inheres in them, and the capability of that force is being drawn out in their daily lives. Those who bear such names also engage in a public act of self-deification. They apotheosize themselves, not merely to be a miniaturized version of Jesus or the Christian God, but to conjure – and share with others – the myth that they share in the divinization of Jesus, the transforming capabilities of His power and the glory, and overall, derive the social and supernatural blessings that accrue from being named with the name of Jesus.

The irony is that in trying to erase the demonic history in their names, they resound its presence and make it resonate even more. As someone remarked tongue in cheek, "How do you address a woman who named her child Esupofo when you abbreviate the name? Do you call her Mama Esu (mother of Esu)? Or Mama Ofo (mother of losses/failure or nothing)?" What seemed like a silly joke about the new names has a point worth pondering. Esu is the Yoruba god of mischief, among other roles, but has been cast in modern Christianity as the equivalent translation of the devil and demons. A name like Esupofo is therefore both a prayer and a declaration of the Christian victory not only over the devil, but also over a pagan past. In actually using the name, they encounter some snafu. Since most people who use other people's names typically abbreviate them for usability, a name like Esupofo, when abridged to either Esu or Pofo, undermines the purpose of identity affirmation and supplications the giver of the name intended. The name is only meaningful when used in full, and others around who use the name toy with the bearer of the name by shortening it. That way, they keep the new convert who changed his/her name down to earth, a form of discontinuity that enforces continuity, a disconnection that ironically also reconnects. Those who bear names like Esupofo *still* bear Esu's name even though their stance antagonizes the deity. In trying to cover up the African demons, they put them in an echo chamber. Each time someone who has replaced his "pagan" name with Jesu mentions the name, those familiar with the culture hear the silence of a family deity that the name bearers have commuted into a demon and strove hard to wash out from their culture and history. There is therefore no permanent erasure in this instance.

While some scholars that I have consulted in the course of this work consider the Jesu pattern an erasure of indigenous culture, particularly the ones that substitute the local gods with Jesus, there is also an expansion. In the world of the Yoruba people where different gods coexist, Jesu- names widen the pantheon to accommodate Jesus as one of their deities. Pentecostal Christians might disagree that Jesus is merely another god in a pantheon and instead argue that he is *the* God. However, because he takes the place that the gods have traditionally occupied in Yoruba names, Jesus too becomes another mythic figure. In the same vein, names that depict family professions and similar characteristics found in names such as Ayan- (for a family of drummers) or Ode- (for a family of hunters) or Oje- (for a family entrusted with egungun masquerade traditions) no longer feature in these patterns. The same development is true for the names that are called *amutorunwa* (literally translated as names given from heaven but means names that have self-selected prior to birth such as the ones given to twins). In fact, as one of the respondents told me, her Jesu name is an amotorunwa name because the inspiration for the name came directly from "heaven above." In her conception, heaven has shifted from the Yoruba idea of where immaterial beings reside to the Christian one occupied by the Trinity – God the Father, Son, and Holy Spirit – and other celestial beings.

Another observation is that the collection does not feature names registering negativity, despair, rebellion, criticism, or even expressing disappointment using proverbial language. The Jesu- names register victory and power, or at least prayer for them. For instance, it was not uncommon for Yorubas to have names like Fatanmi (Ifa deceived me), Matanmi (Do not deceive me.), Ebisemiju (The family offended me too much), and Bekolari (Things did not go as expected). Jesu- names are either determinedly contrived as prayer or describe the joys of being a follower of Jesus. None of the names we came across were critical of the Christian God for whatever reason, unlike what can be found in traditional indigenous names. The curious one, however, was the Fatoyinbo surname that was changed to Jesutoyinbo. While some arguments do arise on the meaning of Yoruba names and their recondite meanings lost to time, development of writing, and the tonality of language, *Fatoyinbo* is translatable to "Ifa is equal to – or up to – the level of the white man," a line of thinking that has been attributed to the kind of relationship "natives" had with the colonial officers. By implication, *Jesutoyinbo* means that Jesus is being equated to the white man where whiteness denotes (colonial) domination and power. However, one defense of such choice by the name bearer is that the translation is less important than the banner of Jesus they bear alongside the name. Thus, the semantic content of the name is not so much in the meaning but in the reason behind the selection.

In naming children with Jesu- names, Pentecostals also express the Christological spirit of the times. In the name of Jesus, they have found power; they perform the power through a series of actions that strengthen their essence as people of power. Names are an important site for this performance because they are given to an individual for others to use, to share, to connect. The name is how they share their self-definition, and also relate the prayers and promises of establishing that identity through life. In naming, they order their being as people of power and do so in relation to others. By saying it is the spirit that names the child, and they do not come by their names as personal effort, they also indicate their belonging to a higher power from whom they draw their identity as people of power. In giving Jesu-names, the spirit facilitates a congruence between individual identity and the values of a society it is reshaping in its own image. Because modern society is heterogeneous and cannot have the ethic coherence of traditional societies like Umuofia, names still plot the graph of the ground that Pentecostal Christianity has won and which will continue to multiply across generations.

Appendix

Abajesude – the one who arrives with Jesus
Abajesude – the one who arrives with Jesus
Abajesurin – the one who walks with Jesus
AgbaraJesu – power of Jesus
Akinjesu – Jesus' warrior/champion
Ayanfejesu – the beloved of Jesus
Ifejesu – the love of Jesus
Ifejesu – the love of Jesus
Jesubukola – Jesus adds to my wealth
Jesubukunmi – Jesus adds to me
Jesubunmi – Jesus has given me this
Jesudairo – Jesus holds this one down
Jesudele – Jesus has arrived home
Jesudele – Jesus has come home
Jesudipe – Jesus supplicated (on my behalf)
Jesudiran – Jesus is multiplied across generations
Jesudola – Jesus has become wealth
Jesudolami – Jesus has become my wealth
Jesudolami – Jesus has become my wealth
Jesudolapofunmi – Jesus condenses different forms of wealth together in this one

Jesudowole – Jesus laid hands on (this one)
Jesudunmomi – Jesus is sweet to me
Jesudunsin – Jesus is sweet/pleasant to serve
Jesudurotimi (abiku name) – Jesus stayed with me
Jesufela – Jesus spreads wealth
Jesufemi – Jesus loves me
Jesufunke – Jesus gave me this one (child) to care for
Jesugbamila – Jesus has delivered/saved me
Jesugbemi – Jesus has benefitted me
Jesugbemi Fajemirokun – Ifa allowed me to sight the ocean
Jesugbemiro – Jesus upholds me
Jesugbohunmi – Jesus heard my voice
Jesugbolahan – Jesus exposes/showcases wealth
Jesugboromiro – Jesus interceded on my behalf
Jesugboye – Jesus has received honor
Jesujaguntolu – Jesus fought the battle like the chief one
Jesujide – Jesus has arisen and arrived
Jesujide – Jesus has arisen/awoken to come (here)
Jesujimade – Jesus arises to nobility
Jesujimi – Jesus entrusts (this) to me
Jesujomiloju – Jesus has surprised me
Jesujuwon – Jesus is bigger than/beyond them
Jesukemi – Jesus has blessed me
Jesukeyede – Jesus brings honor (through this one)
Jesukorede – Jesus has brought goodness
Jesukoya – Jesus has rejected suffering (on my behalf)
Jesulabi – we gave birth to Jesus
Jesulade – Jesus is nobility
Jesulaja – Jesus has settled the strife
Jesulana – Jesus paves the way
Jesulayoayemi – Jesus is the joy of my life
Jesulayomi – Jesus is my joy
Jesulere – there is gain in Jesus
Jesuloba – Jesus is king
Jesulokun – Jesus is the link
Jesulola – Jesus is wealth
Jesulolami – Jesus is my joy
Jesuloluwa – Jesus is Lord
Jesulonimi – Jesus is the one that owns me

Jesulowo – Jesus has honor/is honorable
Jesumoroti – Jesus is the one I stand with
Jesunbo – Jesus is coming back
Jesunbowale – Jesus is coming home
Jesunifemi – Jesus is my love
Jesunimofe – it is Jesus that I want
Jesunipinmi – Jesus is my portion
Jesunitemi – Jesus is mine
Jesuniye – Jesus is life
Jesuniyi – Jesus has honor
Jesupamilerin – Jesus made me laugh
Jesuranti – Jesus remembers
Jesurinde – Jesus has walked back (on foot) (to this world)
Jesusegun – Jesus is victorious
Jesuseun – thanks to Jesus
Jesusina – Jesus opens the way
Jesusogo – Jesus has made (this) glorious
Jesutisomiji – Jesus has quickened me (or animated me)
Jesutola – Jesus is enough as wealth
Jesutosin – Jesus is worthy to be worshipped
Jesutoyinbo – Jesus is equivalent to the white man
Jesutunde – Jesus has arrived again
Jesutunmise – Jesus has refurbished my lot
Jesutunwase – Jesus has refurbished our lot
Jesuwale – Jesus has come home
Jesuwande – Jesus has sought me out
Jesuwole – Jesus has entered the house
Jesuwumi – I desire Jesus
Jesuyemi – Jesus befits me
Jokotijesu – sit with Jesus
Mojokotijesu – I sit with Jesus
Mojokotolajesu – I sit with the wealth of Jesus
Mosadijesu – I hide in Jesus
Mosimilejesu – I rest/rely on Jesus
Obajesu – King Jesus
Obanijesu – Jesus is king
Okiki jesu – the fame of Jesus
Olajesu – the wealth of Jesus
Oogojesu – the glory of Jesus

Oorejesu – gift of Jesus
Oreofejesu – the grace of Jesus
Similejesu – rest/rely on Jesus
Teminijesu – Jesus is mine
Tijesu(ni) – (this child) belongs to Jesus
Wurajesu – Jesus' gold

Conclusion: Power Must Change Hands: COVID-19, Power, and the Imperative of Knowledge

The substantial part of this book was already written when the COVID-19 apocalypse hit and things changed for the whole world. I had already sketched the conclusion to this book. The closing thoughts considered how the paradoxes of Pentecostal power as a dominant force and sometimes as embattled might continue to play out in broader cultural contexts. As the primary means of Pentecostal self-recognition, power aggregates the sum of their worship, habits, values, and collective memories. It is not just external characteristics that define power identity, but also their politics, attitudes, and partisan divides on various cultural issues. In a society like Nigeria, people have been through many years of military dictatorship and have witnessed authoritarian uses of power. The transition to democratic forms of government – despite its initial promises of liberation from state oppression – has fallen short of empowering the people. Subsequently, they have become more prone to seeking supernatural power that would manifest through them in the sociopolitical sphere. My proposed quest was to raise the questions of the constitution and history of power identity, how they interact with other ideological elements that make up the society and the changes that have occurred within the social milieu as people manifest power identity.

The modes of strategic self-differentiation that define Pentecostals, I noted, were best explored through their performances. While Pentecostals, like most Christians, generally balk at the idea that their boisterous worship activity was "a performance," they also understood their actions as processes of producing meanings that ultimately establishes their power identity. Consequently, they are constantly in a performative mode as they position themselves against an *other*. The power identity, unlike identities based on physical characteristics or marked in material ways, cannot be taken for granted because it is frequently challenged and has to be continuously performed power to be sustained. The unceasing will to perform power has broader social implications in a supposedly democratic society like Nigeria because it means power is constantly tested against an *other* to establish its reality.

Power identity is unique because its makeup is performative, and the condition of its existence is based on the continuity of its performance to disrupt an existing order and inaugurate the Pentecostal status before all witnesses. They have to unceasingly mobilize both social and spiritual imaginaries to generate the range of acts that will challenge the social order and confirm their identity. The impossibility of ever standing at ease, their never taking a break from the eternal vigilance of watching over their identity so as not to lose it, defines their social behavior at all levels. Thus, when COVID-19 happened in 2020, it not only tested the claims of Nigerian Pentecostals – particularly its leadership – as the people of power, their actions made me consider how power identity as it is presently constituted could hold up during a world-altering event like the pandemic. It became another transitional phase for a faith whose power identity was already in a process of social transitions.

At first, when the news of a viral disease began to roll in from China in the earlier part of the year 2020, it seemed all too remote for anyone to be anxious. When the first case of COVID-19 got to Nigeria in late February, it was through an Italian worker in a Nigerian company who had flown into the country. Even though there was some panic that the disease had finally berthed, the bigger fears people grappled with were spurred by the well-meaning foreign organizations who kept saying they worried about Africa and their well-known fragile medical system in the face of the disease. The World Health Organization noted that the threat to Africa was "considerable." The billionaire philanthropists, Bill and Melinda Gates, had some unpleasant predictions about the fate of Africa in the coming months. Already, the challenge several European countries faced circulated in the media and Africans rightly agonized about what would become of less-endowed countries like theirs if rich and powerful countries with advanced medical systems could not stand up to the disease. There was so much palpable fear in the minds of people as they tried to discern what was happening, but there was nothing in the way of knowledge or insight they had that adequately responded to such a befuddling moment. Since this book and its writer were caught in the vortex of events, I decided to use this conclusion to offer my reflections on what the COVID-19 pandemic portends for all, especially for Pentecostalism, a faith and cultural movement of people whose identity is power.

One of the earliest interventions from the Pentecostal circuit came from David Elijah of the Glorious Mount of Possibility, who went viral when he claimed he was going to China to "destroy coronavirus." According to him, "Where there is a prophet people cannot die. I cannot be a prophet in this world and China is dying. It is not possible!"[1] He would soon become a meme online and the target of many fake news websites who claimed he had been infected with the virus while praying for people in China. Another, Kingsley Innocent "Talknado," described the virus as a hoax, and the funds budgeted for tackling the disease was simply another means for Nigeria's corrupt political class to release the funds they would eventually embezzle. He even added that coronavirus could never enter Nigeria, and if it ever did, it would be destroyed by "corrosive anointing."[2] At that time, people had begun to worry: these pastors, unable to offer anything more than such self-aggrandizement, appeared rather frivolous.

By the time the number of cases began to multiply and the world's most powerful economies went into a tailspin, people looked around wildly for answers. As the nation started to shut down to slow down the spread of the virus, a people who had long been accustomed to seeking the face of God in puzzling situations and listening to their pastors wanted to know what was happening. Nigerians used to sensationalist prophecies by their pastors at the beginning of every new year could not fathom why the spiritual sensors of their leaders failed to detect one of the most significant historical events of the twenty-first century so far. The apocalypticism of COVID-19 thus exposed not only the vulnerability of our human bodies – both rich and poor alike – and our constructed global economic and political systems, the effects landed on the consortium of Pentecostal pastors too. Nigerians, thoroughly bewildered by the scale of events, turned to their pastors to ask how they could not have seen any of these incidences coming.

In some of the WhatsApp messages shared at that time of great bewilderment, people quoted the Bible, Amos 3:7, where God said he would not do anything without revealing it to his servants, the prophets. They asked themselves how come none of God's prophets

---

[1]   https://wrqk.iheart.com/featured/the-stansbury-show/content/2020-03-09-a-nig erian-pastor-says-he-will-prophetically-destroy-the-coronavirus/
[2]   www.youtube.com/watch?v=6uPl6AWnS9g

saw this coming and forewarned the people of God? How could they not have seen all of the effects of COVID-19 ahead? Where were the power and the anointing that pastors had always boasted to restore the world furiously spinning out of control back on its orbit? By the time people started asking questions and even the most powerful pastors who had previously always claimed access to arcane knowledge came up short, it was clear that the pandemic had demystified the Pentecostal pastorate, their claims of miracles of healing, the foresight of their prophecies, and the unrestricted access pastors say they have to the supernatural realm.

Pentecostals, the people of power, found themselves in dire straits where the power to manipulate signs and symbols to produce meaning did not answer to this world-changing event. Over the years, they had built powerful empires in the forms of huge cathedrals and enterprises, enthroned politicians to become a part of the political elite, and they had been at the forefront of the production of public culture. However, COVID-19 did not respond to the various forms of power they had accumulated and performed for the public. The period of the initial lockdown was a traumatic one in the history of contemporary Nigeria because it showed people who did not have the right divination instruments to interpret the times and were therefore as lost as those deemed powerless. Everything they had flaunted as proof of their power now seemed pretty useless in combatting this life-changing event.

Putting up stunning architectural masterpieces and drawing large crowds are some of the ways churches have established their degree of power within the social culture. For instance, in 1999, Bishop David Oyedepo of Living Faith International (Winners' Chapel) dedicated the Faith Tabernacle, a church building with a capacity to seat up to 50,000 people. By 2015, the Bishop announced they were commencing Faith Theatre, a building that would sit up to 100,000 people. In 2018, Pastor Paul Enenche of Dunamis International Gospel Centre dedicated Glory Dome, a church with the reputed capacity to contain 100,000 people, about the largest in the whole world. In 2019, Pastor Adeboye said during a church program that he would not rest until he had built a church the size of Ibadan (one of the largest cities in Africa with 1,189 square miles). He said, "If anybody tells you Pastor Adeboye is dead, don't believe them because God is going to build us the auditorium as big as Ibadan. Until that is done, I'm not going anywhere." Each time these pastors have put up or have announced they would be putting up these buildings, they draw flak from people who have seen these projects as self-glorification projects. When the pandemic broke, none of those conventional ways of performing power responded to the crisis.

It is not surprising that people ask their pastors for clarity at a crucial moment in history when they were confounded by a crisis of meaning and expect an answer. For centuries, religion has been a source of meaning-making for people as they are caught in events that upend their world. Also, as I showed in Chapters 1 and 2, when Pentecostals say they are a people of power, there is a legitimate basis for that assertion. Abuse by military dictators eroded intellectualism and the trust people should have had in their government and institutions. After the years of corrupt leadership, people have grown thoroughly cynical of their government and eminently distrustful that bureaucratic efforts are sincere enough to improve their lot. Also, trained expertise long ago left the deliberative public square and their spaces mostly taken up by pastors and religious leaders. Some of them, professors of science before they became pastors, still towed the familiar path of mysticism and relentless pursuit of demonic forces. That exchange left Nigeria bereft of critical insights necessary to confront moments such as the one birthed by the COVID-19 virus. The sense of uncertainty became more acute as the days passed and people remained in isolation, fatigued from inactivity. With no sense of clarity of what was happening on a larger scale, and no other sources of information than conspiracy theories forwarded across WhatsApp and other social media networks, people resorted to seeking alternative and unofficial sources of information. The pastors themselves scrambled for answers as the fear of what would befall the country in the face of this unprecedented event hit.

From declaring the pandemic a demonic attack to sharing conspiracy theories, Pentecostal leaders' response to their anxious congregants to provide a moral meaning to the moment fell short of the reassurance the public needed. The world these pastors now operate in, as I showed in much of Chapters 3 and 4, is one where their ability to make meanings and generate myths is also attenuated by the public who easily generate momentum through the force of social media commentary. Consequently, they met the pastor's intervention with ridicule and severe criticism. As the days passed and there was still no more clarity on what the role of pastors would be in the mega-drama unfolding in the world, pastors who could not figure out their roles in this meaning-changing event reached for familiar gimmicks of attributing things to demons and some mystical forces that wanted to institute a new world order.

As I described in both Chapters 1 and 2, Pentecostalism has regularly used the specter of the devil to evoke notions of radical evil and thereby provoke people to pray against contrary situations. As such, when the pandemic hit, the allure of the whole world being embattled by a secret elite group who wanted to take over the world was too powerful to resist. This also circulated in the USA, where some claimed the pandemic was about a coming new world order being instituted by those who wanted to take over the US presidency from the Lord's chosen, Donald Trump. As I also mentioned in Chapter 2, Trump's presidency is important to a subset of Nigerian Christians because he represents the political power they vicariously gained after they lost ground in their own country.

These reactionary tactics were also responses to being routinely ridiculed by people who wondered why they could not re-enact miracles of healing by saving the world from COVID-19. Some people definitely believed that there was indeed a global elite conspiracy afoot, but across social media networks other people gleefully circulated memes, jokes, and long essays about the failure of people who had always claimed to be people of power to rise to a historical moment. They were ridiculed for waiting for scientists to come up with a vaccine for COVID-19 so that they could safely resume their healing miracles. These responses during the pandemic, especially when churches were shut, suggested Pentecostal leaders were trying too hard to wrest control back from the consequences of the pandemic. Unlike the joke factory where they can control the production through their relationship with comedians as I described in Chapter 5, this global event was well beyond their purview.

These roiling issues, the attacks on church institutions and their counter-attacks demonstrate a few developments: first is the fact that Pentecostals might have maintained a power identity over the years, but their claims to supernatural power were demystified even as the established hierarchies were being inverted. The pandemic-induced corrosion was a culmination of many years of the systematic challenge of their role as mediators of meaning. As Chapters 3 and 4 of this book demonstrate, the social media and the various activities that take place on it have been crucial to the "see finish" of these pastors, especially ones who have always claimed special access to divine supernatural power. There has already been the "proletarianization" of power and the incumbent diminution of their authority. The anti-authoritarian impulse of divine revelation that can take place outside the purview of leadership power is already asserting itself in moments such as the *Free the Sheeple* movement and the inherent democratic critique of #MeToo #ChurchToo. When the #ChurchToo moment occurred and people claimed everyone was just as anointed as their leaders, they were already seeking to clip the wings of the powerful leaders. In the past, an anointed man of God telling his congregation that God had revealed to him that the pandemic was a plot against the US president would have stayed largely within the precincts of his church while the effect of that vision on his congregation seeped out into larger the culture. However, these days those messages escape the bounds of their church as soon as they have been delivered. They find their way to social media where a contrarian audience lampoons them, and a believing congregation has to become hyper-defensive on behalf of their faith.

Second is the fact that though they might be a people of power and have established that in various ways, the COVID-19 pandemic showed the limits of the kind of power that they have accumulated. The public opposition to their building another church as big as Ibadan, for instance, is an important criticism, and it testifies to what people desire from formidable institutions such as the church. The churches have already impacted every sphere of the society with its ethos: media, popular culture, politics, education, economic systems, publishing, commerce, and even transnational global flows. There is virtually no area left untouched, and there is no sphere of cultural activity that they are not already involved in, either directly or indirectly.

As I showed in Chapter 6, even newborn children are already imprinted with the name of Jesus and the underlying politics of power demonstration. They will grow up in a society dominated by huge cathedrals, but equipped with scant scientific answers to challenging questions posed by the realities of living in a global world. Critics who say Nigeria needs more factories and not more churches thus reflect a desire to see the Pentecostal church do more in terms of developing a social agenda rather than raising up bigger cathedrals. Pentecostals have acquired immense economic and political resources, and most of the tools of social reproduction now lay within their hands, but COVID-19 showed the limits of that power. Spouting conspiracies theories of 5G technology and a new world order, anti-China sentiments, pro-Trump arguments, devil-blaming rhetoric, and so on, were an attempt to grapple with the apocalyptic moment of COVID-19. They have acquired the power to manipulate signs and symbols to generate even more power, but they were greatly confounded by the event of the pandemic.

So, what might be the way forward for people who identity themselves by power? The response of two pastors to the pandemic particularly interests me here, and they might be pointers to directions worth pursuing. One was Pastor Temitope B. Joshua, the leader of the Synagogue Church of all Nations, who prophesied in the early days of the pandemic that on March 27, 2020, the pandemic would simply "go the way it came": whether a vaccine was developed or not, it would just disappear. Before resorting to preaching conspiracy theories retailed from QAnon, Apostle Johnson Suleman of Omega Fire Ministries International also said God told him that the virus would go the way it came, and it would simply "disappear." He said, "You are going to discover you will not hear about it anymore. Because the same way it came, is how it will go. Everything will return to normal. Don't fear." They made these prophecies early in the pandemic, clearly underestimating its potential impact in the following months. It is quite tempting to dismiss these pastors as merely swinging a bat to hit anything by sheer coincidence, but what they said is actually consistent with scientific understanding of the lifecycle of viruses and diseases. Viruses truly do "disappear" after containment initiatives like social distancing, quarantines, and travel restrictions have slowed down the spread of the disease. Those public health initiatives are deemed to have worked when the transmission chain is broken, the virus can no longer find new vectors, and existing carriers have recovered.

So while they might have masked their response in religious language, in playing the role of epidemiological experts, they still deferred to objective knowledge. If they could do that privately in order to make public prophetic declarations, why mystify knowledge? Why not tell the congregation what science says about viruses and let the people see the secular sleight of hand that underpins such prophecies? The lesson from the pandemic is the imperative of power changing hands. The title of one of the regular programs of the MFM megachurch, *Power Must*

Change Hands, should be regarded as a call to Pentecostals and the wielders of power within its ranks. After years of claiming the power to bend reality and change the course of human affairs, there is a need to face the fact that power needs to change hands from the myth-making prophets whose utterances are based on inspired visions to those who foretell based on informed and rational knowledge.

Why not let power change hands to those of actual scientists who generate this knowledge? In a 2009 *New York Times* article written about the exploits of the African Pentecostal churches in the USA, it was striking to note that one of the pastors, the head of the RCCG church in North America at the time, and a former automotive-design engineer with an M.B.A. and some business experience running a Wendy's franchise, brought all those secular experiences into setting up the church chain in the USA. While many claims can be made about how the power of God instituted diaspora churches, the empirical reality is that worldly business knowledge and techniques also played an important role. Pentecostalism would not have been as successful if the pastors had not been trained up to a certain level of education and expertise. The reality is that much of their power and success came from mastery of secular knowledge, so why is there so much mysticism?

Pentecostalism attained prominence because its proponents claimed a close alliance with supernatural forces. However, beneath the public act of praying for miracles and receiving them, non-spiritual techniques that actually make things work are also applied but mostly redacted making natural phenomena appear as magical. Those who claim ability to manipulate the supernatural to make things happen are treated as a repository of transcendent knowledge. Rather than people seeking to empower themselves, knowledge and understanding are cloaked in mystery. The trouble is that the mystification of scientific knowledge has its limitations for social growth and development. The fact that religious leaders themselves depend on rational techniques shows the imperative of ripping the veil and letting the people see that the wizard behind the curtain is just an ordinary man working a set of machines. There is no supernatural force healing people or rewarding them with an untold wealth that can match the near-endless possibilities engendered by secular knowledge of social development and modern medicine. Approaches to faith practices and power grabbing need evolve to accommodate knowledge. Although the Pentecostal belief in magicality has had its role in propelling Pentecostal movement adherents to great heights, COVID-19 showed the limits of how much the mythologization of temporal concerns and solutions could be sustained. To play in the exacting confines of the secular, there is no other choice than to face up to the long-term powerlessness or irrelevance of the claims of supernatural powers in the affairs of the modern world.

Select Bibliography

Monographs, Journal Articles, and Web-Published Articles

Achebe, Chinua. *Morning Yet on Creation Day: Essays*. Ibadan: Heinemann, 1975.

Achebe, Chinua. *Things Fall Apart*. Ibadan: Heinemann Educational Publisher, 1996.

Achebe, Chinua. Cited in *Listening to the Gentle Voice: Rhetorical Strategies in Things Fall Apart*. Chima Anyadike and Kehinde A. Ayoola, eds. Ibadan: HEBN Publishers, 2012: 311–312.

Achebe, Christie C. "Literary Insights into the 'Ogbanje' Phenomenon." *Journal of African Studies* 7: 1 (1980): 31–38.

Achunike, Hilary C. *The Influences of Pentecostalism on Catholic Priests and Seminarians in Nigeria*. Bloomington: iUniverse, 2019.

Adeboye, O. "Transnational Pentecostalism in Africa: The Redeemed Christian Church of God, Nigeria" in Laurent Fourchard, ed., *Entreprises Religieuses Transnationales En Afrique De L'Ouest*. Paris: Karthala Editions, 2005: 439–465.

Adeboye, Olufunke. "'A Church in a Cinema Hall?' Pentecostal Appropriation of Public Space in Nigeria." *Journal of Religion in Africa* 42: 2 (2012): 145–171.

Adeboye, Olufunke. "Explaining the Growth and Legitimation of the Pentecostal Movement in Africa" in Adeshina Afolayan, Olajumoke Yacob-Haliso, and Toyin Falola, eds., *Pentecostalism and Politics in Africa*. London: Palgrave Macmillan, 2018: 25–39.

Adedeji, Joel A. "The Church and the Emergence of the Nigerian Theatre, 1866–1914." *Journal of the Historical Society of Nigeria* (1971): 25–45.

Adedeji, J. A. "The Church and The Emergence of The Nigerian Theatre: 1915–1945." *Journal of the Historical Society of Nigeria* (1973): 387–396.

Adelakun, Abimbola Adunni. "Pastocracy: Performing Pentecostal Politics in Africa" in Kenneth Kalu, Olajumoke Yacob-Haliso, and Toyin Falola, eds., *Africa's Big Men: Predatory State-Society Relations in Africa*. New York: Routledge, 2018: 1010–1118.

Adelakun, Abimbola. "Pentecostal Panopticism and the Phantasm of 'The Ultimate Power'" in Adeshina Afolayan, Olajumoke Yacob-Haliso, and Toyin Falola, eds., *Pentecostalism and Politics in Africa*. London: Palgrave Macmillan, 2018: 101–118.

Adelakun, Abimbola A. "Black Lives Matter! Nigerian Lives Matter!: Language and Why Black Performance Matters." *Genealogy* 3: 2 (2019).

Adenrele, Adetoro Rasheed. "Boko Haram Insurgency in Nigeria as a Symptom of Poverty and Political Alienation." *IOSR Journal of Humanities and Social Science* 3:5 (2012): 21–26.

Adesokan, Akinwumi. *Postcolonial Artists and Global Aesthetics*. Bloomington: Indiana University Press, 2011.

Adetula, Victor A. O. "Nigeria's Rebased Economy and Its Role in Regional and Global Politics." *E-International Relations* 13 (2014): 1–13.

Adogame, Afe. "Politicization of Religion and Religionization of Politics in Nigeria" in Chima J. Korieh and G. Ugo Nwokeji, eds., *Religion, History, and Politics in Nigeria*. Maryland: University Press of America, 2005: 125–139.

Adogame, Afe. "To God Be the Glory: Home Videos, the Internet, and Religio-cultural Identity in Contemporary African Christianity." *Critical Interventions* 2: 3–4 (2008): 147–159.

Adogame, Afe. *Religion Crossing Boundaries: Transnational Religious and Social Dynamics in Africa and the New African Diaspora*. Leiden: Brill, 2010.

Adogame, Afe. "Transnational Migration and Pentecostalism in Europe." *Penteco-Studies: An Interdisciplinary Journal for Research on the Pentecostal and Charismatic Movements* 9: 1 (2010): 56–73.

Adogame, Afe. "Dealing with Local Satanic Technology: Deliverance Rhetoric in the Mountain of Fire and Miracles Ministries." *Journal of World Christianity* 5: 1 (2012): 75–101.

Adogame, Afe. "The Anthropology of Evil" in Kenneth R. Ross, J. Kwabena Asamoah-Gyadu, and Todd M. Johnson, eds., *Christianity in Sub-Saharan Africa*. Scotland: Edinburgh University Press, 2017: 433–444.

Afolayan, Adeshina. "Hilarity and the Nigerian Condition." *The Journal of Pan African Studies* 6: 5 (2013): 156–174.

Agre, Philip E. "Real-Time Politics: The Internet and the Political Process." *The Information Society* 18: 5 (2002): 311–331.

Agyekum, Kofi. "The Sociolinguistic of Akan Personal Names." *Nordic Journal of African Studies* 15: 2 (2006): 206–235.

Ajayi, J. F. Ade. *Christian Missions in Nigeria, 1841–1891: The Making of a New Elite*. Ibadan: Longman, 1965.

Ajibade, Babson. "'Lady No Be So': The Image of Women in Contemporary Church Posters in Nigeria." *Visual Studies* 27: 3 (2012): 237–247.

Akinade, Akintunde E. *Christian Responses to Islam in Nigeria: A Contextual Study of Ambivalent Encounters.* New York: Palgrave Macmillan, 2014.

Akinade, Akintunde E. "Holy Dilemma: Engaging Prayer and Power in African Pentecostalism." *Journal of World Christianity* 10: 2 (2020): 147–169.

Akinnaso, F. Niyi. "The Sociolinguistic Basis of Yoruba Personal Names." *Anthropological Linguistics* 22: 7 (1980): 278–279.

Akingbe, Niyi. "Saints and Sinners: Protest in Waiting for Angel." *Journal of International Social Research* 3: 11 (2010): 27–32.

Akinola, Olabanji. "Boko Haram Insurgency in Nigeria: Between Islamic Fundamentalism, Politics, and Poverty." *African Security* 8: 1 (2015): 1–29.

Albrecht, Daniel E. *Rites in the Spirit: A Ritual Approach to Pentecostal/Charismatic Spirituality.* Sheffield: Sheffield Academic Press, 1999.

Alford, C. Fred. *What Evil Means to Us.* Ithaca: Cornell University Press, 1997.

Ambrose, Linda M., and Kimberly Alexander. "Pentecostal Studies Face the #MeToo Movement: Introduction." *Pneuma* 41: 1 (2019): 1–7.

Anderson, Allan Heaton. *Spirit-Filled World: Religious Dis/Continuity in African Pentecostalism.* New York City: Springer, 2018.

Apter, Andrew. *The Pan-African Nation: Oil and the Spectacle of Culture in Nigeria.* Chicago: University of Chicago Press, 2008.

Apter, David E. "Politics as Theatre: An Alternative View of the Rationalities of Power" in Jeffrey C. Alexander, Bernhard Giesen, and Jason L. Mast, eds., *Social Performance: Symbolic Action, Cultural Pragmatics, and Ritual.* Cambridge: Cambridge University Press, 2006: 218–256.

Asaju, Dapo F. "Noise, Fire and Flame: Anointing and Breakthrough Phenomena among the Evangelicals" in David O. Ogungbile and Akintunde E. Akinade, eds., *Creativity and Change in Nigerian Christianity.* Lagos: Malthouse Press, 2010: 95–108.

Asamoah-Gyadu, J. Kwabena. "Anointing through the Screen: Neo-Pentecostalism and Televised Christianity in Ghana." *Studies in World Christianity* 11: 1 (2005): 9–28.

Asamoah-Gyadu, J. Kwabena. ""Get on the Internet!" Says the LORD': Religion, Cyberspace and Christianity in Contemporary Africa." *Studies in World Christianity* 13: 3 (2007): 225–242.

Asamoah-Gyadu, J. Kwabena. "Mediating Spiritual Power: African Christianity, Transnationalism and the Media" in Afe Adogame and Jim Spickard, eds., *Religion Crossing Boundaries: Transnational Religious and Social Dynamics in Africa and the New African Diaspora.* Leiden: Brill, 2010: 87–103.

Asamoah-Gyadu, J. Kwabena. "Spirit, Mission and Transnational Influence: Nigerian-Led Pentecostalism in Eastern Europe." *PentecoStudies* 9: 1 (2010): 74–96.

Asamoah-Gyadu, J. Kwabena. *Contemporary Pentecostal Christianity: Interpretations from an African Context.* Oregon: Wipf and Stock Publishers, 2013.

Asamoah-Gyadu, J. Kwabena. "Pentecostalism and the Transformation of the African Christian Landscape" in Martin Lindhardt, ed., *Pentecostalism in Africa: Presence and Impact of Pneumatic Christianity in Postcolonial Societies.* Leiden: Brill, 2015: 100–114.

Awortu, Beatrice E. "Boko Haram Insurgency and the Underdevelopment of Nigeria." *Research on Humanities and Social Sciences* 5: 6 (2015): 213–220.

Ayandele, Emmanuel Ayankanmi. *The Missionary Impact on Modern Nigeria, 1842–1914: A Political and Social Analysis.* Ibadan: Longman, 1966.

Ayantayo, Jacob Kehinde. "The Phenomenon of Change of Name and Identity in Yorùbá Religious Community in the Light of Social Change." *ORITA: Ibadan Journal of Religious Studies* 42: (2010): 1–16.

Ayantayo, Jacob K. "Prosperity Gospel and Social Morality: A Critique" in D. O. Ogungbile and A. E. Akinade, eds., *Creativity and Change in Nigerian Christianity.* Lagos: Malthouse Press, 2010: 201–218.

Ayegboyin, Deji. "A Rethinking of Prosperity Teaching in the New Pentecostal Churches in Nigeria." *Black Theology* 4: 1 (2006): 70–86.

Banjo, Omotayo. "What Are You Laughing At? Examining White Identity and Enjoyment of Black Entertainment." *Journal of Broadcasting & Electronic Media* 55: 2 (2011): 137–159.

Bappah, Habibu Yaya. "Nigeria's Military Failure Against the Boko Haram Insurgency." *African Security Review* 25: 2 (2016): 146–158.

Barish, Jonas A., and Jonas Alexander Barish. *The Antitheatrical Prejudice.* Berkeley: University of California Press, 1981.

Baruh, Lemi. "Mediated Voyeurism and the Guilty Pleasure of Consuming Reality Television." *Media Psychology* 13: 3 (2010): 201–221.

Beard, Mary. *Laughter in Ancient Rome: On Joking, Tickling, and Cracking Up.* Berkeley: University of California Press, 2014.

Berger, Peter L. *The Sacred Canopy: Elements of a Sociological Theory of Religion.* New York: Integrated Media, 2011.

Bernal, Victoria. "Please Forget Democracy and Justice: Eritrean Politics and the Powers of Humor." *American Ethnologist* 40: 2 (2013): 300–309.

Bhatia, Nandi. *Acts of Authority/Acts of Resistance: Theater and Politics in Colonial and Postcolonial India.* Ann Arbor: University of Michigan Press, 2010.

Bial, Henry, and Sara Brady, eds. "Introduction" to *The Performance Studies Reader*, 1–4. London: Psychology Press, 2004.

Blanes, Ruy, and Diana Espirito Santo, eds. *The Social Life of Spirits*. Chicago: University of Chicago Press, 2013.

Bloch, Ruth H. *Visionary Republic: Millennial Themes in American Thought, 1756–1800*. Cambridge: Cambridge University Press, 1988.

Bogad, Larry. *Tactical Performance: Serious Play and Social Movements*. New York: Routledge, 2016.

Botterweck, G. Johannes, Helmer Ringgren, and Heinz-Josef Fabry, eds. *Theological Dictionary of the Old Testament*. Vol. 14. Michigan: Wm. B. Eerdmans Publishing, 2004.

Bowler, Kate, and Wen Reagan. "Bigger, Better, Louder: The Prosperity Gospel's Impact on Contemporary Christian Worship." *Religion and American Culture* 24: 2 (2014): 186–230.

Bozzini, David M. "The Catch-22 of Resistance: Jokes and the Political Imagination of Eritrean Conscripts." *Africa Today* 60: 2 (2013): 39–64.

Brasher, Brenda E. *Give Me that Online Religion*. New Jersey: John Wiley & Sons, 2001.

Brassett, James. "British Comedy, Global Resistance: Russell Brand, Charlie Brooker and Stewart Lee." *European Journal of International Relations* 22: 1 (2016): 168–191.

Brooks, Daphne. *Bodies in Dissent: Spectacular Performances of Race and Freedom, 1850–1910*. Durham: Duke University Press, 2006.

Bunt, Gary R. *iMuslims: Rewiring the House of Islam*. Chapel Hill: University of North Carolina Press, 2009.

Burgess, Sarah K. "Between the Desire for Law and the Law of Desire: #MeToo and the Cost of Telling the Truth Today." *Philosophy & Rhetoric* 51: 4 (2018): 344–5.

Butler, Melvin L. "'Nou kwe nan Sentespri' (We believe in the Holy Spirit): Music, Ecstasy, and Identity in Haitian Pentecostal Worship." *Black Music Research Journal* (2002): 85–125.

Butticci, Annalisa. *African Pentecostals in Catholic Europe*. Cambridge: Harvard University Press, 2016.

Campbell, Heidi. "Challenges Created by Online Religious Networks." *Journal of Media and Religion* 3: 2 (2004): 81–99.

Campbell, Heidi. "Spiritualising the Internet: Uncovering Discourses and Narratives of Religious Internet Usage." *Online–Heidelberg Journal of Religions on the Internet* 1: 1 (2005). https://doi.org/10.11588/heidok .00005824

Campbell, Heidi. *When Religion Meets New Media*. New York: Routledge, 2010.

Campbell, Heidi A. "Religious Authority and the Blogosphere." *Journal of Computer-Mediated Communication* 15: 2 (2010): 251–276.

Capps, Donald. *A Time to Laugh: The Religion of Humor*. London: A&C Black, 2005.

Capps, Donald. "Religion and Humor: Estranged Bedfellows." *Pastoral Psychology* 54: 5 (2006): 413–438.

Carl, Florian. "Music, Ritual and Media in Charismatic Religious Experience in Ghana" in Thomas Wagner & Anna Nekola, eds., *Congregational Music-Making and Community in a Mediated Age*. Surrey: Ashgate, 2015: 45–60.

Carlson, Marvin. *The Haunted Stage: The Theatre as Memory Machine*. Ann Arbor: University of Michigan Press, 2003.

Carlson, Marvin. *Theatre & Islam*. New York: Macmillan International Higher Education, 2019.

César, Waldo. "From Babel to Pentecost: A Social-Historical-Theological Study of the Growth of Pentecostalism" in Andre Corten and Ruth Marshall-Fratani, eds., *Between Babel and Pentecost: Transnational Pentecostalism in Africa and Latin America*. Bloomington: Indiana University Press, 2001: 22–40.

Cherry, Stephen M., and Helen Rose Ebaugh, eds. *Global Religious Movements across Borders: Sacred Service*. New York: Routledge, 2016.

Challies, Tim. *The Next Story: Life and Faith after the Digital Explosion*. Grand Rapids, MI: Zondervan, 2011.

Chatora, Arthur. "Encouraging Political Participation in Africa the Potential of Social Media Platforms." *Situation Report*. Institute for Security Studies, 2012.

Cheruiyot, David, and Charu Uppal. "Pan-Africanism as a Laughing Matter: (Funny) Expressions of African Identity on Twitter." *New Media and Processes of Social Change in Contemporary Africa*. Gothenburg: Nordicom, 2018.

Chitando, Ezra. "Theology from the Underside: The Case of African Christian Names in Zimbabwe." *Journal of Theology for Southern Africa* 101 (1998): 23–34.

Chitando, Ezra. "Signs and Portents? Theophoric Names in Zimbabwe." *Word and World* 21: 2 (2001): 144–151.

Childers, Jana. *Performing the Word: Preaching as Theatre*. Nashville: Abingdon Press, 1998.

Claassens, L. Juliana M. "Laughter and Tears: Carnivalistic Overtones in the Stories of Sarah and Hagar." *Perspectives in Religious Studies* 32: 3 (2005): 295–308.

Clarke, Clifton. "Call and Response: Towards an African Pentecostal Theological Method" in Clifton Clarke, ed., *Pentecostal Theology in Africa*. Oregon: Pickwick, 2014. Kindle.

Cleary, Edward L. *Power, Politics, and Pentecostals in Latin America*. New York: Routledge, 2018.

Coben, Lawrence A., & Takeshi Inomata. *Archaeology of Performance: Theaters of Power, Community, and Politics*. Lanham: Rowman Altamira, 2006.

Codone, Susan. "Megachurch Pastor Twitter Activity: An Analysis of Rick Warren and Andy Stanley, Two of America's Social Pastors." *Journal of Religion, Media and Digital Culture* 3: 2 (2014): 1–32.

Coleman, Simon. *The Globalisation of Charismatic Christianity*. Vol. 12. Cambridge: Cambridge University Press, 2000.

Coleman, Stephen. "Elections as Storytelling Contests." *Contemporary Theatre Review* 25: 2 (2015): 175.

Collins, Jane, and Andrew Nisbet, eds. *Theatre and Performance Design: A Reader in Scenography*. New York: Routledge, 2010.

Collins, Patricia Hill. *Black Feminist Thought: Knowledge, Consciousness, and the Politics of Empowerment*. New York: Routledge, 2002.

Comaroff, Jean. "Pentecostalism, Populism and the New Politics of Affect" in D. Freeman, ed., *Pentecostalism and Development. Non-Governmental Public Action*. New York: Palgrave Macmillan, 2012: 41–66.

Comaroff, Jean, and John L. Comaroff. "Occult Economies and the Violence of Abstraction: Notes from the South African Postcolony." *American Ethnologist* 26: 2 (1999): 279–303.

Comaroff, Jean, and John Comaroff. "Privatizing the Millennium New Protestant Ethics and the Spirits of Capitalism in Africa, and Elsewhere." *Africa Spectrum* 35: 3 (2000): 293–312.

Comolli, Virginia. *Boko Haram: Nigeria's Islamist Insurgency*. Oxford: Oxford University Press, 2015.

Compagnone, Vanessa, and Marcel Danesi. "Mythic and Occultist Naming Strategies in Harry Potter." *Names* 60: 3 (2012): 127–134.

Conze, Linda, Ulrich Prehn, and Michael Wildt. "Photography and Dictatorships in the Twentieth Century: Introduction." *Journal of Modern European History* 16: 4 (2018): 453–462.

Corten, André, and Ruth Marshall-Fratani. *Between Babel and Pentecost: Transnational Pentecostalism in Africa and Latin America*. Bloomington: Indiana University Press, 2001.

Cox, Harvey. *Fire from Heaven: The Rise of Pentecostal Spirituality and the Reshaping of Religion in the 21st Century*. Massachusetts: Da Capo Press, 2009.

Crawley, Ashon. "Let's Get It On!" Performance Theory and Black Pentecostalism." *Black Theology* 6: 3 (2008): 308–329.

Dawson, Michael C. "Black Power in 1996 and the Demonization of African Americans."*PS: Political Science & Politics* 29: 3 (1996): 456–461.

Davies, Christie. "Exploring the Thesis of the Self-Deprecating Jewish Sense of Humor." *Humor: International Journal of Humor Research* 4: 2 (1991): 189–210.

Dean, Jodi. "Why the Net Is Not a Public Sphere." *Constellations* 10: 1 (2003): 95–112.

DeFrantz, Thomas F., and Anita Gonzalez, eds. "Introduction" to *Black Performance Theory*. Durham: Duke University Press, 2014.

Devlieger, Clara. "Rome and the Romains: Laughter on the Border between Kinshasa and Brazzaville." *Africa* 88: 1 (2018): 160–182.

Dowd, Robert Alfred. *Christianity, Islam and Liberal Democracy: Lessons from Sub-Saharan Africa*. Oxford: Oxford University Press, 2015.

Dox, Donnalee. *Reckoning with Spirit in the Paradigm of Performance*. Ann Arbor: University of Michigan Press, 2016.

Drescher, Elizabeth. *Tweet If You [Heart] Jesus: Practicing Church in the Digital Reformation*. New York: Morehouse Publishing, 2011.

Dubberley, William S. "Humor as Resistance." *International Journal of Qualitative Studies in Education* 1: 2 (1988): 109–123.

Edelman, Lee. *No Future: Queer Theory and the Death Drive*. Durham: Duke University Press, 2004.

Edelman, Joshua, Claire Maria Chambers, and Simon du Toit, eds. "Introduction: The Public Problem of Religious Doings" in *Performing Religion in Public*. Houndmills, Basingtoke: Palgrave Macmillan, 2013.

Ellcessor, Elizabeth. "'One Tweet to Make So Much Noise': Connected Celebrity Activism in the Case of Marlee Matlin." *New Media & Society* 20: 1 (2018): 257.

Ellis, Iain. *Humorists vs. Religion: Critical Voices from Mark Twain to Neil DeGrasse Tyson*. North Carolina: McFarland, 2018.

El-Nawawy, Mohammed. *Islam dot com: Contemporary Islamic Discourses in Cyberspace*. New York: Springer, 2009.

Evans, Michael S. "Who Wants a Deliberative Public Sphere?" *Sociological Forum* 27: 4 (2012): 872–895.

Fakuade, Gbenga, Joseph Friday-Otun, and Hezekiah Adeosun. "Yoruba Personal Naming System: Traditions, Patterns and Practices." *Sociolinguistic Studies* 13: 2–4 (2019): 251–271.

Faleye, Olukayode Abiodun. "Religious Corruption: A Dilemma of the Nigerian State." *Journal of Sustainable Development in Africa* 15: 1 (2013): 170–185.

Falola, Toyin. *A Mouth Sweeter than Salt: An African Memoir*. Ann Arbor: University of Michigan Press, 2005.

Faseke, Babajimi Oladipo. "Nigeria and the Organization of Islamic Cooperation: A Discourse in Identity, Faith and Development, 1969–2016." *Religions* 10: 3 (2019): 156.

Fawole, W. Alade. "Voting without Choosing: Interrogating the Crisis of 'Electoral Democracy' in Nigeria" in Tukumbi Lumumba-Kasongo, ed., *Liberal Democracy and Its Critics in Africa: Political Dysfunction and the Struggle for Social Progress.* London: Zed Books, 2005: 149–171.

Freeman, Lisa A. *Antitheatricality and the Body Public.* Philadelphia: University of Pennsylvania Press, 2016.

Gaiya, Musa A. B. *The Pentecostal Revolution in Nigeria.* Copenhagen: Centre of African Studies, University of Copenhagen, 2002.

Garlick, Harry. *The Final Curtain: State Funerals and the Theatre of Power.* Amsterdam: Rodopi, 1999.

Geybels, Hans, and Walter Van Herck, eds. *Humour and Religion: Challenges and Ambiguities.* London: Bloomsbury Publishing, 2011.

Gharavi, Lance, ed. "Introduction" to *Religion, Theatre, and Performance: Acts of Faith.* New York: Routledge, 2012.

Gifford, Paul. "Persistence and Change in Contemporary African Religion." *Social Compass* 51: 2 (2004): 169–176.

Gilbert, Lysias Dodd. "Prolongation of Boko Haram Insurgency in Nigeria: The International Dimensions." *Research on Humanities and Social Sciences* 4: 11 (2014): 150–156.

Gilmore, David D. "Some Notes on Community Nicknaming in Spain." *Man* 17: 4 (1982): 686–700.

Gilroy, Paul. *Against Race: Imagining Political Culture beyond the Color Line.* Massachusetts: Harvard University Press, 2000.

Goffman, Erving. *The Presentation of Self in Everyday Life.* Middlesex: Harmondsworth, 1978.

Goldstein, Donna M. *Laughter Out of Place: Race, Class, Violence, and Sexuality in a Rio Shantytown.* Berkeley: University of California Press, 2003.

Grant, August E., Amanda FC Sturgill, Chiung Hwang Chen, and Daniel A. Stout, eds. *Religion Online: How Digital Technology Is Changing the Way We Worship and Pray.* Santa Barbara: ABC-CLIO, 2019.

Guenther, Katja M. "The Politics of Names: Rethinking the Methodological and Ethical Significance of Naming People, Organizations, and Places." *Qualitative Research* 9: 4 (2009): 411–421.

Hackett, Rosalind I. J. "The Gospel of Prosperity in West Africa" in Richard H. Roberts, ed., *Religion and the Transformations of Capitalism: Comparative Approaches.* New York: Routledge, 1995: 199–214.

Hackett, Rosalind I. J. "The New Virtual (inter) Face of African Pentecostalism." *Society* 46: 6 (2009): 496–501.

Hackett, Rosalind. "Is Satan Local or Global? Reflections on a Nigerian Deliverance Movement" in Afe Adogame, ed., *Who Is Afraid of the Holy Ghost? Pentecostalism and Globalization in Africa and Beyond.* New Jersey: Africa World Press, 2011: 111–131.

Hackett, R. & Benjamin F. Soares, eds. *New Media and Religious Transformations in Africa.* Bloomington: Indiana University Press, 2015.

Hall, Mark David. *Did America Have a Christian Founding?: Separating Modern Myth from Historical Truth.* Nashville: Thomas Nelson, 2019.

Halliwell, Stephen. "The Uses of Laughter in Greek Culture." *The Classical Quarterly* 41: 2 (1991): 279–296.

Hammerman, Joshua. *thelordismyshepherd.com: Seeking God in Cyberspace.* Deerfield Beach, FL: Simcha, 2000.

Hammett, Daniel. "Resistance, Power and Geopolitics in Zimbabwe." *Area* 43: 2 (2011): 202–210.

Hart, Keith. "*The Hit Man's Dilemma.*" Chicago: University of Chicago Press, 2005.

Haynes, Jonathan. *Nollywood: The Creation of Nigerian Film Genres.* Chicago: University of Chicago Press, 2016.

Haynes, Naomi. "Pentecostalism and the Morality of Money: Prosperity, Inequality, and Religious Sociality on the Zambian Copperbelt." *Journal of the Royal Anthropological Institute* 18: 1 (2012): 123–139.

Helmy, Mohamed M., and Sabine Frerichs. "Stripping the Boss: The Powerful Role of Humor in the Egyptian Revolution 2011." *Integrative Psychological and Behavioral Science* 47: 4 (2013): 450–481.

Herzog, Rudolph. *Dead Funny: Humor in Hitler's Germany.* New York: Melville House, 2011.

Heuser, Andreas. "Charting African Prosperity Gospel Economies." *HTS Theological Studies* 72: 4 (2016): 8.

Hillenbrand, Fritz Karl Michael. *Underground Humour in Nazi Germany, 1933–1945.* New York: Routledge, 2002.

Hipps, Shane. *The Hidden Power of Electronic Culture: How Media Shapes Faith, the Gospel, and Church.* Michigan: Zondervan, 2005.

Horton, Robin. "African Conversion." *Africa* 41: 2 (1971): 85–108. http://doi.org?/10.2307/1159421.

Howard, Robert Glenn. *Digital Jesus: The Making of a New Christian Fundamentalist Community on the Internet.* New York: New York University Press, 2011.

Hund, Emily, and Lee McGuigan. "A Shoppable Life: Performance, Selfhood, and Influence in the Social Media Storefront." *Communication Culture & Critique* 12: 1 (2019): 18–35.

Hutchings, Tim. "The Dis/embodied Church: Worship, New Media and the Body" in E. Obinna and G. Vincett, eds., *Christianity in the Modern World*. New York: Routledge, 2016: 37–58.

Ihejirika, Walter C. "Media and Fundamentalism in Nigeria." *Media Development* 52: 2 (2005): 38–44.

Ilechukwu, Sunny T. C. "Ogbanje/Abiku: a Culture-Bound Construct of Childhood and Family Psychopathology in West Africa: the Ogbanje/Abiku Syndrome: a Case Study of an Interface between a Culture-Bound Concept and Modern Psychiatry." *Psychopathologie Africaine* 23: 1 (1990): 19–60.

Ilechukwu, Sunday T. C. "Ogbanje/Abiku and Cultural Conceptualizations of Psychopathology in Nigeria." *Mental Health, Religion and Culture* 10: 3 (2007): 239–255.

Ilesanmi, Simeon O. "From Periphery to Center: Pentecostalism Is Transforming the Secular State in Africa." *Harvard Divinity Bulletin* 35: 4 (2007).

Imo, Edward Egbo. "Stand-Up Comedy as Impetus for Evangelism in Nigeria: The Example of Aboki4Christ's Medicinal Laughter." *International Review of Humanities Studies* 3: 1 (2018). https://doi.org/10 .7454/irhs.v3i1.32.

Ivie, Robert L., and Oscar Giner. "Hunting the Devil: Democracy's Rhetorical Impulse to War." *Presidential Studies Quarterly* 37: 4 (2007): 580–598. http://doi.org/10.1111/j.1741-5705.2007.02615.x.

Jagsi, Reshma. "Sexual Harassment in Medicine – #MeToo." *New England Journal of Medicine* 378: 3 (2018): 209–211.

Jedlowski, Alessandro, Jyoti Mistry, Jordache A. Ellapen et al. *Global Nollywood: The Transnational Dimensions of an African Video Film Industry*. Bloomington: Indiana University Press, 2013.

Jenkins, Philip. *The Next Christendom: The Coming of Global Christianity*. Oxford: Oxford University Press, 2011.

Johnson, Samuel. *The History of the Yorubas: From the Earliest Times to the Beginning of the British Protectorate*. Cambridge: Cambridge University Press, 1966.

Kadenge, Maxwell, Patricia Ruramisai Mabugu, Esther Chivero, and Rejoice Chiwara. "Anthroponyms of Albinos among the Shona People of Zimbabwe." *Mediterranean Journal of Social Sciences* 5: 27 (2014): 1230.

Kalu, Ogbu U. "Safiyya and Adamah: Punishing Adultery with Sharia Stones in Twenty-First-Century Nigeria." *African Affairs* 102: 408 (2003): 389–408.

Kalu, Ogbu. "Sharia and Islam in Nigerian Pentecostal Rhetoric, 1970–2003." *Pneuma* 2 (2004): 242–261.

Kalu, Ogbu. *Power, Poverty, and Prayer: The Challenges of Poverty and Pluralism in African Christianity, 1960–1996.* Trenton, NJ: Africa World Press, 2006.

Kalu, Ogbu. *African Pentecostalism: An Introduction.* Oxford: Oxford University Press, 2008.

Kalu, Ogbu U. "Holy Praiseco: Negotiating Sacred and Popular Music and Dance in African Pentecostalism." *Pneuma* 32: 1 (2010): 16–40.

Kantorowicz, Ernst. *The King's Two Bodies: A Study in Medieval Political Theology.* Princeton: Princeton University Press, 2016.

Kaoma, Kapya. *Colonizing African Values: How the US Christian Right Is Transforming Sexual Politics in Africa.* Political Research Associates, 2012.

Kaplan, Justin, Anne Bernays, and Kaplan Educational Centers. *Language of Names: What We Call Ourselves and Why It Matters.* New York: Simon & Schuster, 1997.

Kasule, Samuel. *Resistance and Politics in Contemporary East African Theatre: Trends in Ugandan Theatre Since 1960.* London: Adonis & Abbey Publishers, 2013.

Katsaura, Obvious. "Theo-urbanism: Pastoral Power and Pentecostals in Johannesburg." *Culture and Religion* 18: 3 (2017): 232–262.

Kenny, Joseph. "Sharīa and Christianity in Nigeria: Islam and a 'Secular' State." *Journal of Religion in Africa* 26: 4 (1996): 338–364.

Kershaw, Baz. *The Politics of Performance: Radical Theatre as Cultural Intervention.* New York: Routledge, 2002.

Kilde, Jeanne Halgren. *When Church Became Theatre: The Transformation of Evangelical Architecture and Worship in Nineteenth-Century America.* Oxford: Oxford University Press, 2002.

Klein, Christina. *Cold War Orientalism: Asia in the Middlebrow Imagination, 1945–1961.* Berkeley: University of California Press, 2003.

Knibbe, Kim. "'We Did Not Come Here as Tenants, but as Landlords': Nigerian Pentecostals and the Power of Maps." *African Diaspora* 2: 2 (2009): 133–158.

Komolafe, Sunday Babajide. "The Changing Face of Christianity: Revisiting African Creativity." *Missiology* 32: 2 (2004): 217–238.

Komori, Yuri. "Trends in Japanese First Names in the Twentieth Century: A Comparative Study." *International Christian University Publications, Asian Cultural Studies* 28 (2002): 67–82.

Kotsko, Adam. *The Prince of This World.* California: Stanford University Press, 2016.

Kotsko, Adam. *Neoliberalism's Demons: On the Political Theology of Late Capital.* California: Stanford University Press, 2018.

Kuhlmann, Jenny. "Zimbabwean Diaspora Politics and the Power of Laughter: Humour as a Tool for Political Communication, Criticism and Protest." *Journal of African Media Studies* 4: 3 (2012): 295–314.

Kukah, Matthew Hassan. *Religion, Politics and Power in Northern Nigeria*. Ibadan: Spectrum Books, 1993.

Kumwenda, Grace. "The Portrayal of Witchcraft, Occults and Magic in Popular Nigerian Video Films." PhD thesis, University of the Witwatersrand (2008).

Latour, Bruno. "When Things Strike Back: A Possible Contribution of 'Science Studies' to the Social Sciences." *The British Journal of Sociology* 51: 1 (2000): 113–114.

Laude, Patrick. *Divine Play, Sacred Laughter, and Spiritual Understanding*. New York: Springer, 2005.

Lee, Shayne. "Prosperity Theology: TD Jakes and the Gospel of the Almighty Dollar." *CrossCurrents* 57 (2007): 227–236.

Lewison, Elsie. "Pentecostal Power and the Holy Spirit of Capitalism: Re-imagining Modernity in the Charismatic Cosmology." *Symposia* 3: 1 (2011): 31–54.

Lipsitz, George. *The Possessive Investment in Whiteness: How White People Profit from Identity Politics*. Philadelphia: Temple University Press, 2006.

MacKenzie, Iain, Fred Francis, and Krista Bonello Rutter Giappone. *Comedy and Critical Thought: Laughter as Resistance*. Washington, DC: Rowman and Littlefield International, 2018.

Maduka, Chidi T. "African Religious Beliefs in Literary Imagination: Ogbanje and Abiku in Chinua Achebe, JP Clark and Wole Soyinka." *The Journal of Commonwealth Literature* 22: 1 (1987): 17–30.

Makoni, Busi, Sinfree Makoni, and Pedzisai Mashiri. "Naming Practices and Language Planning in Zimbabwe." *Current Issues in Language Planning* 8: 3 (2007): 437–467.

Marishane, Jeffrey. "Prayer, Profit and Power: US Religious Right and Foreign Policy." *Review of African Political Economy* 18: 52 (1991): 73–86.

Marshall, Ruth. "Power in the Name of Jesus." *Review of African Political Economy* 52 (1991): 21–37. Accessed June 19, 2020. www.jstor.org/sta ble/4005954.

Marshall, Ruth. "Power in the Name of Jesus: Social Transformation and Pentecostalism in Western Nigeria 'Revisited'" in Terence Ranger and Olufemi Vaughan, eds., *Legitimacy and the State in Twentieth-Century Africa*. New York: Palgrave Macmillan, 1993: 213–246.

Marshall, Ruth. "God Is Not a Democrat: Pentecostalism and Democratisation in Nigeria" in Paul Gifford, ed., *The Christian*

Churches and the Democratisation of Africa. Leiden: Brill, 1995: 239–260.

Marshall, Ruth. *Political Spiritualities: The Pentecostal Revolution in Nigeria*. Chicago: University of Chicago Press, 2009.

Marshall, Ruth. "The Sovereignty of Miracles: Pentecostal Political Theology in Nigeria 1." *Constellations* 17: 2 (2010): 197–223.

Marshall, Ruth. "Destroying Arguments and Captivating Thoughts: Spiritual Warfare Prayer as Global Praxis." *Journal of Religious and Political Practice* 2: 1 (2016): 92–113.

Marti, Gerardo, and Gladys Ganiel. *The Deconstructed Church: Understanding Emerging Christianity*. Oxford: Oxford University Press, 2014.

Mason, David V. *The Performative Ground of Religion and Theatre*. New York: Routledge, 2018.

Maxwell, David. "'Delivered from the Spirit of Poverty?': Pentecostalism, Prosperity and Modernity in Zimbabwe." *Journal of Religion in Africa/Religion en Afrique* 28: 3 (1998): 350.

Maxwell, David. "Christianity without Frontiers: Shona Missionaries and Transnational Pentecostalism in Africa." *Christianity and the African Imagination: Essays in Honour of Adrian Hastings* (2002): 295–332.

Mayfield, Alex R. "The Question of Power in African Pentecostalism." *Spiritus: ORU Journal of Theology* 3: 1 (2017): 87–107.

Mbah, Peter, Chikodiri Nwangwu, and Herbert C. Edeh. "Elite Politics and the Emergence of Boko Haram Insurgency in Nigeria." *TRAMES: A Journal of the Humanities & Social Sciences* 21: 2 (2017):181.

Mbembe, Achille. "The Banality of Power and the Aesthetics of Vulgarity in the Postcolony." *Public Culture* 4: 2 (1992): 1–30.

Mbembe, Achille. *On the Postcolony*. Berkeley: University of California Press, 2001.

McCabe, Douglas. "Histories of Errancy: Oral Yoruba 'Àbíkú' Texts and Soyinka's 'Abiku.'" *Research in African Literatures* (2002): 45–74.

McCauley, John F. "Africa's New Big Man Rule? Pentecostalism and Patronage in Ghana." *African Affairs* 112: 446 (2013): 1–21.

McCauley, John F. "Pentecostalism as an Informal Political Institution: Experimental Evidence from Ghana."*Politics and Religion* 7: 4 (2014): 761–787.

McClendon, Gwyneth H., and Rachel Beatty Riedl. *From Pews to Politics: Religious Sermons and Political Participation in Africa*. Cambridge: Cambridge University Press, 2019.

McDonald, Marianne, and Michael Walton, eds. *The Cambridge Companion to Greek and Roman Theatre.* Cambridge: Cambridge University Press, 2007.

Merrill, Lisa. "Feminist Humor: Rebellious and Self-Affirming." *Women's Studies: An Interdisciplinary Journal* 15: 1–3 (1988): 271–280.

Meyer, Birgit. "'Praise the Lord': Popular Cinema and Pentecostalite Style in Ghana's New Public Sphere." *American Ethnologist* 31: 1 (2004): 92–110.

Meyer, Birgit. "Pentecostalism and Neo-Liberal Capitalism: Faith, Prosperity and Vision in African Pentecostal-Charismatic Churches." *Journal for the Study of Religion* 20: 2 (2007): 5–28.

Meyer, Birgit. "Aesthetics of Persuasion: Global Christianity and Pentecostalism's Sensational Forms." *South Atlantic Quarterly* 109: 4 (2010): 741–763.

Meyer, Birgit. "How Pictures Matter" in Øivind Fuglerud and Leon Wainwright, eds., *Objects and Imagination: Perspectives on Materialization and Meaning.* New York: Berghahn Books, 2015: 160–182.

Meyer, Birgit. "Picturing the Invisible: Visual Culture and the Study of Religion." *Method & Theory in the Study of Religion* 27: 4–5 (2015): 333–360.

Mintz, Lawrence E. "Stand-up Comedy as Social and Cultural Mediation." *American Quarterly* 37: 1 (1985): 75.

Miller, Donald E., Kimon H. Sargeant, and Richard Flory, eds. *Spirit and Power: The Growth and Global Impact of Pentecostalism.* Oxford: Oxford University Press, 2013.

Morgan, David. *Visual Piety: A History and Theory of Popular Religious Images.* Berkeley: University of California Press, 1999.

Mudasiru, Surajudeen Oladosu. "Ethnicity and the Voting Pattern in Nigeria's 2015 General Elections: The Case of Lagos State." *The Electorate Institute Abuja* (2015): 15.

Ngong, David. "African Pentecostal Pneumatology" in Clifton Clarke, ed., *Pentecostal Theology in Africa*, Eugene, OR: Pickwick Publications, 2014. Kindle.

Ngwira, Emmanuel, and Ken Junior Lipenga. "A Country Laughing at Itself: Malawian Humour in the Digital Age." *English Studies in Africa* 61: 2 (2018): 21–35.

Niebylski, Dianna C. *Humoring Resistance: Laughter and the Excessive Body in Latin American Women's Fiction.* New York: SUNY Press, 2012.

Normand, Linn. *Demonization in International Politics: A Barrier to Peace in the Israeli-Palestinian Conflict.* New York: Springer, 2016.

North, John David. *God's Clockmaker: Richard of Wallingford and the Invention of Time.* London: A&C Black, 2005.

Nwanosike, Dominic, Ugbor Kalu, Jonathan Emenike Ogbuabor, Benedict Uzoechina, and Gabriel Ebenyi. "Economic Development Dynamics in Nigeria: Evidence from 1914–2014." *Saudi Journal of Business and Management Studies* 1: 4 (2016): 154–161.

Obadare, Ebenezer. "Democratic Transition and Political Violence in Nigeria." *Africa Development* 24: 1 (1999): 199–220.

Obadare, Ebenezer. "Pentecostal Presidency? The Lagos-Ibadan 'Theocratic Class' & the Muslim 'Other.'" *Review of African Political Economy* 33: 110 (2006): 665–678.

Obadare, Ebenezer. "The Uses of Ridicule: Humour, 'Infrapolitics' and Civil Society in Nigeria." *African Affairs* 108: 431 (2009): 241–261.

Obadare, Ebenezer. "The Muslim Response to the Pentecostal Surge in Nigeria: Prayer and the Rise of Charismatic Islam." *Journal of Religious and Political Practice* 2: 1 (2016): 75–91.

Obadare, Ebenezer. "'Raising Righteous Billionaires': The Prosperity Gospel Reconsidered." *HTS Theological Studies* 72: 4 (2016): 1–8.

Obadare, Ebenezer. "The Charismatic Porn-Star: Social Citizenship and the West-African Pentecostal Erotic." *Citizenship Studies* 22: 6 (2018): 603–617.

Obadare, Ebenezer. "On the Theologico-Theatrical: Explaining the Convergence of Pentecostalism and Popular Culture in Nigeria." *Africa at LSE*. Last Modified: October 7, 2020. (2018). http://eprints.lse.ac.uk/id/eprint/91276.

Obadare, Ebenezer. *Pentecostal Republic: Religion and the Struggle for State Power in Nigeria*. London: Zed, 2018.

Odom, Glenn. *Yorùbá Performance, Theatre and Politics: Staging Resistance*. New York: Springer, 2015.

Oduyoye, Mercy A. *Hearing and Knowing: Theological Reflections on Christianity in Africa*. Eugene, OR: Wipf and Stock Publishers, 2009.

Ogbaa, Kalu. "Names and Naming in Chinua Aehebe's Novels." *Names* 28: 4 (1980): 267–289.

Ogie, Ota. "Edo Personal Names and Worldview." *New Perspectives in Edoid Studies: Essays in Honour of Ronald Peter Schaefer*. Book Series 20. Centre for Advanced Studies of African Society, 2002.

Ogunyemi, Chikwenye Okonjo. "An Abiku-Ogbanje Atlas: A Pre-Text for Rereading Soyinka's *Aké* and Morrison's *Beloved*." *African American Review* 36: 4 (2002): 663–678.

Ojo, John Sunday. "Looting the Looters: The Paradox of Anti-Corruption Crusades in Nigeria's Fourth Republic (1999–2014)." *Canadian Social Science* 12: 9 (2016): 1–20.

Ojo, Matthews A. "The Church in the African State: The Charismatic/Pentecostal Experience in Nigeria." *Journal of African Christian Thought* 1: 2 (1998): 25–32.

Ojo, Matthews A. "Pentecostalism and Charismatic Movements in Nigeria: Factors of Growth and Inherent Challenges." *The WATS Journal: An Online Journal from West Africa Theological Seminary* 3: 1 (2018): 74–94.

Okagbue, Osita. *Resistance and Politics in Contemporary East African Theatre*. London: Adonis & Abbey Publishers, 2013.

Okoli, Al Chukwuma, and Philip Iortyer. "Terrorism and Humanitarian Crisis in Nigeria: Insights from Boko Haram Insurgency." *Global Journal of Human Social Science-GJHSS-F* 14: 1 (2014): 39–50.

Okome, Onookome. "Nollywood: Spectatorship, Audience and the Sites of Consumption." *Postcolonial Text* 3: 2 (2007): 1–21.

Okoye, Chukwuma. "Technologies of Faith Performance: Theatre/Performance and Pentecostalism in Africa." *African Performance Review* 1: 1 (2007): 80–95.

Olanisebe, Samson O. "Elimination by Substitution: The Travesty of Changing Cultural Names to Biblical Names by Pentecostals in Southwestern Nigeria." *Ilorin Journal of Religious Studies* 7: 2 (2017): 107–124.

Olomola, Isola. "Contradictions in Yoruba Folk Beliefs Concerning Post-Life Existence: The Ado Example." *Journal des Africanistes* 58: 1 (1988): 107–118.

Olubitan, A. A. "Pluralism and Christianity in Recent Drama of Yoruba Nollywood." *Uniilorin e-Journals, The Performer* 14: 3 (2012): 159–170.

Olupona, Jacob K. "The Changing Face of African Christianity: Reverse Mission in Transnational and Global Perspectives" in M. Okome, ed., *Transnational Africa and Globalization*. New York: Palgrave Macmillan, 2011: 79–194.

Olupona, Jacob. *City of 201 Gods: Ilé-Ifè in Time, Space, and the Imagination*. Berkeley: University of California Press, 2011.

Omenma, J. Tochukwu, J. Chisolum Onu, and Z. Onyinyechi Omenma. "Factors Limiting Nomination of Women Candidates for Elections in Nigeria." *Mediterranean Journal of Social Sciences* 7: 5 (2016): 202–211.

Omoloso, Rahim Kajogbola. "A Speech Act Analysis of Selected Yoruba Anthroponyms." *Dialectologia: Revista Electrònica* 15 (2015): 117–135.

Omotola, J. Shola. "Godfathers and the 2007 Nigerian General Elections." *Journal of African Elections* 6: 2 (2007): 134–154.

O'Neill, Kevin Lewis. "I Want More of You: The Politics of Christian Eroticism in Postwar Guatemala." *Comparative Studies in Society and History* 52: 1 (2010): 131–156.

O'Neill, Kevin Lewis. *City of God: Christian Citizenship in Postwar Guatemala*. Berkeley: University of California Press, 2010.

Onapajo, Hakeem. "Politics and the Pulpit: The Rise and Decline of Religion in Nigeria's 2015 Presidential Elections." *Journal of African Elections* 15: 2 (2016): 112–135.

Orie, Ọlanikẹ Ọla. "Yoruba Names and Gender Marking." *Anthropological linguistics* 44: 2 (2002): 115–142.

Oseni, Z. I. *"A Guide to Muslim Name, with Special Reference to Nigeria."* Islamic Publications Bureau, 1981.

Osinulu, Adedamola. "The Road to Redemption: Performing Pentecostal Citizenship in Lagos" in M. Diouf and R. Frederick, eds., *The Arts of Citizenship in African Cities*. New York: Palgrave Macmillan, 2014: 115–135.

Osundare, N. *African Literature and the Crisis of Post-Structuralist Theorising*. Options Book and Information Services, 1993.

Oyěwùmí, Oyèrónkẹ. *What Gender Is Motherhood?: Changing Yoruba Ideals of Power, Procreation, and Identity in the Age of Modernity*. New York: Springer, 2016.

Palacios, Joy. "Introduction: Performing Religion." *Performance Matters* 3: 1 (2017): 1–6.

Palmié, Stephan. *Wizards and Scientists: Explorations in Afro-Cuban Modernity and Tradition*. Durham: Duke University Press, 2002.

Papacharissi, Zizi. "The Virtual Sphere: The Internet as a Public Sphere." *New Media & Society* 4: 1 (2002): 9–27.

Patsiaoura, Evanthia. "Transcending Distinctions between Religious and Secular Musicianship: Nigerian Pentecostals across Popular Performance Settings." *Popular Music and Society* (2019): 1–23.

Peacock, Louise. *Slapstick and Comic Performance: Comedy and Pain*. New York: Springer, 2014.

Pearce, Katy, and Adnan Hajizada. "No Laughing Matter: Humor as a Means of Dissent in the Digital Era: The Case of Authoritarian Azerbaijan." *Demokratizatsiya* 22: 1 (2014): 67.

Pfukwa, Charles, and Lawrie Barnes. "Negotiating Identities in Guerrilla War Names in the Zimbabwean War of Liberation." *African Identities* 8: 3 (2010): 209–219.

Pierce, Steven. *Moral Economies of Corruption: State Formation and Political Culture in Nigeria*. Durham: Duke University Press, 2016.

Poster, Mark. "Cyberdemocracy: Internet and The Public Sphere." *Internet Culture* (1997): 201–218.

Provine, Robert R. "Laughter as an Approach to Vocal Evolution: The Bipedal Theory." *Psychonomic Bulletin & Review* 24: 1 (2017): 238–244.

Pype, Katrien. "The Liveliness of Pentecostal/Charismatic Popular Culture in Africa" in Martin Lindhardt, ed., *Pentecostalism in Africa*. Leiden: Brill, 2015: 345–378 .

Pype, Katrien. *The Making of the Pentecostal Melodrama: Religion, Media and Gender in Kinshasa*. New York: Berghahn Books, 2012.

Pype, Katrien. "Funerary Comedies in Contemporary Kinshasa: Social Difference, Urban Communities and the Emergence of a Cultural Form." *Africa: The Journal of the International African Institute* 85: 3 (2015): 457–477.

Radde-Antweiler, Kerstin, and Xenia Zeiler, eds. *Mediatized Religion in Asia: Studies on Digital Media and Religion*. New York: Routledge, 2018.

Rasmussen, Lissi. *Christian-Muslim Relations in Africa: The Cases of Northern Nigeria and Tanzania Compared*. London: British Academic Press, 1993.

Rasmussen, Terje. "Internet and the Political Public Sphere." *Sociology Compass* 8: 12 (2014): 1326.

Robert, Dana. "Shifting Southward: Global Christianity Since 1945." *International Bulletin of Missionary Research* 24 (2000): 50–58.

Ryan, Jennifer. "Negotiations of Faith and Space in Memphis Music" in Reily, Suzel Ana, and Jonathan M. Dueck, eds., *The Oxford Handbook of Music and World Christianities*. Oxford University Press, 2016: 449–468.

Sanneh, Lamin O., and Joel A. Carpenter, eds. *The Changing Face of Christianity: Africa, the West, and the World*. Oxford: Oxford University Press, 2005.

Sarajlic, Eldar. "The Ethics and Politics of Child Naming." *Journal of Applied Philosophy* 35 (2018): 121–139.

Sautter, Cia. *The Performance of Religion: Seeing the Sacred in the Theatre*. Oxfordshire: Taylor & Francis, 2017.

Schafer, Elizabeth. *Theatre & Christianity*. New York: Macmillan International Higher Education, 2019.

Scott, James C. *Weapons of the Weak: Everyday Forms of Peasant Resistance*. New Haven: Yale University Press, 2008.

Schechner, Richard. "What Is Performance Studies." *Rupkatha Journal on Interdisciplinary Studies in Humanities* 5: 2 (2013): 3.

Scott, James C. *Weapons of the Weak: Everyday Forms of Peasant Resistance*. New Haven: Yale University Press, 2008.

Shapiro, Stephen, and Philip Barnard. *Pentecostal Modernism: Lovecraft, Los Angeles, and World-Systems Culture*. London: Bloomsbury Publishing, 2017.

Shepherd, Simon. *The Cambridge Introduction to Performance Theory*. Cambridge: Cambridge University Press, 2016.

Shipley, Jesse Weaver. "Comedians, Pastors, and the Miraculous Agency of Charisma in Ghana." *Cultural Anthropology* 24: 3 (2009): 523–552.

Slaughter, Joseph R. "'A Mouth with Which to Tell the Story': Silence, Violence, and Speech in Chinua Achebe's *Things Fall Apart*" in Harold Bloom, ed., *Chinua Achebe's* Things Fall Apart. New Jersey: Africa World Press, 2009: 69–98.

Smiley, CalvinJohn, and David Fakunle. "From 'Brute' to 'Thug:' The Demonization and Criminalization of Unarmed Black Male Victims in America." *Journal of Human Behavior in the Social Environment* 26: 3–4 (2016): 350–366.

Smith, Daniel Scott. "Child-Naming Practices, Kinship Ties, and Change in Family Attitudes in Hingham, Massachusetts, 1641 to 1880." *Journal of Social History* 18: 4 (1985): 541–566.

Sofola, J. A. *African Culture and the African Personality: What Makes an African Person African.* Ibadan: African Resources Publishers, 1978: 110–111.

Spivak, Gayatri Chakravorty. "Religion, Politics, Theology: A Conversation with Achille Mbembe." *Boundary 2* 34: 2 (2007): 149–170.

Stevenson, Jill. *Sensational Devotion: Evangelical Performance in Twenty-First-Century America.* Ann Arbor: University of Michigan Press, 2013.

Stewart, Katherine. *The Power Worshippers.* New York: Bloomsbury, 2020.

Sorensen, Majken Jul. "Humor as a Serious Strategy of Nonviolent Resistance to Oppression." *Peace & Change* 33: 2 (2008): 167–190.

Soyinka, Wole. *Death and the King's Horseman.* New York: WW Norton & Company, 2002.

Sulaiman, Nahidh Falih. "Theatre of Exorcism: Evoking the Past to Control the Present." *Journal of Language Studies* 3: 1 (2019): 176–192.

Stolow, Jeremy, ed. *Deus in Machina: Religion, Technology, and the Things in Between: Religion, Technology, and the Things in Between.* New York: Fordham University Press, 2013.

Stott, Andrew. *Comedy.* New York: Routledge, 2014.

Sule, Babayo, Mohd Azizuddin Mohd Sani, and Bakri Mat. "Godfatherism and Political Party Financing in Nigeria: Analysing the 2015 General Election." *Geografia-Malaysian Journal of Society and Space* 14: 1 (2018): 1–14.

Suzman, Susan M. "Names as Pointers: Zulu Personal Naming Practices." *Language in Society* 23: 2 (1994): 253–272.

Taiwo, Olatunde O. "From Jagua to Ali Baba: Humour in Contemporary Nigeria." *AGOGO: Journal of Humanities* 3 (2017): 26–31.

Taiwo, Olufemi. *How Colonialism Preempted Modernity in Africa.* Bloomington: Indiana University Press, 2010.

Tatarchevskiy, Tatiana. "The 'Popular' Culture of Internet Activism." *New Media & Society* 13: 2 (2011): 297–313.

Taylor, Diana. *Disappearing Acts: Spectacles of Gender and Nationalism in Argentina's "Dirty War"*. Durham: Duke University Press, 1997.

Taylor, Diana. *The Archive and the Repertoire: Performing Cultural Memory in the Americas*. Durham: Duke University Press, 2003.

Taylor, Mark Lewis. "Bringing Noise, Conjuring Spirit" in Anthony B. Pinn, ed., *Noise and Spirit: The Religious and Spiritual Sensibilities of Rap Music*. New York: New York University Press, 2003: 107–130.

Thurston, Robert W. "Social Dimensions of Stalinist Rule: Humor and Terror in the USSR, 1935–1941." *Journal of Social History* 24: 3 (1991): 541–562.

Togarasei, Lovemore. "The Pentecostal Gospel of Prosperity in African Contexts of Poverty: An Appraisal." *Exchange* 40: 4 (2011): 336–350.

Ukachi, Austen C. *The Best Is Yet to Come: Pentecostal and Charismatic Revivals in Nigeria from 1914 to 1990s*. Florida: Xulon Press, 2013.

Ukah, Asonzeh. "Advertising God: Nigerian Christian Video-Films and the Power of Consumer Culture." *Journal of Religion in Africa* 33: 2 (2003): 203–231.

Ukah, Asonzeh F. K. "Pentecostalism, Religious Expansion and the City: Lessons from the Nigerian Bible-Belt" in Peter Probst and Gerd Spittler, eds., *Between Resistance and Expansion: Explorations of Local Vitality in Africa*. New Jersey: Transaction Publishers, 2004: 415–441.

Ukah, Asonzeh F. K. "Those Who Trade with God Never Lose: The Economics of Pentecostal Activism in Nigeria" in Toyin Falola and J. D. Y. Peel, eds., *Christianity and Social Change in Africa: Essays in Honor of JDY Peel*. Durham: Carolina Academic Press, 2005: 253–274.

Ukah, Asonzeh. "Piety and Profit: Accounting for Money in West African Pentecostalism (Part 1)." *Stellenbosch Theological Journal* 48: 3–4 (2007): 621–632.

Ukah, Asonzeh. "Piety and Profit: Accounting for Money in West African Pentecostalism (Part 2)." *Dutch Reformed Theological Journal= Nederduitse Gereformeerde Teologiese Tydskrif* 48: 3–4 (2007): 633–648.

Ukah, Asonzeh Franklin-Kennedy. *A New Paradigm of Pentecostal Power: A Study of the Redeemed Christian Church of God in Nigeria*. Trenton, NJ: Africa World Press, 2008.

Ukah, Asonzeh F. K. "Roadside Pentecostalism: Religious Advertising in Nigeria and the Marketing of Charisma." *Critical Interventions* 2: 1–2 (2008): 125–141.

Ukah, Asonzeh. "God Unlimited: Economic Transformations of Contemporary Nigerian Pentecostalism" in Lionel Obadia and

Donald Wood, eds., *The Economics of Religion: Anthropological Approaches*. Bingley: Emerald Group Publishing Limited, 2011: 187–216.

Ukah, A. F. K. "Prophets for Profit: Pentecostal Authority and Fiscal Accountability among Nigerian Churches in South Africa" in A. Adogame, M. Echtler & O. Freiberge, eds., *Alternative Voices: A Plurality Approach for Religious Studies*. Gottingen: Vandenhoek & Ruprecht, 2013: 134–159.

Ukah, Asonzeh. "The Midwife or the Handmaid? Religion in Political Advertising in Nigeria" in Joachim Küpper, Klaus W. Hempfer, Erika Fischer-Lichte, eds., *Religion and Society in the 21st Century*. Berlin/Boston: Walter de Gruyter, 2014: 87–114.

Ukah, Asonzeh. "Building God's City: The Political Economy of Prayer Camps in Nigeria." *International Journal of Urban and Regional Research* 40: 3 (2016): 524–540.

Ukah, Asonzeh. "God, Wealth & The Spirit of Investment: Prosperity Pentecostalism in Africa" in Sabine Dreher and Peter J. Smith, eds., *Religious Activism in the Global Economy: Promoting, Reforming, or Resisting Neoliberal Globalization*. Lanham: Rowman & Littlefield International, 2016: 73–90.

Ukah, Asonzeh. "Emplacing God: The Social Worlds of Miracle Cities–Perspectives from Nigeria and Uganda." *Journal of Contemporary African Studies* 36: 3 (2018): 351–368.

Van Dijkhuizen, Jan Frans. *Devil Theatre: Demonic Possession and Exorcism in English Renaissance Drama, 1558–1642*. Cambridge: DS Brewer, 2007.

Vasconcelos, João. "Homeless Spirits: Modern Spiritualism, Psychical Research, and the Anthropology of Religion in the Late Nineteenth and Early Twentieth Centuries" in Frances Pine and João Pina-Cabral, eds., *On the Margins of Religion*. New York: Berghahn, 2008: 13–38.

Vaughan, Olufemi. *Religion and the Making of Nigeria*. Durham: Duke University Press, 2016.

Vengeyi, Obvious. "'Zimbabwean Poverty Is Man-Made!' Demystifying Poverty by Appealing to the Prophetic Book of Amos: General." *Scriptura: International Journal of Bible, Religion and Theology in Southern Africa* 107: 1 (2011): 223–237.

Voloshinov, Valentin Nikolaevich, and Michail M. Bachtin. *Marxism and the Philosophy of Language*. Massachusetts: Harvard University Press, 1986.

Wald, Kenneth D., and Allison Calhoun-Brown. *Religion and Politics in the United States*. Lanham: Rowman & Littlefield, 2014.

Wamitila, Kyallo Wadi. "What's in a Name: Towards Literary Onomastics in Kiswahili Literature." In *Swahili Forum VI* (1999): 35–44.

Wariboko, Nimi. "Counterfoil Choices in the Kalabari Life Cycle." *African Studies Quarterly* 3: 1 (1999).

Wariboko, Nimi. "Pentecostal Paradigms of National Economic Prosperity in Africa" in Katherine Attanasi and Amos Yong, eds., *Pentecostalism and Prosperity: The Socio-Economics of a Global Charismatic Movement.* New York: Palgrave Macmillan, 2012: 35–59.

Wariboko, Nimi. *The Pentecostal Principle: Ethical Methodology in New Spirit.* Michigan: Wm. B. Eerdmans Publishing, 2012.

Wariboko, Nimi. "African Pentecostalism: A Kinetic Description" in Annalisa Butticci, ed., *Na God: Aesthetics of African Charismatic Power.* Padua: Grafiche Turato Edizioni, 2013: 21–23.

Wariboko, Nimi. *Methods of Ethical Analysis: Between Theology, History, and Literature.* Oregon: Wipf and Stock Publishers, 2013.

Wariboko, Nimi. *The Charismatic City and the Public Resurgence of Religion: A Pentecostal Social Ethics of Cosmopolitan Urban Life.* Springer, 2014.

Wariboko, Nimi. "Faith Has a Rate of Return" in *Economics in Spirit and Truth*, 87–104. Palgrave Macmillan, 2014: 87–104.

Wariboko, Nimi. "The King's Five Bodies: Pentecostals in the Sacred City and the Logic of Interreligious Dialogue." *Journal of Africana Religions* 2: 4 (2014): 477–501.

Wariboko, Nimi. *Nigerian Pentecostalism.* New York: University of Rochester, 2014.

Wariboko, Nimi. "West African Pentecostalism: A Survey of Everyday Theology" in Vinson Synan, Amos Yong, and Kwabena Asamoah-Gyadu, eds., *Global Renewal Christianity: Spirit-Empowered Movements, Past, Present and Future, Africa and Diaspora.* Lake Mary: Charisma House Publishers, 2016: 1–18.

Wariboko, Nimi. "Christian-Muslim Relations and the Ethos of State Formation in West Africa" in Evelyne A. Reisacher, ed., *Dynamics of Muslim Worlds: Regional, Theological and Missiological Perspectives.* Illinois: InterVarsity Press, 2017: 57–81.

Wariboko, Nimi. "Pentecostalism in Africa." In *Oxford Research Encyclopedia of African History.* October 26, 2017. https://doi.org/10.1093/acrefore/9780190277734.013.120.

Wariboko, Nimi. "African Pentecostal Political Philosophy: New Directions in the Study of Pentecostalism and Politics" in Adeshina Afolayan, Olajumoke Yacob-Haliso, and Toyin Falola, eds., *Pentecostalism and Politics in Africa.* London: Palgrave Macmillan, 2018: 385–417.

Wariboko, Nimi. *The Split God: Pentecostalism and Critical Theory*. New York: SUNY Press, 2018.

Wariboko, Nimi. *Ethics and Society in Nigeria: Identity, History, Political Theory*. New York: University of Rochester Press, 2019.

Wariboko, Nimi. *Transcripts of the Sacred in Africa: Beautiful, Monstrous, Ridiculous*, Forthcoming Bloomington: Indiana University Press 2022.

Weitz, Eric. *Theatre and Laughter*. New York: Macmillan International Higher Education, 2015.

Weeraratne, Suranjan. "Theorizing the Expansion of the Boko Haram Insurgency in Nigeria." *Terrorism and Political Violence* 29: 4 (2017): 610–634.

White, Dr P., Fortune Tella, and Mishael Donkor Ampofo. "A Missional Study of the Use of Social Media (Facebook) by Some Ghanaian Pentecostal Pastors." *Koers* 81: 2 (2016): 1–8.

Willems, Wendy. "Comic Strips and "the Crisis": Postcolonial Laughter and Coping with Everyday Life in Zimbabwe." *Popular Communication* 9: 2 (2011): 126–145.

Wise, Jennifer. *Dionysus Writes: The Invention of Theatre in Ancient Greece*. Ithaca: Cornell University Press, 2000.

Yong, Amos. "A Typology of Prosperity Theology: A Religious Economy of Global Renewal or a Renewal Economics?" in Katherine Attanasi and Amos Yong, eds., *Pentecostalism and Prosperity: The Socio-Economics of a Global Charismatic Movement*. New York: Palgrave, 2012: 15–33.

Yong, Amos. "On Binding, and Loosing, the Spirits: Navigating and Engaging a Spirit-Filled World" in V. Kärkkäinen, K. Kim, A. Yong, eds., *Interdisciplinary and Religio-Cultural Discourses on a Spirit-Filled World*. New York: Palgrave Macmillan, 2013: 1–12.

Yonge, Charlotte Mary. *History of Christian Names*. New York: Macmillan and Company, 1884.

York, Peter. *Dictator Style: Lifestyles of the World's Most Colorful Despots*. San Francisco: Chronicle Books, 2006.

Web and Social Media Links

"About us." National Theatre, Iganmu, Surulere, Lagos, Nigeria.

"Actor thinks comedy has no place in church." *Pulse.ng*. December 12, 2016. www.pulse.ng/entertainment/celebrities/mike-bamiloye-actor-thinks-comedy-has-no-place-in-church/7vrglqk.

Adeboye, Enoch (Pastor E. A. Adeboye) "When we built the first auditorium, on this camp, 100 metres by 50 metres, it was the biggest auditorium in Africa, and my people ... " Facebook, September 20, 2019. www.facebook.com/PastorEAAdeboye/videos/440082256608686/.

Adegoke, Yinka. "Nigeria's 'frivolous' anti-social media bill just won't go away." Quartz Africa. Quartz, March 21, 2016. https://qz.com/africa/635647/nigerias-frivolous-anti-social-media-bill-just-wont-go-away/.

Ade-Rufus, Adedayo, "'But Christians have died too' – Adeboye sparks debate with coronavirus comment." *TheCable Newspaper*. March 18, 2020. https://lifestyle.thecable.ng/adeboye-sparks-debate-with-coronavirus-comment/.

Ade-Rufus, Adedayo. "'Why should we praise him?' – Reactions as rumour of Oyedepo approving N650 m for road repairs booms." *TheCable.ng*, October 26, 2019. https://lifestyle.thecable.ng/reactions-as-rumour-of-oyedepo-approving-n650 m-for-road-repairs-booms/.

Adejobi, Adedayo. "I started stand-up comedy in the church." *ThisDay Newspapers*. October 1, 2016. www.thisdaylive.com/index.php/2016/10/01/i-started-stand-up-comedy-in-the-church/.

Adelaja, Sunday. "Pastors like TB Joshua who sell anointing oil are turning Christians into pagans." YouTube. February 13, 2019. Video, 7: 09. www.youtube.com/watch?v=pyQyFZeq3t0.

Adepegba, Adelani. "COZA rape allegation: Fatoyinbo remains in police custody as he seeks bail perfection." *The Punch Newspaper*. August 27, 2019. https://punchng.com/coza-rape-allegation-fatoyinbo-remains-in-police-custody-as-he-seeks-bail-perfection/.

Agency Report. "COZA: CAN speaks on rape allegation against Fatoyinbo." *Premium Times*. June 29, 2019. www.premiumtimesng.com/news/headlines/337880-coza-can-speaks-on-rape-allegation-against-fatoyinbo.html.

Akinkahunsi, Timileyin. "COZA pastor, Fatoyinbo, denies rape allegation, threatens to sue." *The Punch Newspaper*. June 29, 2019. https://punchng.com/coza-pastor-fatoyinbo-denies-rape-allegation-threatens-to-sue/.

Akinkuotu, Eniola. "Court fines Busola Dakolo N1 m, dismisses case against Fatoyinbo." *The Punch Newspaper*. November 14, 2019. https://punchng.com/court-fines-busola-dakolo-n1 m-dismisses-case-against-fatoyinbo/.

Akinkuotu, Eniola. "Why we invited Dakolo, wife – Police." *The Punch Newspaper*. July 21, 2019. https://punchng.com/why-we-invited-dakolo-wife-after-aisha-buharis-tweet-police/.

Akinkuotu, Eniola. "Feminists at war with Adeboye over birthday message to wife." *The Punch Newspaper*. July 14, 2020. https://punchng.com/feminists-at-war-with-adeboye-over-birthday-message-to-wife/.

Akinloye, Dimeji. "Ex-minister writes on 'John Kerry's unadulterated garbage.'" *Pulse News* online. August 25, 2016. www.pulse.ng/news/loc

al/fani-kayode-ex-minister-writes-on-john-kerrys-unadulterated-garbage
/fbrp3rd.

Akinnola, Richard. "Pastor Bosun Emmanuel: The political red herring."
Vanguard Media online. November 29, 2014. www.vanguardngr.com/2
014/11/pastor-bosun-emmanuel-political-red-herring/.

Akinola, Christopher. "Pastor Bosun, Buhari's 'Jihad' and Christianity in
Nigeria." *P.M. News* online. April 18, 2015. www.pmnewsnigeria.com/
2015/04/18/pastor-bosun-buharis-jihad-and-christianity-in-nigeria/

Akpororo. "Akpororo Live Comedy @ the Experience 2018 #TE13 |
Nigerian Comedy." *Life Entertainment TV*. December 10, 2018. Video,
14: 48. www.youtube.com/watch?v=SFpXSt7hiHo.

"Akpororo tells Pastor Biodun his Church resembles a CLUB the church
explodes | Coza Global." Siderz Entertainment TV. Video, 8: 27. www
.youtube.com/watch?v=L_AXLJZCjXI.

Aku, Summer. "Nigerian pastors unite against Daddy Freeze |The full
compilation of pastors' responses (tithe drama)." YouTube. Summer
Aku Vlogs, April 18, 2018. www.youtube.com/watch?v=KzB2l3 J-q38.

Aku, Summer. Blind. No More. *Teespring, Inc.* https://teespring.com/blind-
no-more?cross_sell=true&cross_sell_format=none&count_cross_sell_
products_shown=3&pid=212&cid=5839. Accessed June 15, 2020.

Arenyeka, Laju. "I hawked bread, pure water to pay my school fees – Holy
Mallam." *Vanguard Media*. August 17, 2013. www.vanguardngr.com/2
013/08/i-hawked-bread-pure-water-to-pay-my-school-fees-holy-mallam/

"Arms smuggling jet caught with $10million in South Africa linked to CAN
President, Ayo Oritsejafor." *Sahara Reporters* online. Last modified
September 15, 2014. http://saharareporters.com/2014/09/15/arms-
smuggling-jet-caught-10million-south-africa-linked-can-president-ayo-
oritsejafor.

Ameh, Comrade Godwin. "You lied, it is not a sin to invite comedians to
church – Enenche Enenche replies Mike Bamiloye." *Daily Post – Nigeria
News*. December 13, 2016. https://dailypost.ng/2016/12/13/lied-not-sin-
invite-comedians-church-enenche-enenche-replies-mike-bamiloye/

Bamiloye, Mike. "Does anyone take notice of the trending world news?
Jerusalem was declared capital of Israel … " Facebook. December 9,
2017. Retrieved on July 9, 2020. www.facebook.com/MIKEBAMILOYE/
posts/10154880867671831.

Bankole, Idowu. "Trump's rally: IPOB commends US over Kanu's VIP
invitation." *Vanguard Media* online. February 3, 2020. www.vanguardngr
.com/2020/02/ipob-commends-us-over-kanus-vip-invitation-to-trumps-
rally-says-leader-not-a-terrorist/.

Bee. "God have mercy! COZA pastor goes worldly; Flaunts bag worth over
1 million naira." *BlueNews Media* online. September 6, 2016. http://blue

news.com.ng/god-mercy-coza-pastor-goes-worldly-flaunts-bag-worth-1-million-naira.

"Best of Still Ringing Comedian" StreamComLive. November 2, 2016. Video, 8: 24. www.youtube.com/watch?v=tCaVCC0hWnw.

"Bishop Oyedepo shares testimony of his photo 'speaking in tongues and saving kidnap victims;' Uti Nwachukwu, Beverly Osu and Daddyy Freeze react (video)." *LindaIkeji.* December 8, 2019. www.lindaikejisblog.com/2019/12/bishop-oyedepo-shares-testimony-of-his-photo-speaking-in-tongues-and-saving-kidnap-victims-uti-nwachukwu-beverly-osu-and-daddyy-freeze-react-video-2.html.

"Buhari sacks official whose actions led to Adeboye's exit as RCCG leader." *Premium Times.* January 9, 2017. www.premiumtimesng.com/news/head lines/220007-breaking-buhari-sacks-official-whose-actions-led-adeboyes-exit-rccg-leader.html.

Bundle of Joy. "Evil islamic plans for Nigeria and Africa." YouTube. July 8, 2014. Video, 1:29:42. www.youtube.com/watch?v=5FhYpKBKusQ.

Cadwalladr, Carole. "Cambridge Analytica's ruthless bid to sway the vote in Nigeria." *Guardian News* online. Last modified on October 2, 2018. www.theguardian.com/uk-news/2018/mar/21/cambridge-analyticas-ruthless-bid-to-sway-the-vote-in-nigeria.

"CBN Governor, Sanusi Lamido accuses Pastor Adeboye of aiding corruption." *Pointblank News* online. Last modified January 14, 2014. http://pointblanknews.com/pbn/exclusive/cbn-governor-sanusi-lamido-accuses-pastor-adeboye-of-aiding-corruption/.

"Coronavirus: Pastor Adeboye reveals those who will die." *P.M. News.* March 30, 2020. www.pmnewsnigeria.com/2020/03/30/coronavirus-pastor-adeboye-reveals-those-who-will-die/.

"COZA – The journey so far!!!" COZATV. July 24, 2015. Video, 7: 28. www.youtube.com/watch?v=mTcSy8iSx2o

Daddy Freeze and Bro Ayilara. "Bro Ayilara speaks of his unpleasant experience at the RCCG school RCBC." Daddy Freeze. Video, 1:24:17. www.youtube.com/watch?v=eIaOy4AZqR8

"Evangelicals love Donald Trump for many reasons, but one of them is especially terrifying end times." *Mother Jones and the Foundation for National Progress* online. January 23, 2020. www.motherjones.com/polit ics/2020/01/evangelicals-are-anticipating-the-end-of-the-world-and-trump-is-listening/.

Dias, Elizabeth. "Christianity will have power." *The New York Times* online. Accessed August 9, 2020. www.nytimes.com/2020/08/09/us/evan gelicals-trump-christianity.html?smid=fb-share

Dimas, David. "Should we continue to have stand-up comedy in church?" *Premium Times.* August 4, 2017. https://opinion.premiumtimesng.com/2

017/08/04/should-we-continue-to-have-stand-up-comedy-in-church-by-david-dimas/

Emediegwu, Lotanna. "Pst Paul Enenche introduces Pst Kumuyi at the Glory Dome." YouTube. December 1, 2018. Video, 11: 46. www.youtube.com/watch?v=801IOJ-uzTw.

Ezeh, Fred. "Alleged rape: Pastor Fatoyinbo responds, says 'I never raped even as unbeliever.'" *The Sun Nigeria*. June 28, 2019. www .sunnewsonline.com/alleged-rape-pastor-fatoyinbo-responds-says-i-neve r-raped-even-as-unbeliever/.

Felix-Adejumo, Funke. "'Your suffering is loading': Pastor Funke Felix-Adejumo Slams Daddy Freeze." Moregist 81blog. November 22, 2017. Video, 2: 18. www.youtube.com/watch?v=1pTML1YcHXY.

Gaffey, Conor. "Nigeria: Christian group rails against John Kerry for 'divisive' visit." *Newsweek Digital*. August 26, 2016. www.newsweek.com/nigeria-christian-group-rails-against-john-kerry-divisive-visit-493796.

Gray, Rosie. "Firm founded by David Axelrod worked in Nigerian election as recently as December." February 9, 2015. *Buzzfeed News* online. www .buzzfeednews.com/article/rosiegray/firm-founded-by-david-axelrod-worked-in-nigerian-election-as.

Holy Mallam. "Value of Worship, Praise and Comedy | Holy Mallam." He Lives Bible Church Milton Keynes. November 24, 2012. Video, 36: 20. www.youtube.com/watch?v=nCoux0Oz3dQ.

"Hunger pushed me to start comedy – Akpororo." *Tori.ng*. July 11, 2015. www.tori.ng/news/4103/hunger-pushed-me-to-start-comedy-akpororo.html.

"If a girl cannot pray for one hour, don't marry her, says Adeboye." *TheCable.ng*, January 2, 2018. www.thecable.ng/girl-cannot-pray-one-hour-dont-marry-says-adeboye.

"I'll query any pastor who hosts comedian in church – Okoroafor, Assemblies of God head." *The Punch Newspaper*. April 21, 2019. https://punchng.com/ill-query-any-pastor-who-hosts-comedian-in-church-okoroafor-assemblies-of-god-head/.

Iroanusi, QueenEsther, National Assembly, and Wole Soyinka Centre for Investigative Journalism. "Nigerian senate reintroduces bill to regulate social media use." *Premium Times Nigeria*, November 6, 2019. www .premiumtimesng.com/news/headlines/361199-nigerian-senate-reintroduces -bill-to-regulate-social-media-use.html.

Kazeem, Yomi. "Nigeria's lawmakers are about to pass a bill which could gag citizens on social media." *Quartz Africa*. Quartz, December 4, 2015. https://qz.com/africa/565754/nigerias-lawmakers-are-about-to-pass-a-bil l-which-could-gag-citizens-on-social-media/.

Kenechukwu, Stephen. "'We need factories the size of Ibadan, not churches' – Daddy Freeze tackles Adeboye." *TheCable Newspaper*.

December 15, 2019. https://lifestyle.thecable.ng/we-need-factories-the-size-of-ibadan-not-churches-daddy-freeze-tackles-adeboye/

Kperogi, Farooq. "BMC trolls think they can get me fired from my job." *farooqkperogi.com*. January 2, 2020. www.farooqkperogi.com/2020_01 _02_archive.html

Lee, Morgan. "The Christian case for Nigeria's new Muslim president." *Christianity Today* online. April 1, 2015. www.christianitytoday.com/new s/2015/april/christian-case-for-nigeria-new-muslim-president-buhari.html.

Maclean, Ruth and Eromo Egbejule. "How 'Nigeria's #MeToo moment' turned against rape accuser." *Guardian News & Media*. August 6, 2019. www.theguardian.com/global-development/2019/aug/06/nigeria-metoo-moment-accuser-busola-dakolo.

Marx, Karl. "The power of money." Economic and Philosophic Manuscripts of 1844. www.marxists.org/archive/marx/works/1844/manuscripts/powe r.htm. Last accessed August 15, 2020.

Matika, Peter, "'We don't sell blood of Jesus!'" *The Sunday News* online. August 20, 2017. www.sundaynews.co.zw/we-dont-sell-blood-of-jesus /.

Mike-Bamiloye, Damilola. "Abejoye Season 2; The Peace maker part 1." YouTube. September 23, 2019. Video, 1:46:30. www.youtube.com/watc h?v=axcxui10wYA.

Mount Zion FM Information. "Agbara Nla Part 4." YouTube. Video, 2:04:13. www.youtube.com/watch?v=zLrqn6GJxso.

"'My messages are not for everybody' – Pastor." *Pulse.ng*. August 16, 2016. www.pulse.ng/communities/religion/enoch-adeboye-my-messages-are-not-for-everybody-pastor/g472ew7.

"My worry for this generation of Christians – Adeboye." Excerpts from online chat between the General Overseer of the Redeemed Christian Church of God, RCCG, Pastor Enoch Adejare Adeboye and Pastor Poju Oyemade. *Vanguard Media* online. April 6, 2020. www.vanguardngr.com /2020/04/my-worry-for-this-generation-of-christians-adeboye/.

"Nigerian pastor sells coronavirus anointing oil for $100 online." *Oyo Gist* online. May 14, 2020. https://oyogist.com/2020/05/nigerian-pastor-sells-coronavirus-anointing-oil-for-100-online/.

"Nigerian pastors unite against Daddy Freeze |The Full Compilation of Pastors' Responses(Tithe Drama)." Summer Aku Vlogs. April 18, 2019. Video, 12;58. www.youtube.com/watch?v=KzB2l3 J-q38.

"Nigerian president to lead 30,000 Christian pilgrims to Israel." October 15, 2013. *Algemeiner.com*. www.algemeiner.com/2013/10/15/nigerian-president-to-lead-30000-christian-pilgrims-to-israel/.

"Nigeria storm over social media bill." *BBC* online. December 4, 2015. www .bbc.com/news/world-africa-35005137.

"Nigeria's Goodluck Jonathan: Officials back Boko Haram." January 8, 2012. *BBC* online. www.bbc.com/news/world-africa-16462891.

Nuel, Nonny. "Biodin Fatoyinbo of COZA rocks N1 m Gucci supreme tote bag." *EchoNaija*. September 5, 2016. https://echonaija.com.ng/biodin-fatoyinbo-coza-rocks-n1m-gucci-supreme-tote-bag/.

Obadare, Ebenezer. "The New Name? It's a Prayer!" *Reverberations New Directions in the Study of Prayer*. August 29, 2013. https://forums.ssrc.org /ndsp/2013/08/29/the-new-name-its-a-prayer/.

Ochonu, Moses E., "Unraveling the 'Mystery' of Nigerian Trump supporters.' *Premium Times* online. November 4, 2016. https://opinion .premiumtimesng.com/2016/11/04/unraveling-mystery-nigerian-trump-supporters-moses-e-ochonu/

Odion, Okonofua. "Busola Dakolo shares update on rape case against COZA pastor Biodun Fatoyinbo." *Pulse.ng*. April 6, 2020. www .pulse.ng/entertainment/celebrities/busola-dakolo-shares-update-on-case-against-coza-pastor-biodun-fatoyinbo/qtsezlc.

Odoba-Yacham. "Between Pastor Biodun Fatoyinbo and Barrister Isaac Danladi, who is more classy? (Pictures)." *Opera News Kenya*. July, 2020. https://ke.opera.news/ke/en/entertainment/3c3f4eaba5a781ec65 b2e32e2df63d61?news_entry_id=t7d61232a200627en_ke.

Oduah, Chika. "Nigeria's Biafra separatists see hope in Trump." *VOA* online. November 14, 2016. www.voanews.com/africa/nigerias-biafra-separatists-see-hope-trump.

Ogundipe, Samuel. "Adeboye speaks on rape scandal, gives advice to pastors ." *Premium Times*. July 6, 2019. www.premiumtimesng.com/news/top-news/ 339180-adeboye-speaks-on-rape-scandal-gives-advice-to-pastors.html.

Ohlheiser, Abby. "Uganda's new anti-homosexuality law was inspired by American activists." *The Atlantic* online. December 20, 2013. www .theatlantic.com/international/archive/2013/12/uganda-passes-law-punishes -homosexuality-life-imprisonment/356365/.

Okoduwa, Gabriel. "Do not pay tithe by Pastor Abel Damina." YouTube, October 28, 2017. www.youtube.com/watch?v=aqtFS8ll02o.

Oladeji, Bayo. "Nigeria: Aso Villa Church – God used Obasanjo – Chaplaincy." *AllAfrica* online. Last modified November 19, 2010. https:// allafrica.com/stories/201011220110.html.

Olafusi, Ebunoluwa. "Oyedepo: Why I accompanied Atiku to Obasanjo's residence." *TheCable News* online. October 15, 2018. www.thecable.ng /oyedepo-why-i-accompanied-atiku-to-obasanjos-residence.

Olowoniyan, Tope, and Daddy Freeze. "If you don't want to stop paying tithe, then don't watch our explosive interview with Daddy Freeze." LindaIkeji TV. September 30, 2017. Video, 55: 59. www.youtube.com/w atch?v=ZWPjBzau_W8.

Onyeji, Ebuka. "Living Faith Church reacts to video showing founder, Oyedepo, urging members to 'kill.'" *The Premium Times* online. January 14, 2017. www.premiumtimesng.com/news/top-news/220482-living-faith-church-reacts-video-showing-founder-oyedepo-urging-members-kill.html.

Orjinmo, Nduka. "Enoch Adeboye sexism row: Why the Nigerian pastor is so popular." *BBC* online. August 12, 2020. www.bbc.com/news/world-africa-53488921

Owolabi, Femi. "EXTRA: I'm the best dressed pastor in town, says Fatoyinbo." *TheCable*. November 21, 2020. www.thecable.ng/extra-im-the-best-dressed-pastor-in-town-says-fatoyinbo.

Oyemade, Poju (@pastorpoju). "I have read it in scriptures but now i have seen it; a united church in prayer governs world affairs. Evangelicals were united for Trump." Twitter. November 9, 2016. https://twitter.com/pastorpoju/status/796295987010617344.

Oyero, Kayode. "US election: Trump hails parade in Nigeria, says 'great honour.'" *The Punch Newspaper* online. November 3, 2020. https://punchng.com/us-election-trump-hails-parade-in-nigeria-says-great-honour/.

"Pastor begins sales of 'holy oil' to protect members from coronavirus." *Vanguard Media* online. February 6, 2020. www.vanguardngr.com/2020/02/pastor-begins-sales-of-holy-oil-to-protect-members-from-coronavirus/.

"Pastor Funke Adejumo joins the tithes controversy in this ranting speech." *NijaBox*. June 11, 2018. www.facebook.com/nijabox/videos/222444281690137/.

"Pastor insists Jonathan bribed CAN with 7 billion Naira." *Sahara Reporters* online. February 25, 2015. https://saharareporters.com/2015/02/25/pastor-insists-jonathan-bribed-can-7-billion-naira.

"Pastor Sam Adeyemi says the practice of tithing has expired, no Christian should feel guilty for not tithing." *BlackChristianNews*, March 1, 2018. https://blackchristiannews.com/2018/03/pastor-sam-adeyemi-says-the-practice-of-tithing-has-expired-no-christian-should-feel-guilty-for-not-tithing/.

"Pay your tithes willingly and not out of fear – Bishop Mike Okonkwo ." *BellaNaija*, March 7, 2018. www.bellanaija.com/2018/03/pay-tithes-willingly-mike-okonkwo/.

Pham, John-Peter. *Boko Haram's evolving threat*. Africa Center for Strategic Studies, 2012.

Phillips, Barnaby. "Church of the 50,000 Faithful." *BBC* online. Last modified November 30, 1999. http://news.bbc.co.uk/2/hi/africa/542154.stm.

Ricketts, Olushola. "Why I slammed Akpororo for performing shirtless – Sammie Okposo." *The Punch Newspaper*. April 7, 2019. https://punchng.com/why-i-slammed-akpororo-for-performing-shirtless-sammie-okposo/.

SaharaReporters. "'#SayNoToIntimidation', Aisha Buhari responds to SaharaReporters' story on police invasion of Dakolo's residence." *Sahara Reporters*. July 20, 2019. http://saharareporters.com/2019/07/20/%E2%80%98saynotointimidation%E2%80%99-aisha-buhari-responds-saharareporters-story-police-invasion-dakolo

Salu, Jide. "How Nigeria presidential challenger Buhari went from 'ruthless ex-dictator' to 'weak leader.'" *Quartz Media* online. March 24, 2015. https://qz.com/368219/how-nigeria-challenger-buhari-went-from-ruthless-dictator-to-weak-leader/.

Sanchez, Rebecca Lee. "How American evangelicals made life unbearable for gays in Uganda." *GlobalPost/PRX* online. November 15, 2013. www.pri.org/stories/2013-11-15/how-american-evangelicals-made-life-unbearable-gays-uganda.

"Still ringing: Bishop Oyedepo falls from his seat after watching this comedian." *Complete Tv*. September 6, 2015. Video, 4: 40. www.youtube.com/watch?v=RAioInibFxw.

Suleman, Johnson. "Apostle Johnson Suleman reveals deep secret of this virus." *Omega Fire Ministries* New York. Video, 7: 49. www.youtube.com/watch?v=GtnMUvNz0LI&feature=youtu.be

Tellitall. "How I discovered I could make people laugh – Holy Mallam." *Gistmania Naijapals*. June 1, 2014. www.gistmania.com/talk/topic,206840.0.html.

Temple-West, Patrick. "Democrats working both sides of Nigeria's presidential election." *Politico* online. February 14, 2015. www.politico.com/story/2015/02/nigeria-presidential-election-goodluck-jonathan-muhammadu-buhari-115190.

The Associated Press. "Nigerian protests erupt in violence." *New York Times* online. July 6, 1993. www.nytimes.com/1993/07/06/world/nigerian-protests-erupt-in-violence.html?auth=login-email.

The Associated Press. "Rioting in Nigeria kills at least 11." *New York Times* online. July 7, 1993. www.nytimes.com/1993/07/07/world/rioting-in-nigeria-kills-at-least-11.html.

The Stansbury Show. "A Nigerian Pastor says he will "prophetically destroy" the coronavirus." *iHeartMedia*. March 9, 2020. wrqk.iheart.com/featured/the-stansbury-show/content/2020-03-09-a-nigerian-pastor-says-he-will-prophetically-destroy-the-coronavirus/.

The World Staff. "'More amusing than disgusting': Why Trump is so popular in Nigeria." *PRX*. December 26, 2019. www.pri.org/stories/2019-12-26/more-amusing-disgusting-why-trump-so-popular-nigeria.

Thandiubani. "Photos of the flamboyant lifestyle of Pastor Biodun Fatoyinbo." *Tori.ng*. July 12, 2019.

Tukur, Sani. "Governor Nyako accuses Jonathan administration of genocide against Northern Nigeria." *The Premium Times* online. April 19, 2014. www .premiumtimesng.com/news/159014-governor-nyako-accuses-jonathan-administration-genocide-northern-nigeria.html.

Udodiong, Inemesit. "'Any pastor who takes tithe from the poor is putting his family under a curse' - OAP teaches." *Pulse.ng*. November 11, 2018. www.pulse.ng/communities/religion/daddy-freeze-any-pastor-who-takes-tithe-from-the-poor-is-putting-his-family-under-a/jk1sdnp.

Udodiong, Inemesit. "Religious activist insists that Jesus is against tithing, seed sowing." *Pulse.ng*. September 25, 2018. www.pulse.ng/communities/religion/daddy-freeze-religious-activist-insists-that-jesus-is-against-tithing-seed-sowing/wdwr10z.

Ujah, Emma. "We'll conquer Goliaths – Jonathan." *Vanguard Media* online. September 26, 2011. www.vanguardngr.com/2011/09/we-ll-conquer-goliaths-jonathan/.

Uzodinma, Emmanuel. "US election: Nnamdi Kanu writes open letter to Trump." *Daily Post – Nigeria News*. November 11, 2016. https://daily post.ng/2016/11/11/us-election-nnamdi-kanu-writes-open-letter-trump/.

Wahab, Bayo. "Coronavirus: Adeboye says God told him world will be on compulsory holiday." *Pulse.ng*. March 22, 2020. www.pulse.ng/news/local/coronavirus-adeboye-says-god-told-him-world-will-be-on-compulsory-holiday/m7tk3zf.

Weber, Jeremy. "Why Nigeria's president just visited (almost) every pilgrimage site in Israel." *Christianity Today* online. October 28, 2013. www.christianitytoday.com/news/2013/october/nigeria-president-israel-pilgrimage-jonathan-goodluck.html.

"Worshippers pay N1,000 to enter Oyakhilome's church." *P.M. News* online. January 5, 2011. www.pmnewsnigeria.com/2011/01/05/worshippers-pay-n1000-to-enter-oyakhilomes-church/.

Wootson Jr., Cleve R., Vanessa Williams, Dan Balz, and Scott Clement. "Black Americans are deeply pessimistic about the country under Trump, whom more than 8 in 10 describe as 'a racist,' Post-Ipsos poll finds." *The Washington Post* online. January 17, 2020. www.washingtonpost.com/politics/black-americans-deeply-pessimistic-about-country-under-president-who-more-than-8-in-10-describe-as-a-racist-post-ipsos-poll-finds/2020/01/16/134b705 c-37de-11ea-bb7b-265f4554af6d_story.html.

Yesufu, Deji. "Evangelicals' support of Donald Trump." Last modified December 22, 2019. http://mouthpiece.com.ng/evangelicals-support-of-donald-trump/.

Yost, Lauren. "The speech act of naming in context: A linguistic study of naming in the Old Testament." *Linguistics Senior Research Projects*, 17 (2018). https://digitalcommons.cedarville.edu/linguistics_senior_projects/17

Xenab, success. "Meet the Best Dressed Pastor in Nigeria, COZA's Abiodun Fatoyinbo – PHOTOS." *Gistmania Naijapals*. August 29, 2018. www.gistmania.com/talk/topic,365651.0.html.

Index

disempowered, 22
disempowered, the, 18, 51
disempowerment, 49
disenfranchised, the, 183
dissent, 20, 141, 147, 161
doctrine, 2, 147, 149, 155, 156, 159, 174, 197
dominance, 184
dominion theology, 75
drama, 10
drama ministers, 47–48
dramatization, 47
Dunamis International Gospel Centre, 239

economy, 54, 238, 242
Edelman, Joshua, 9
Edelman, Lee, 216
Egypt, 1
Ekwefi, 217–222
election, 76
  2011 (Nigeria), 76, 80
  2015 (Nigeria), 67, 71, 83
  2020 (USA), 71
Elijah, David, 238
Ellis, Iain, 187
Elton, Sydney G., Rev., 21
embodiment, 9, 11, 23, 121
Emmanuel, Bosun, 85
employment, 202
empowerment, 3, 5, 12, 28, 50, 52, 59, 89, 174, 183, 201
Enenche, Paul, Pastor, 239
entertainment, 9, 11, 43, 148, 176, 177
eroticism, 119–120, 127
ethical comedy, 191
ethics, 133
ethnicity, 2, 3, 25, 27, 69
Europe, 61
evangelical, 71, 85, 89, 100, 101
evangelization, 89
Eve, 214
evil, 30, 42, 45, 50, 56, 64
exorcism, 25, 39, 45, 50, 73, 114

Facebook, 92, 95, 101, 124, 144, 166
Faith Tabernacle, 74, 239
Faith Theatre, 239
fake news, 71, 95, 171

Fatoyinbo, Biodun, 102–103, 110, 125, 132
fear, 49, 51, 64, 73, 99, 110, 146, 159, 179, 237, 240
feminism, 135, 168
finances, 151
Financial Regulatory Council of Nigeria (FRCN), 169
Fourth Republic, 26, 53, 143
free markets, 53
Free the Sheeple, 145–148, 149–159, 161, 169, 170, 173, 174, 175, 242
freedom, 53, 54, 141, 151, 157, 172
Freud, Sigmund, 158
Fulani, 80, 87

Gates, Bill and Melinda, 237
gender, 2, 3, 133
Ghaddafi, Muammar, 88
Ghana, 204
Gharavi, Lance, 28
Gifford, Paul, 55
globalization, 96, 140, 143, 204, 242
Glorious Mount of Possibility, 238
Glory Dome, 239
God, 10, 13, 22, 40, 42, 45, 47, 53, 57, 60, 62, 63, 80, 111, 112, 118, 119, 124, 134, 149, 173, 174, 190, 226
Goldstein, Donna, 182
gospel comedians, 27
gossip, 102, 188, 189, 196
Gowon, Yakubu, 17
Graham, Billy, 82
Greece, 1

Habila, Helon, 51
Hart, Keith, 199
Hausa, 80
Haynes, Naomi, 59
He Lives Bible Church, 191
hell, 61, 176
hierarchy, 16, 62, 106, 198, 241
History of the Yorubas, The, 223
Holy Ghost, 63
Holy Mallam, 186, 191
Holy Spirit, 12, 28, 159, 173, 209
homosexuality. *See also* same-sex marriage

Milton Keynes UK
Ingram Content Group UK Ltd.
UKHW052015100923
428442UK00015B/56